THE AFRICAN AMERICAN
GUIDE TO WRITING
AND PUBLISHING
NONFICTION

ALSO BY JEWELL PARKER RHODES

Free Within Ourselves: Fiction Lessons for Black Writers

Voodoo Dreams

Magic City

THE
AFRICAN AMERICAN
GUIDE TO WRITING
AND PUBLISHING
NONFICTION

Jewell Parker Rhodes

BROADWAY BOOKS / NEW YORK

BROADWAY

Broadway Books titles may be purchased for business or promotional use or for special sales. For information, please write to: Special Markets Department, Random House, Inc., 1540 Broadway, New York, NY 10036.

BROADWAY BOOKS and its logo, a letter B bisected on the diagonal, are trademarks of Broadway Books, a division of Random House, Inc.

PRINTED IN THE UNITED STATES OF AMERICA

Visit our website at www.broadwaybooks.com

Permissions can be found on pages 349-50.

LIBRARY OF CONGRESS CATALOGING-IN-PUBLICATION DATA
Rhodes, Jewell Parker.
The African American guide to writing and publishing nonfiction / Jewell Parker Rhodes.—1st ed.
    p. cm.
Includes bibliographical references.
1. Authorship—Marketing. 2. Authorship. 3. Autobiography—Authorship. 4. American literature—African American authors.
I. Title.
PN161 .R45 2001
808'.02'08996073—dc21
2001037714
ISBN 0-7679-0578-4

Book design by Richard Oriolo

FIRST EDITION

1 3 5 7 9 10 8 6 4 2

ACKNOWLEDGMENTS

I deeply appreciate having had the pleasure of working with Janet Hill, Vice President and Executive Editor of Doubleday and Harlem Moon. Visionary, creative, meticulous, Janet is an author's best partner. My thanks, too, to Miriam Goedrich, Jane Dystel, and Jo Fagan of Jane Dystel Literary Management. Three righteous and brilliant women who help guide my career. Special thanks to Tayari Jones, my friend and research assistant, who is launching her own book, *Leaving Atlanta*. And, finally, hugs and kisses to my family—Brad, Kelly, and Evan— who inspire and prove that love is the best support for a writer.

CONTENTS

Contents

PART III

MEMOIR

PART IV

BEYOND MEMOIR AND AUTOBIOGRAPHY: WITNESSING AND THE PERSONAL ESSAY

PART V

BREAKING INTO PRINT

We build our temples for tomorrow, as strong as we know how and we stand on top of the mountain, free within ourselves.

—Langston Hughes, *"The Negro Artist and the Racial Mountain,"*
  The Nation, *1926*

THE AFRICAN AMERICAN
GUIDE TO WRITING
AND PUBLISHING
NONFICTION

PREFACE

The Art of Nonfiction Writing: Celebrating Self and Community

Everyone dreams of telling stories about their life and experiences. This need to communicate is the heart of our humanity. Sharing ourselves, we affirm the self, bear witness to memory, and leave a legacy that outwits our mortality.

The best writing comes from knowing who you are, in the fullest sense, and understanding how the very essence of you is rooted in and sustained by a cultural heritage. As African Americans, we have a rich history of words—both oral and written—that freed and shaped a new culture, a new people in America.

Words are powerful. They mirror, critique, reveal, and affirm who we are both as individuals and as a people. Words are our enduring testament that we have survived and thrived, spiritually and creatively.

Listen to the spirit, the rhythm, the unique quality of self in the following examples:

"Hold your back up, now! Deenie, keep still! Put your head so!" Scratch, scratch. "When last you wash your hair? Look the dandruff!" Scratch, scratch, the comb's truth setting my teeth on edge. Yet, these were some of the moments I missed most sorely when our real wars began.

I remember the warm mother smell caught between her legs, and the intimacy of our physical touching nestled inside of the anxiety/pain like a nutmeg nestled inside its covering of mace.

The radio, the scratching comb, the smell of petroleum jelly, the grip of her knees and my stinging scalp all fall into—*the rhythms of a litany, the rituals of Black women combing their daughters' hair.*

—Audre Lorde, *Zami: A New Spelling of My Name*

In the thronging lobby, I saw some of the real Roxbury hipsters eyeing my zoot, and some fine women were giving me that look . . .

Hamp's band was working, and that big, waxed floor was packed with people lindy-hopping like crazy. I grabbed some girl I'd never seen, and the next thing I knew we were out there lindying away and grinning at each other. It couldn't have been finer.

—Malcolm X, *The Autobiography of Malcolm X*

I still be performing. Read poetry in the hole. The other fellows get real quiet and listen. Sing down in there too.

Nothing else to do, so we entertain each other. They always asking me to sing or read. "Hey, Wideman. C'mon man and do something." Then it gets real quiet while they waiting for me to start. Quiet and it's already dark. You in your own cell and can't see nobody else. Barely enough light to read by. The other fellows can hear you but it's just you and them walls so it feels like being alone much as it feels like you're singing or reading to somebody else.

—John Edgar Wideman, *Brothers and Keepers*

This is a love story like every love story I had always known, like no love story I could ever have imagined. It's everything beautiful—bright colors, candle-scented rooms, orange silk, and lavender amethyst. It's everything grotesque, disfigured. It's long twisting wounds, open and unhealed, nerves pricked raw, exposed.

This is a love story, awake and alive. It's a breathing document, a living witness. It's human possibility, hope, and connection. It's a gathering of the Spirit, the claiming of dreams. It's an Alvin Ailey dance, *a rainbow roun' mah shoulder.* It's a freedom song, a 12-string guitar, a Delta blues song. This story is a reprieve.

—asha bandele, *The Prisoner's Wife*

Good writing isn't simply organizing words on a page. Good—possibly great—writing requires you to open your heart wide, to feel intensely, and to reflect on how the "I" crystallizes the "We" of a community.

This book is meant to help you on your journey to becoming a better writer. Unlike my previous book, *Free Within*

Ourselves: Fiction Lessons for Black Authors, the guiding principle is not to write creative fiction but *to write nonfiction more creatively.*

Even in writing the "truth," one has to engage the senses, be attuned to diction (what words mean and how they sound), to narrative shape, and how fictional techniques of dialogue, description, and setting can enhance the quality, credibility, and persuasiveness of what you say.

Because black people are infinitely varied, our voices, arguments, and questions about ourselves and our world are infinitely varied. But the core of being ourselves, being what Langston Hughes called "free within ourselves," is our celebration of the African American tradition.

Each time you commit words to a page, you are drawing upon the creative and cathartic acts of our people. When you write "I," you are exclaiming, celebrating, "I am here, and here I intend to stay" for all of us—the living and the long dead.

To be truly "free within ourselves," each of us needs to engage fully in life:

- engage imaginatively, dreaming of the past and the future;

- engage passionately, experiencing the reality of the here and now;

- engage in celebrating our capacity for weaving both joy and heartache into art!

As a writer, you have the opportunity to explore what it means to be human, to conjure through words those passions, those spirits which are important to you and which echo the legacy of our people.

As a writer, you have the opportunity to turn "your story" into "our story." Your memories stir remembrances in others, reminding us all of both the glory and the bittersweet wonder of being alive. Your testimony resonates and calls upon readers to lift their voice to testify and bear witness. The personal *is* political. Free, celebrate yourself through writing, and you will build a bridge and everlasting bond with readers. The personal engenders community. *Celebrate yourself, and you celebrate us all!*

Good writers probe themselves and their world; good writers laugh and cry; good writers observe; good writers don't just talk about writing, they write.

PART I

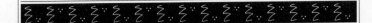

CELEBRATING OURSELVES

O N E

FINDING YOUR VOICE

Whether it's the first time, the hundredth or the thousandth time, give yourself permission to speak, *to write your heart and soul down on paper.*

Always believe—there is no better voice than your own unique voice. No better story than the one you need to write.

Select a journal—a three-ring binder, a legal pad, a leather-bound blank book, whatever's most comfortable for you. This journal is your life line to writing more effectively and productively. Select a special pen—a felt tip, roller ball, fountain pen, or a profusion of rainbow gels. Journal writing should be a tactile experience, alive with the joy of your hand moving across the page, of leaving colored markings that speak about your self and the world at large.

On page one, write:

I Am (*your name)*
I Believe in Myself
I Have Something to Say

When you feel doubtful about your voice, reread the first page of your journal. Remind yourself that this journal is your song, your celebration of how you observe and experience the world. It is your private practice field. You'll collect ideas and feelings, but you'll explore how best to express them—*how best to sing your song, speak your mind, and say what needs to be said!*

A journal is for shouts and whispers, cries and laughter. It is never a place for silence. With each sentence you write in your journal, you affirm and improve your voice, the power of your words.

Just as musicians play scales to strengthen their rhythm and tone, to limber their fingers, hands, and mouths, so, too, a writer must practice the basics of writing prose. Observation, clarity, description, voice, sentence structure, and rhythm are all essential skills that require continual practice.

Don't try to do the following exercises all at once. Take time between exercises to experience, observe, reflect, and revise. If you're struggling with an exercise, repeat it. Move on when you feel your writing is improving. By doing the exercises in this book, you'll be allowed to make mistakes and to explore thoughts and feelings. After practicing these exercises, when you *do* sit down to write an essay or book, you'll be much better prepared to succeed.

MY BEST ADVICE

Treasure your journal. A journal begins the process of crafting ideas into art.

For those of you who are new to writing, this chapter will help limber your skills of observing, listening, recording, and assembling portraits of your world. For those of you who have been writing for a while, these opening exercises will give you the opportunity to sharpen your skills and reflect again how heritage can influence and deepen your writing.

In either case, don't hurry your growth. *Writing is a process.* Nothing is discrete; everything is interconnected. Who you are, what subjects you select, what skills you learn, and what nonfiction you choose to write are integrated, much like single grains of sand shaping a shoreline.

REMEMBER: There are many trails to follow as a writer, but the main toll road is the same—*a willingness to explore who you are and a belief that your voice matters.*

When you're anxious or filled with self-doubt, remember: the collective spirit of our people is with you. Your journey to discover the power of voice, your words are an affirmation of all of us. Your journal is your life line, life support, and key to finding your voice!

Open your journal. Take a deep breath. The adventure begins.

EXERCISE 1

EXPERIENCING A
COMMUNITY EVENT

Like a cub reporter, go out and observe an event worth celebrating. It can be a political rally, church services, a family reunion, or lunchtime at your community park. Write quickly for twenty minutes; don't edit.

When you've finished, reread your description and ask yourself: Is it specific? Are there sounds in your description? Are there colors, textures, smells, tastes? What did you fail to observe? What did you leave out? What did you write just right?

For twenty minutes, rewrite the description, adding more details.

Compare the two versions and decide which one you like best, which conveys the more complete picture.

EXERCISE 2

EXPERIENCING THE FOLK

Look for a person to describe, someone worth focusing on and writing about. It can be someone you know, a trusted teacher, a performance poet, or young girl playing defense in a pick-up game of basketball. Write quickly for twenty minutes; don't edit.

When you've finished, reread your description. How well did you describe the person? Would I recognize them if I saw them on the street, saw them in action? How does your person dress, talk, move? What do they feel—joy, anger, exhilaration? How can you tell? What outward signs, what actions best express personality? How do they react to others? How do they react to touch, sight, taste, and sound?

What makes this person special to you? What about them are you highlighting?

Revise your description for twenty minutes, adding new details.

Compare the two versions and decide which one you like best. Which version is more accurate? The most vibrant and "lifelike?"

EXERCISE 3

TALKING THAT TALK:
COMMUNITY STORYTELLERS

Storytelling is a fundamental human activity—some stories are short (leaving you breathless for more), some are long and twisting, some teach, some give praise, some slander, some help you imagine a time and place where you've never lived. In Africa, the *griot* was honored as master storyteller, responsible for maintaining the stories and legends of the tribe. The *griot* tradition did not die with the advent of American slavery. Indeed, cultural storytelling kept the past alive and sustained a newly born people. Slaves were not "blank slates" but a community who mirrored, shaped, celebrated, informed, and inspired themselves through stories.

Many of us when we hear or see the word "story" immediately think fiction, think only of stories as untrue, created out of the imagination. Not necessarily so. *Stories can be true, drawn from concrete reality.* But even while you may be recording a "true story," you'll want to write it as interesting as fiction—you'll want to capture sensory details, characterization, and the voice of the storyteller!

Go out and find a storyteller—a former diva who used to sing for Motown, a young adult remembering the glamor of prom night, a grandmother on the front porch spinning stories about her childhood and her family's migration north. Go to the local barbershop or beauty salon and talk to the elders or the most colorful person in the room.

Listen to the voice of this storyteller, the rhythms in his or her speech. Is the talk slow and meandering or fast and focused? Is the voice loud or soft, rough or smooth? Is the voice conversational or formal? Write a page in the "voice" of the storyteller you've studied. Try to recapture their story—feel free to elaborate, to improve upon your memory. The important thing is to keep writing the "voice" of the storyteller you've heard. To keep imitating the rhythm, sounds, and speech.

Reread your writing. Can you hear the storyteller's voice? Rewrite any sentences that don't sound like your storyteller.

Repeat this exercise with two other people. If you first wrote a young man's tale of valor, try capturing the scratchy cadences of a deejay or the ebullient voice of a teenager. Stretch yourself—look for a variety of voices to challenge you. If you haven't heard enough good storytellers, don't underestimate the power of simply asking: "Please, tell me a story. Tell me about something that happened to you." You'll be surprised by the "truths" you may hear.

Once you've captured three storytellers, list the differences among the three "voices." Which "voice" did you capture best? Who told the best story? Why was it the best? How did the voice make the story more interesting?

Over time you'll train yourself to hear nuances of speech, differences of grammar, word choice, rhythm, and sound.

For now, listen up! As a writer, you need daily practice in listening to people talk—becoming more in tune with the full range of human sounds.

For one week, listen more and talk less. Record your experiences in your journal.

EXERCISE 4

TALKING THAT TALK:
FAMILY TALES

Our ancestors shape our family's stories. Talk to an aunt, a grandparent, a second cousin, about your family's heritage. Ask to see pictures, mementos, genealogy charts, family Bibles. What stories are attached to these objects? What do these stories reveal about the African American spirit in your family? What makes them dramatic and intriguing?

Certain stories are easily passed down through the generations within families. Other stories are told in whispers, with long silences between incidents. Listen for the "gaps" in one of your family's stories. Listen for the silences, for what might be left unsaid, the secrets, then—*explore, investigate.*

For an hour, write the family tale you found; write the story just as your family member told it.

Next, put a star by all the points in the story where you *don't* know what happened. These starred points represent opportunities for research.

For example, in my family, my mother often told how her grandmother was a slave owned by a Georgia planter with the surname Wright:

> *"When Master decided to sell Grandmother, she begged to be sold with her husband and infant. Master agreed; and years later, when the family was emancipated, they kept the Wright name."*

Mother's tale has been passed down for three generations; nonetheless, I wasn't sure the tale was entirely true. Having a slave family sold intact was highly unusual. And while many slaves kept their masters' names, why did my ancestors keep the Wright name? Was it an expression of appreciation? Had they refused to adopt the name of their last owner? Why didn't they just adopt an entirely new name for a new life of freedom?

Research can include interviewing relatives, friends, even family doctors and lawyers who may have knowledge about a family's history. Clues, too, can be found in family journals, letters, baby books, Bibles, slave records, and community newspapers. Rummaging through attic boxes, through both my mother's and grandmother's belongings, I discovered photos, diary scraps, and, ultimately, a poster, framed, declaring:

SLAVE AUCTION
**Various goods and animals to be auctioned,
including one healthy male,
a woman (good cook), and child.
Wright Plantation
Respectable offers only**

Researching, I had begun creating the basic bones for a family history. Such histories about bloodlines have rich potential to be incorporated in an essay for a family reunion, in a memoir about my life and heritage, or even in a historical document about slave history and African American migrations.

Now revise your family story, filling in the "gaps" with investigation and research.

Compare your two tales—the one told to you and your revision. How has your research deepened your story? Is the second version more compelling? More satisfying to you as a reader? What other research could you do to further enhance your story?

Reread all the writing in your journal. You've written description, detailed portraits of people, researched history, and conveyed your own unique sense of what is special about your family and community—all the things a good writer does!

Celebrate! You're on your way!

TWO

LITERARY ANCESTORS

O black and unknown bards of long ago,
How came your lips to touch the sacred fire?
How, in your darkness, did you come to know
The power and beauty of the minstrel's lyre?

—James Weldon Johnson,
"O Black and Unknown Bards"

Forbidden to read or write, African Americans echoed their pain in spirituals, folk and work songs, and in stories orally passed down through the generations. Art, with its cathartic power, undoubtedly preserved lives, preserved sanity, and preserved a legacy for African American artists to build upon.

Ever since the eighteenth century, black people also contrived to create a written record, to create literature. While folk and oral traditions are splendid, the word *writ large*—printed for posterity—has a different resonance. Beyond serving as a record to be responded to, discussed, and analyzed for generations, a written record allows a particular person's experience to resonate for us all. The specific life, paradoxically, with all its distinctive particulars, illuminates the more general human and cultural condition.

To be defiant—to write a life story in the American era of slavery—was a supremely personal and political act. Slaves understood that words bound in a book had the potential to assert their existence as rational humans. Writing was, literally, a way of scribing themselves into being, argue Henry Louis Gates, Jr., and Charles T. Davis in the introduction to their edited collection, *The Slave's Narrative.*

Gates and Davis also point out the tragic irony of slaves believing only whites had access to "talking books":

[My master] used to read prayers in public to the ship's crew every Sabbath day; and when I first saw him read, I was never so surprised in my life, as when I saw the book talk to my master, for I thought it did, as I observed him to look upon it, and move his lips. I wished it would do so with me. As soon as my master had done reading, I followed him to the place where he put the book, being mightily delighted with it, and when nobody saw me, I opened it, and put my ear down close upon it, in great hopes that it would say something to me; but I was very sorry, and greatly disappointed, when I found that it would not speak. This thought immediately presented itself to me, that everybody and everything despised me because I was black.

—*A Narrative of the Most Remarkable Particulars in the Life of James Albert Ukawsaw Gronniosaw, An African Prince, As Related By Himself (1770)*

Because the Western text could not *see* or *hear* the slave's presence or voice, the black self went unrecognized. Thus, the slave Gronniosaw was moved to speak and write a text that recognized his presence and spoke his voice as a black man. Gates and Davis found that, in addition to James Gronniosaw in 1770, at least three other black eighteenth-century authors (John Marrant in 1785, Ottobah Cugoano in 1787, Olaudah Equiano in 1789) argued that for blacks to be recognized as human beings, the book must be made to speak for, about, and with the voice of black people. The association of literacy with freedom and self-validation was born. The tradition of African American autobiography had begun.

Another compelling irony is that multilingual, multivoiced Africans had to learn English and Western literary conventions in order to re-create themselves, in print, as a new people: African Americans. While thousands of slaves, dating back to the eighteenth century, told their stories in oral form, many, despite prohibitions against reading and writing, created a textual mirror, a quintessentially new American literature—the slave narrative.

Frederick Douglass's 1845 *Narrative of the Life of Frederick Douglass, An American Slave, Written by Himself* is justifiably the most famous of the narratives. Beginning with the famous phrase "I was born . . ." Douglass represents himself as a man of reason, "rebirthing" himself into existence despite a prejudiced white populace:

> *"If you give a nigger an inch, he will take an ell. A nigger should know nothing but to obey his master—to do as he is told to do. Learning would spoil the best nigger in the world . . ."*

These words sank deep into my heart, stirred up sentiments that
lay slumbering, and called into existence an entirely new train of
thought. It was a new and special revelation, explaining dark
and mysterious things, with which my youthful understanding
had struggled in vain. I now understood what had been to me a
most perplexing difficulty—to wit, the white man's power to
enslave the black man. It was a grand achievement and I prized
it highly. From that moment, I understood the pathway from
slavery to freedom . . . Though conscious of the difficulty of
learning without a teacher, I set out with high hope, and a fixed
purpose, at whatever cost or trouble, to learn how to read.

In his introduction to Douglass's *Narrative* (Penguin,
1982), Houston A. Baker, Jr., argues that unique to slave narratives were: 1) the depiction of the slave's experience; 2) the
escape from bondage to freedom; 3) the recognition that reading and writing were critical in defining the self; and 4) the
commitment to abolitionist goals. Thus, historically, within the
African American tradition, autobiography has spiritual, physical, emotional, as well as political significance.

AUTOBIOGRAPHY—***Autos*** (self), ***bios*** (life), and ***graphe***
(writing) = the slave's journey of establishing an identity
subject to his or her own control.

If a life is written down, it has authority. The bound book
suggests truth of the highest order. *It also has persuasive appeal.*
When the slave succeeds in the slave-owner's literate realm, he
manipulates the language and logic of the slave-holder to
prove himself a man in the slave-holder's eyes. By learning a

new tongue, by becoming "double-voiced" (fluent in both black dialect and standard English), black people embody what W.E.B. DuBois called a "double consciousness."

But while Douglass explored the literary terrain of what makes a slave a man, Harriet Jacobs, in her slave narrative, *Incidents in the Life of a Slave Girl (1861),* explored the impact of racism and sexism upon black women.

Unlike Douglass, Jacobs felt compelled to write under a pseudonym—Linda Brent—thus reflecting a nineteenth century more comfortable with assertions of masculinity (even those of a slave) than with black women asserting their claim to be viewed as respectable, nurturing mothers in control of their sexual and reproductive destiny.

Jacobs wanted to "arouse the women of the North to a realizing sense of the condition of two millions of women at the South, still in bondage, suffering what I suffered, and most of them far worse." Literary theorist Hazel Carby argues that Jacobs was making a direct appeal to the cross-racial sisterhood of all women. However, in her narrative, Jacobs points out white women's cruelty and betrayal when they blame and abuse slave women for their husband's sexual overtures and dominance. Jacobs, through her fictional character, Linda Brent, highlights scene after scene in which the white mistress, instead of aiding a slave woman, blames her for her own victimization. Like Douglass, she begins her narrative with "I was born a slave . . ." but details how puberty led to "The Trials of Girlhood":

> But I now entered upon my fifteenth year—a sad epoch
> in the life of a slave girl. My master began to whisper
> foul words in my ear. Young as I was, I could not remain

ignorant of their import. I tried to treat them with indifference or contempt. The master's age, my extreme youth, and the fear that his conduct would be reported to my grandmother, made him bear this treatment for many months. He was a crafty man, and resorted to many means to accomplish his purposes . . . He tried his utmost to corrupt the pure principles my grandmother had instilled. He peopled my young mind with unclean images, such as only a vile monster could think of.

—Harriet Jacobs, *Incidents in the Life of a Slave Girl*

Sexual victimization, maternity, and motherhood added another lens to slave narratives. While male narratives emphasized the man's "heroic journey," women's narratives, like Jacobs's, lifted the veil on sexual exploitation, which, in theory, should have allied all women.

But just as Douglass's autobiography inspired such writers as James Baldwin, Richard Wright, Ralph Ellison, Malcolm X, John Edgar Wideman, and Brent Staples, Jacobs's veiled autobiography generated a parallel tradition, one that would inspire Zora Neale Hurston, Ida B. Wells, Lorraine Hansberry, Maya Angelou, Angela Davis, and Jill Nelson, among others.

Critics maintain that a key feature of African American literature is "intertexuality"; that is, black writers engage in a literary dialogue across the generations. Zora Neale Hurston's celebration of folk culture spoke to Alice Walker; Alice Walker responded in her essays and stories celebrating Southern culture and ancestral heritage. Nathan McCall's *Makes Me Wanna Holler* opens a dialogue with Richard Wright about what makes a man. While racism may have blunted Bigger

Thomas's life, McCall argues forcefully that personal responsibility is a powerful tool against many demeaning aspects of prejudice.

As a writer, you too are engaging in a great literary tradition. You are answering, echoing ideas set forth by our literary ancestors. You are carrying forward our cultural dialogue to a new generation.

Writing, you bear witness to your inner voice and feelings. But your words also bear witness to common ideas and themes that herald and influence our lives today.

MY BEST ADVICE

*Read our literary ancestors. Their voices nurture
and shape your artistry.*

To be a good writer, read, then read some more. There are twelve months in a year. In your journal, commit to reading three new books a month—more if you can. (Appendix A is a good starting point.) Most important, *expand your horizons.* If you only read contemporary authors, read your nineteenth-century sisters and brothers! If you like political essays, read biographies. If you like historical texts, read spiritual affirmations. Self-help books, memoirs, histories, essays on social and political issues, books on finance, food, and much, much more have been written, and written well, by black authors.

**Read first *for sheer enjoyment.* Read second *for
craft and technique.***

A writer *always* learns from reading. Even if you think a prose piece isn't well done, reading it will refine your sense of literature, what you value, how you approach writing.

Look at this selection from James Baldwin's essay "Notes of a Native Son":

> *The day of my father's funeral had also been my nineteenth birthday. As we drove him to the graveyard, the spoils of injustice, anarchy, discontent, and hatred were all around us. It seemed to me that God himself had devised, to mark my father's end, the most sustained and brutally dissonant of codas. And it seemed to me, too, that the violence which rose all about us as my father left the world had been devised as a corrective for the pride of his eldest son. I had declined to believe in that apocalypse which had been central to my father's vision; very well, life seemed to be saying, here is something that will certainly pass for an apocalypse until the real thing comes along. I had inclined to be contemptuous of my father for the conditions of his life, for the condition of our lives. When his life had ended I began to wonder about that life and also, in a new way, to be apprehensive about my own.*

When you read this paragraph, you are immediately struck by the stark commingling of life and death. "Funeral" and "birthday" joined together are a sad irony; but Baldwin heightens the anguish when he tells us that the *son* who should be celebrating his birth is bearing witness to his *father's* death. All the joy associated with birthdays is undercut by the rituals of grief. From this highly personal vantage point, Baldwin expands the focus to include social disorder: "As we drove him to the graveyard, the spoils of injustice, anarchy, discontent, and hatred were all around us." While Baldwin doesn't specifically describe the "spoils," the reader is encouraged to imagine them.

"As we drove him to the graveyard" opens the landscape and encourages readers to think about a community's devastation so widespread that, while driving through town to the graveyard, it is visible everywhere. The words "injustice, anarchy, discontent, and hatred" have an emphatic rhythm and the words imply deep-rooted social, political, and emotional disorder.

Baldwin widens his focus yet again:

> It seemed to me that God himself had devised, to mark my father's end, the most sustained and brutally dissonant of codas. And it seemed to me, too, that the violence which rose all about us as my father left the world had been devised as a corrective for the pride of his eldest son.

By repeating "it seemed to me," Baldwin makes clear his particular perception that personal and social roles are linked to a religious world view. Indeed, in Baldwin's mind, God takes an active role in both his life and his father's death. "Brutally dissonant of codas" resonates with suggestions of inharmonious music, a violent requiem inappropriate to his father's life. "Corrective for pride" implies that Baldwin believes God is chastising him for rejecting his father's faith and for judging the father too harshly. The word "apocalypse" encourages comparison of the biblical prophetic visions of "end of the world" with visions of a present-day, riot-torn city. Among this disorder, Baldwin's words suggest guilt, a riot of emotions, and a personal disorder in thought and values.

"When his life had ended I began to wonder about that life and also, in a new way, to be apprehensive about my own" underscores perfectly the interconnection between a father's life and his son's, between a father's death and the potential for a son's metaphorical rebirth. As the essay continues, Baldwin weaves his personal remembrances with the political condition of being the black (not the white) son of America.

Baldwin's writing is celebrated because he is not afraid to invest his words with passion, nor is he afraid of linking the particular incidents of his life with the grand scale of social upheaval and change. Baldwin knows the two are inextricably linked. The personal *is* political. There are no vague abstractions in his prose. Everything is detailed. Consequently, Baldwin enables us to think and respond complexly to his multiplicity of emotions and ideas.

A writer's job is to make prose seem effortless. As a reader/artist, your job is to read for technique. *Why do the sentences flow so smoothly? How do details reflect the period, the values of an era? Why does description heighten credibility? Is the author trying to write objectively or subjectively? Does it matter?*

Like magicians, writers create marvelous effects. But behind each effect is a decision made by an author. Writers have a multitude of choices—choices that help them create art.

In your journal, commit to writing a paragraph about each essay or book you read. Don't simply write, "I liked it." Narrow your comments; be specific. What makes the essay wonderful? The topic? Descriptive detail? Rhythm and repetition? The voice of the writer? A cogent argument?

Studying other writers not only improves your writing, it also makes you a better editor of your own work. Besides inspiration, good writing requires skill—an attention to details and an awareness that the best writing comes from rewriting, from questioning the choices you make about the words you use.

Literary ancestors are your foundation. We all have a responsibility to know our literary heritage and to understand that our work is part of a larger continuum of voices entertaining, loving, praising, and sometimes criticizing our people. By engaging in an artistic dialogue with our literary forefathers and foremothers, you'll help to reshape what it means to be "free within ourselves." Perhaps, even more important, you'll discover new ways of chronicling our history, telling our stories—that will inspire and reverberate among generations of writers to come.

Read. Good writing depends on exposure to other voices. Read all you can.

EXERCISE 1

READING IMMERSION

Immerse yourself in reading. Just as you can't breathe without inhaling *and* exhaling, you can't develop as a writer without being a devoted reader.

Go to the bookstore or library and select three new and varied books reflecting our culture. You'll have great fun browsing, uncovering new authors. In your journal, begin a **"What to Read Next List"** to remind you of authors and titles to try in the future. (Clearly, books by all authors are potentially valuable to you as a writer. But, for now, focus on our African American heritage. Once you've become well acquainted with your own literary tradition, proceed to any and all books you're interested in.)

You may not read three books in a month, but try. Substitute reading time for television, housecleaning, or laundry. Carry a book everywhere—on the train, to the hairdresser's or doctor's office. Order "take-out" and curl up with a book instead of a hot stove and dirty dishes.

Browse, buy, or borrow terrific books from your local bookstore, a used bookstore, or a library. If you're strapped for time, look for collections of essays. June Jordan, bell hooks, Derrick Bell, and others, have written fabulous books with terrific and challenging essays. African American literature anthologies often include substantial sections on slave narratives and other nonfiction. Audiotapes are another resource. You'll find many autobiographies, memoirs, collections of essays, and spiritual guidance texts recorded for posterity. Listen closely for how the author unfolds his or her point of view and argument. Later, try to compare what you heard with the written word. Do the sentences have the same passion as the voice on the audiotape?

When selecting books, focus on variety. Mix male and female authors. Mix genres. Mix time periods. Eldridge Cleaver's *Soul on Ice* (1968) reflects the angry political rhetoric of the 1960s; Elaine Power's *A Taste of Power: A Black Woman's Story* (1994) is a more contemporary memoir, reflecting the author's belief that the Black Panther Party repressed women. These two books juxtaposed make for an interesting dynamic. Likewise, contrast the formal, moderating tone of Booker T.

Washington's *Up from Slavery* (1900–01) with the passionate, analytical tone of Ellis Cose's *The Rage of the Privileged Class* (1995).

If you buy or borrow more than three books this month, bravo! Be inspired by the books available—and remember, each time you read a book, you are pursuing your goal of becoming and being a better writer.

Select your first book and read for pleasure, both intellectual and emotional. When you've finished, move on to Exercise 2.

EXERCISE 2

READING AS A WRITER, STAGE ONE

Once you've finished reading your first book, pick up your journal and write a one-page response to the book. Be specific.

Was the book interesting? Exciting? Enlightening? Intellectually challenging? Dull? What made it so?

What ideas and feelings was the writer trying to communicate? Was she or he effective?

What did you like best? The author's message? Description? Narration? Viewpoint? Historical elements? Contemporary focus? Memories? Dialogue? Recreation of events?

What didn't you like?

Don't hesitate to write any response you think is relevant. The key is to focus on *your thoughts* about the book.

Read the book again. You can skim passages, but plan on spending an hour or two studying the book. As you're moving from page to page, mark with a highlighter those passages you thought were particularly good, particularly well written. You might highlight a lovely descriptive paragraph. Or a remembered dialogue scene between the main characters. You might highlight a mother-daughter scene, a courtroom scene, the introduction of a new character, the concluding paragraph, or an especially eloquent sentence.

As with a magnifying glass, you're isolating elements that make the book a success. Truly, all fine books are greater than the sum of their parts. But learning to write well is an incremental process—learning, bit by bit, what elements contribute to good writing and learning how to execute those aspects well.

When you thoughtfully reread a book, contemplating why a passage, a scene, or sentence is well done, you are training yourself to read for technique—the "how" of good writing.

With each element you highlight, ask: "Why do I like it?" "What makes this good writing?" "What did the writer choose to do or not to do?"

By developing the habit of more thoughtful reading, you'll acquire the habit of more thoughtful and skilled writing!

EXERCISE 3

READING AS A WRITER, STAGE TWO

For further study, select one of the passages you marked in the preceding exercise. Read it both silently and aloud. Study the passage, asking again: "Why do I like it? What makes this good writing? What did the author do to make it effective?"

Finally, ask, "What is the author teaching me about good writing?" In your journal, write at least three specific answers.

For example, one of my favorite essays is Alice Walker's "Beauty: When the Other Dancer Is the Self." It recounts how, at the age of eight, Alice Walker is blinded in one eye by a BB gun. The "accident" alters Walker's self-image and self-esteem. Ultimately, the words of her three-year-old daughter, who is a fan of the PBS program *Big Blue Marble,* helps to heal Walker's wounded self:

One day when I am putting Rebecca down for a nap, she suddenly focuses on my eye. Something inside me cringes, gets ready to try to protect myself. All children are cruel about physical differences, I know from experience, and that they don't always mean to be is another matter. I assume Rebecca will be the same.

But no-o-o-o. She studies my face intently as we stand, her inside and me outside her crib. She even holds my face maternally between her dimpled little hands. Then, looking every bit as serious and lawyerlike as her father, she says, as if it may possibly have slipped my attention: "Mommy, there's a world in your eye." (As in, "Don't be alarmed, or do anything crazy.") And then, gently, but with great interest: "Mommy, where did you get that world in your eye?"

For the most part, the pain left then . . .

That night I dream I am dancing to Stevie Wonder's song "Always" (the name of the song is really "As," but I hear it as "Always"). As I dance, whirling and joyous, happier than I've ever been in my life, another bright-faced dancer joins me. We dance and kiss each other and hold each other through the night. The other dancer has obviously come through all right, as I have done. She is beautiful, whole, and free. And she is also me.

Walker brilliantly evokes her own vulnerability and the grace of her daughter's love. But how, as a writer, does she achieve this? Read the above paragraphs again. Note how Walker establishes the expectation of being hurt. "Something inside me cringes . . ." Alice, the mother, expects, from experience, that a child might be cruel about physical differences. By establishing what she thinks will happen between her and her daughter, Walker positions herself and her readers for a surprise. The predictable becomes unpredictable. Rebecca, the child, acts as the wise mother.

Walker conjures the picture of Rebecca "maternally" holding her face with her "dimpled little hands." "Serious and lawyerlike as her father" also shows how the child is acting without childish self-interest. Indeed, Rebecca during this critical scene has reversed roles with her mother.

"But no-o-o," Walker writes, imitating the sound of a child. This sentence fragment serves as the critical transition between what Walker expects and the unexpected response from Rebecca. Likewise, the line "her inside and me outside her crib" heightens the tension between mother and child, the very tension that will be released by the child's actions and words.

Hearing Rebecca's voice come alive is critical to the emotional power of the scene. If Walker had left out the dialogue, left out the italicizing of "world" and "get," readers would miss the charm of the child's believing her mother had a world in her eye and had especially arranged it so.

In the final paragraph, the mother dreams she is dancing with another. The split self suggests, perhaps, that the mother is dreaming of Rebecca, who has radiated such love. But, again, unexpectedly, the "other dancer" is the self—the adult Walker, now "beautiful, whole, and free," realizing the dancer "is also me."

Descriptive visual details of Alice, Rebecca, and the other dancer enhance this prose. Active words, like "cringes," "whirling and joyous," make the scene come alive. Hearing the characters' voices—Alice Walker as narrator and Rebecca as wise child—makes the reader feel as though they're overhearing this critical scene. The suggestion of Stevie Wonder's music evokes melody, song, and dance.

The central thesis, *I love myself,* is made richer because Walker, instead of telling us, *shows* us how she came to this profound acceptance of self. The fact that her own child leads her to self-love engenders delight and empathy among her readers.

In my journal, I might write:

What is Walker teaching me about good writing?

ANSWER: Good writing means altering expectations, writing about what is unique, unexpected. (Walker not only challenges the stereotypical roles of mother and daughter, wise elder and ignorant child, but also challenges herself to see the beauty within herself.)

Good writing means not just telling, but re-creating significant events. It means using strong, descriptive language and dialogue. It is more effective for a reader to see, hear, and feel the characters than not.

Good writing means having something worthwhile to say. A strong thesis, an argument, a point of view are all essential to communicating with an audience.

In my journal, I might translate all of the above as reminders to:

- Show rather than tell my argument, my thesis.

- Re-create scenes when possible.

- Use strong, descriptive language. Contrasts in behavior and actions can help illuminate the unexpected.

- Dialogue, colloquial narration can help readers hear and empathize with characters.

- Use strong, active words. The characters are behaving now, in the present. They are active, not passive.

Remember, even if you don't have a degree in English or writing, you *can,* through thoughtful reading and analyzing, become a better writer. Take time to study books, essays, and articles, and they will become wonderful guides for you in creating better prose.

For each of the three books (or more!) you read during your month-long immersion, repeat Exercises 1 through 3. During this month, you'll train yourself to read like a working writer—you'll become more conscious of *what* you're reading, *how* the author constructed the work, and you'll become more articulate in describing what kinds of writing you like and why.

* * *

Keep your commitment to read at least three books a month, to highlight and study specific passages, and to record in your journal what the authors teach you about writing.

Enjoy expanding your literary horizons!

THREE

GATHERING IDEAS, GATHERING SUBJECTS

A good nonfiction writer actively gathers material for potential subjects. Subjects can be widely or narrowly focused, highly intellectual or emotional, or a combination of both. The key is to gather ideas and information consciously from the world around you. Everything you read, see, hear, or experience is a potential subject. Every idea, intuition, or ancestral tie you investigate helps you to become a better, more thoughtful writer.

Writing a memoir, autobiography, or personal essay may seem to require no research. After all, it's your life, isn't it? But *living your life* means being open to ideas and experiences, being intellectually and emotionally curious. Research—whether a formal library search or an informal interview—can bolster, expand, and deepen the significance of your personal perspective and experiences.

REMEMBER: Solid research is essential for quality prose. Sometimes your research needs may be minimal; other times, your needs will be critical. Writing a personal essay about learning to play the piano may encourage you to wonder why it is so much harder for a forty-two-year-old than a seven-year-old. Research on brain networks and motor skills will provide answers. You may write a paragraph on brain physiology that not only makes your essay more comprehensive but provides the key to make your writing transcend "good" and become excellent. Or maybe you're writing a memoir about your grandfather's tales as a Tuskegee airman. Further research about military warfare and discrimination may provide a social and political context for your grandfather's tales. Maybe you can arrange a reunion of surviving airmen and tape their stories. And you may discover that, among his peers, your grandfather's stories become even more vivid and emotionally stirring. Likewise, unearthing a photo of your grandfather as a twenty-two-year-old airman may fundamentally alter your view of the "old man."

PLAIN FACT: Being more knowledgeable never hurt anyone! Research is another word for investigating what interests you.

Just like writing, research can and should be a continuing process.

In addition to your writing-exercise journal, **get a set of index cards, multicolored or plain.** Carry them everywhere in your purse, briefcase, or tote bag so that you can record ideas or connections between ideas. These cards will serve as your intellectual capital, your road map for the issues and subjects that interest you.

For example, you may read in the *Washington Post* that a political campaign lacks issues. On an index card cite the article, section, and page reference and list what issues you think the campaign should be about. Or you may hear a luncheon speaker talking of a woman's need to understand financial management. Jot down the speaker's name, contact number, and your response to her main ideas.

But most important, consider what makes the issue significant for you or for your family or community. How does it connect to your views, opinions, and attitudes toward life?

Second, establish files. Purchase an elaborate teak filing cabinet, if you choose, but, in truth, a cardboard box will serve, if it is well organized with folders and labels.

Your files should hold your index cards, magazine clippings, newspaper excerpts, photographs, essays and articles, Internet and CD-ROM-based materials—in short, anything and everything that stimulates your intellectual and emotional passions.

Divide your files into categories. Be attuned to what these categories *reveal about you*. Files with categories like "Finances," "Environmental Issues," "Elder Care," and "Race and Economics" are vastly different from files labeled "Spiritual Awakenings," "Genealogy," "African Masks," and "Scott Joplin." All of us have interests, but only those we're most intellectually and emotionally intrigued by represent the finest material for our writing projects.

Every few months, revisit your filing system. Do you need to broaden or narrow your categories? Are your files accessible, easy to retrieve? Can they be better organized?

Also, never be afraid to obsess about a category. For a time, you may be interested only in information about shaman rituals in the Caribbean and African American cultures. By all means—*obsess*—you may very well be collecting the material for an important essay or book. Conversely, don't be afraid to have one category with only one sheet of information!

MY BEST ADVICE

Ask questions and delight in the search for answers.
Pursue your passions and celebrate your desire to understand
yourself and your world.

If a subject stirs your soul, it is worth saving. You never know when you might turn it into an essay, article, or even a book.

Don't worry about being an information pack rat! Every few years you may want to re-examine your files and toss any items you've lost interest in. But if something still holds sway over your heart, keep it! For over ten years, I kept a newspaper article about the 1921 Tulsa Race Riot before I ever typed a word of my historical novel, *Magic City.* I still have files on Brazilian folk myths, on Reggae, slave narratives, witchcraft and sorcery, on Marie Laveau, slave folk songs, vampires, Frederick Douglass, and Alexander Dumas, to name a few.

While many subjects will grip your heart, none is more intense and more intimate than *you*—your own life and family history. You may never wish to write about yourself and your specific heritage; so be it! But life creeps up on all of us, and what you've sworn you'd never do, you may one day be tempted to do.

Growing older inspires reflection, a reconsideration of your life and how it fits the pattern of your ancestors' lives. Letters, photographs, family scrapbooks you've once lost or neglected, you now miss and regret. Maybe, too hurriedly, you cleared away the mementos of a loved one's life. Perhaps your son's wedding makes you long for more baby pictures, graduation certificates, and the Mother's Day card he wrote when he was five.

Illness, a traumatic accident, thoughts on our own mortality can well make us long to write a memoir, testifying to life's struggles and rewards. You may write to cauterize the pain of poverty and abuse. Or you may wish to celebrate the bittersweet joys of matrimony, as Shirlee Taylor Haizlip did, in her book *In the Garden of Our Dreams: Memoirs of a Marriage.* You may even want to share family recipes, along with stories about how each entree was created.

Whether your life events are pleasurable or sad, tangible items—letters, journals, photos, videos—help to refresh memories, making them concrete again, sensual.

Even if you're uncertain now about writing a memoir or autobiography, I urge you to cherish all items that illuminate how you and your family live. Letters, photos, diaries can be truly special. Save your children's journals. Save the letter your father wrote to you when you went away to college. Save your love letters, the first "serious" Valentine you received. Catalog videos of key family events—a graduation party, a reunion, an aunt's ninety-second birthday, your daughter's triumphant finish of the Boston Marathon.

Take time to record your family elders speaking of their lives and memories. Keep a diary of your own thoughts. Each Thanksgiving, audiotape your family expressing what you're thankful for—what they remember as blessings, as fond memories from the year.

Remember: All fine writing, to a degree, is about the self. Your unique view of the world colors each of your perceptions. But your viewpoint should never be based on prejudice or unsubstantiated facts. Rather, with an open heart and an open mind, seek new information, new experiences, new ideas to think, feel, and write about.

Great writers are continually curious, continually developing.

Gather your note cards and prepare for a trip to the library, cyberspace, your family home, and community archives. Your goal is to become comfortable with exploring resources and developing familiarity with texts, electronic and historical materials, oral histories, and photographic and historical archives.

EXERCISE 1

EMBRACING THE WORLD
IN PRINT AND MEDIA

Take an afternoon and visit the reference and periodical sections of a great library. Although regional libraries are wonderful, sometimes your community library's central branch has more complete offerings as well as a helpful staff to assist in your search for information and ideas.

A university or college library can be a real treasure trove. Many, like those at the University of Colorado, UCLA, Howard University, Spelman College, and Chicago State University, have special collections on the African diaspora, folk history, the Harlem Renaissance, westward migrations, and much more. Call or visit your local community, university, and college libraries, and inquire about resources.

If it is within your means, consider traveling to great libraries. You will be awed by the knowledge and resources housed in the Library of Congress in Washington. If you're ever near or in New York, don't pass up a chance to visit Harlem's Schomburg Center for Research in Black Culture. It is truly a marvelous, soul-inspiring place. Also, the Fisk University Library in Tennessee has broad resources, and Tulane University is a must-stop for anyone interested in Amistad history.

If you live in a small town or rural community, check whether your local library has loan privileges with a consortium of statewide and national libraries. You'll be amazed at how electronic access and interlibrary loans have made a multitude of libraries, hundreds of miles away, seem just around the corner.

Spend a day (that's right, a day! Brown-bag your lunch, if you have to) sifting through national papers such as the *New York Times,* the *Washington Post,* the *Chicago Tribune,* the *LA Times,* as well as such international papers as the *London Times.* Look, too, for community and regional papers with an emphasis on African American issues. Some are the *Detroit Metro News,* the *Informant* in Arizona, the *Atlanta Daily World,* and the Harlem-based *Amsterdam News.*

Familiarize yourself with magazines. *Upscale, Today's Black*

Woman, Essence, Jet, Ebony, and the new *Savoy* focus clearly on African American community issues. And there is a dizzying array of magazines specializing in everything from archeology to photography to geography to New Age spiritualism to children's literature to hideaway islands around the world. Others, like the *Oxford American, National Geographic, Smithsonian, Civilization,* and *Archeology,* have superb in-depth coverage of a variety of general and regional topics.

Don't forget to explore university and independent journals. *Black Renaissance, Renaissance Noir, Callaloo, Obsidian II,* as well as *The Seattle Review, African American Literature Review, Dialogue* all offer nonfiction on a range of topics.

If your research is successful and bears fruit, you'll want to visit the library day after day. One goal, however, should be to discover an enriching magazine, a journal, or a newspaper subscription you simply must have!

If you can, subscribe to a few magazines, journals, or newspapers. Don't stop visiting the library, but there's nothing more glorious than having your very own copy of a magazine, journal, or paper to savor! Don't just subscribe to magazines that reflect your current ideas and interests; look for magazines that challenge and stretch you intellectually and emotionally.

Before you leave the library, fill your index cards with at least *three research ideas* you're interested in writing about. On an index card for each idea, note the subject, why it appeals to you, and what you'd like to know more about. Then list a minimum of three print-based research sources that could provide further information. For example, on index cards I may write:

African Americans in the West

⚡ Interested in writing an essay or book about my family history.

⚡ Interested in why some of my family migrated west in the 1950s. Those who remained in the northeastern industrial belt experienced poverty, declining city services and school systems. Those who went west leaped into middle-class suburbia, enjoying home values and solid public education system.

⚡ What is the history of African American migrations?

⚡ When did African Americans first go west? Why is so little written about westward migrations compared with southern to northern migrations?

⚡ What social, racial, and political conditions did blacks encounter in their migrations?

SEE: *In Search of the Racial Frontier: African Americans in the American West, 1528–1990,* by Quintard Taylor (W. W. Norton, 1998).

SEE: *African Americans in the West: A Bibliography of Secondary Studies,* by Bruce A. Glasrud (Alpine Texas: Center for Big Bend Studies, 1998).

SEE: *African Americans on the Western Frontier,* ed. by Billington and Hardaway (University Press of Colorado).

SEE: *The Black West,* by William Loren Katz (Touchstone/ Simon & Schuster, 1990).

Many libraries now stock media resources and photos, slides, and microfilms of newspapers, maps, and census materials. Since media and archival materials are rarely loaned out, you should begin searching the media resources of the libraries in your community. Select a public library, a university library, and a special subject museum to visit. For example, I would visit the Scottsdale Public Library, Arizona State University, and the Arizona Historical Society for media and archival materials. To my research cards on "westward migrations," I might add:

ASU photographs of early settlers, black cowboys; VHS on "African Americans in the West" (KAET Production); "The Story of Lt. Henry O. Flipper" (PBS Video).
Arizona Historical Museum: microfiche newspapers from Arizona and neighboring states; photos, slides, land-use and population maps, etc.

Later, as I become more involved with my research, I may expand my media and archival search to include libraries and historical museums in western states. Through a phone call or a computer catalog search of libraries, I may discover that the Los Angeles Public Library has the most extensive collection of early western photos and African American newspapers from the 1800s.

Select one of your research index cards (it can be the same or different from the research idea you used earlier). Visit your public and university libraries and special subject museums for media and archival resources. Remember, you don't have to spend hours on research. For now, you're jotting down leads for your research topic and exploring resources available to you. A week, month, or even a year from now, when you're ready to write an essay or book, you'll be grateful for your index cards. You'll also be more at ease in exploring library and historical museum resources.

EMBRACING THE WORLD ELECTRONICALLY

As with print materials, it helps to become familiar with information available in the exploding mediums of cyberspace and CD-ROM.

I am a true fan of Encarta's *Africana* and of other electronic reference encyclopedias, such as Collier's and the World Book. Many reference CD-ROMs are available through libraries, but you may want to purchase one for home use. For example, the *National Geographic* has *all* of its magazine issues on CD; you can search for subjects in numerous cross-references.

On-line, there are many electronic representations of typical print magazines and newspapers, like *Time, Newsweek, Black Issues Book Review, USA Today,* and the *New York Times.* But on-line resources have their own cyberspace life too. The Internet offers a slew of national and international resources. There are literally hundreds of sites on health, women's issues, Caribbean studies, adventure travel, African American history, home remodeling, and so on. I'm convinced that you can pick almost any subject, add www—*fill in the blank*—dot.com, and you'll find immediate information.

Search engines like Altavista, Giggle, Dogpile, Yahoo, and AOL Keyword make it easy to sort, shift, and select information on almost any topic. Web sites like Africana.com, NetNoir, and BlackVoices.com are also excellent resources.

If you're new to the world of computers, it is worthwhile to invest in a course on computer use. But, again, check out the community bulletin board of your library. Often squeezed in among Children's Story Hour and Reading Groups, you'll find short courses on computer research methods. If your library doesn't offer such a course, try requesting it. Supportive, technologically literate librarians can help get you started, but don't be ashamed of trial and error. A computer is a tool, and, as with all such tools, you become more expert with practice.

Whether you're an experienced or inexperienced computer user, spend an hour investigating at least three new search engines, Web links, and CD-ROM-based reference materials. **Make certain to computer "bookmark" or list in your journal search engine addresses and Web links that seem most helpful.** While electronic-based information is growing exponentially, not all sites are equally efficient or informative.

Next, select one of your research index cards from Exercise One and try to gather electronically more information about your topic. For example, selecting my research topic of African American's westward migration, I would key "westward migration" into an Internet search engine to see what pops up. Undoubtedly, there will be dead ends, but there will also be some rewarding avenues for further research.

To my index card on African Americans in the West, I would now add the following research leads:

African Americans in the West

SEE: Internet research sources—e.g., Africana.com; net.noir; look for Internet connections to libraries, societies, and professional organizations devoted to western studies.

Once your index card is filled with print and electronic-based leads, you are ready to launch into further research to support your writing.

Next, try another two searches. You may use your remaining two research cards or search for something entirely new. For example, using Altavista.com, you might type in "folk medicine" and see what you uncover. Or "African Americans in golf history," or "slave work songs," or any other three interests, and see what your computer's search engines yield.

With practice, you'll become comfortable with computer searches, and you'll be able to open the door to new methods of knowing and understanding the world of ideas. Don't worry if you become frustrated. Learning to use the computer in small, concentrated doses can be more effective than endless, random surfing. Bookmark what's interesting and potentially useful to you and pass on the rest!

EXERCISE 3

EMBRACING THE WORLD
IN YOUR NEIGHBORHOOD

Libraries and computers are valuable resources, but you also need to know how to gather information through interviews, records, and archives. In your community, you live among expert witnesses. Neighbors, family, community workers, postal workers, ministers, mechanics, and nurses, all have significant knowledge that you can gather simply by asking questions. Asking questions about trends, events, issues, and values affecting the community can bring you an incredible wealth of specific and personal knowledge. Ask any elder about their memories, and you'll likely be inspired to write histories, folk tales, or essays about our changing world.

While a neighbor's tales may not have the most objective, wide-angled view of "truth," such personal tales can inspire a sense of dramatic immediacy and empathy. A neighbor's recounting of his participation in civil rights marches in Selma may seem narrow in its scope and range, but nonetheless, his personal history can convey differing truths from those printed in textbooks.

Search out someone who has lived in your community for at least ten years. Ask him or her to tell you about any community changes witnessed firsthand. Chances are you'll open a storehouse of local news touching on such varying issues as education, population, crime, political upsets, family structure, health, transit, and business concerns.

* * *

Consider: has anything you've heard about in your community piqued your curiosity? Are there some events, details you'd like to investigate further? Write down specific questions, concerns, clarifications you believe might be worthwhile to pursue.

Ask two neighbors about your questions and concerns. Is the second person's knowledge and perspective similar to or dissimilar from the first neighbor's? What do you think accounts for any differences? Any similarities?

Neighboring churches, mosques, and temples can be a fount of information regarding a community's spiritual development and values. They are also great repositories for rituals of celebration, such as marriage and baptism, as well as for rituals of grief, such as memorial and funeral services.

Even the church's worship services open windows into the nature of the parishioners. Is the organist's playing restrained? Is the choir dominated by enthusiastic young people? What is the mood of the church? Its tone? How does art—statues, stained glass, paintings, icons—contribute to the parishioners' spiritual identity?

If you can, ask the pastor/priest/minister what types of information they gather and keep. What changes has the church/temple/mosque/meeting house undergone and why? You may be surprised by what you'll uncover. Even the spirituals sung over the years may give you insight into how a congregation has reacted to the world. Are there distinct differences between the songs sung during the 1960s' civil rights era and the songs sung during the 1990s' era of relative economic optimism? How have prior church leaders influenced social and community activism?

Discover at least one issue you'd like to pursue in depth. Write it on an index card, along with your questions and ideas for research. (Alternatively, you can select one of the research ideas you wrote down for Exercise One.)

In your wider neighborhood, look for community groups—professional associations like a blues musicians' group, art gallery, coffeehouse poetry series, theater or dance troupe. Consider, too, local chapters of organizations like the NAACP, One Hundred Black Men Alpha Phi Alpha, Delta Sigma Theta, or Jack and Jill. Ask questions about the mission and history of the organization or association. Request to review any print or electronic materials that may show the development and changing character of the group. Interview the president, owner, curator, or artistic director; interview a member, employee, visitor, or artist.

You should uncover at least one issue you'd like to explore further. For example, a local musicians' group might provide insight not only about changing musical styles but also about issues of "artistic growth vs. economic survival" or "drug abuse and the blues."

Last, come full circle and search for new knowledge and information in your familial home. Perhaps you'll visit a great-aunt or your parents or grandparents and ask to see their records—the family bible, genealogies, diaries, letters, artifacts, antiques, quilts—that tell chapters of your family's history you didn't know or barely knew. On an index card, write down the issues you'd have to investigate if you were writing a memoir or an article about a relative.

* * *

You should now feel more at ease in gathering information and choosing potential subjects to write about. Now that you're alert to your world, alert to your own thirst for knowledge, you should feel as though the entire planet is "host" to your curiosity.

You cannot write about what you don't know.

- Research your world using various mediums, electronic and print, CD ROM-based and Internet-based.

- Talk with people, ask questions, interview them. Most folks (me included) love to tell tales.

- Uncover community histories through the local church, historical societies, museums, etc.

- Be attuned to how events are influenced by and reveal human history and drama.

- Explore how things—concrete items, like a painting stored in the attic, an embroidered tablecloth, an old diary—have histories, too, and mirror a personal or wider social significance.

Your files and your index cards are ways to map *your knowledge of yourself and how you experience your world.*

You've taken another step in your journey to become a better writer. Celebrate!

FOUR

PURSUING DREAMS:
Bruised Egos and Hard Work

Is writing hard work? Absolutely!
But has anything you ever really desired to accomplish been easy? More important, would you want it to be easy? Easy gains mean easy satisfaction. Hard work requiring sweat and concentration often yields profound satisfaction.

Most writers experience, at one time or another, sheer terror and overwhelming frustration. Some days you'll lie in bed, emphatically convinced you'll never write a decent sentence. Other days, you'll soar, feeling your words energizing you, leading you to greater understanding of yourself and the world around you.

Most writers write because they must. The process, unfortunately, sometimes locks you in misery and can undermine the creativity you need to excel. By accepting painful aspects of the process as a natural extension of life, you'll find some ease and comfort. You'll also feel an ecstatic thrill that will sustain you for days, even months, when you've written an essay particularly well.

MY BEST ADVICE

Believe in yourself—always. Accept your imperfections, but don't accept the possibility of failing.

Composing words is similar to composing a meaningful life. There are good days and bad days, but, always, your aim is to search for joy, beauty, harmony, and grace to add to your life. Composing literature—*trying to compose literature*—is a glorious calling.

Even when you make mistakes or belittle yourself for actual or imagined flaws and faults, remember to cheer yourself onward. Struggling to reach the mountaintop is infinitely preferable to staying at the bottom, too afraid to make the climb.

We tell our children, relations, and friends "to do the best you can," "to enjoy what you're doing." How often do we forget to give ourselves the same advice? The thoughtful nurturing you give to a friend, spouse, or child you must remember to give to yourself.

I spent years berating myself for not writing more . . . for not writing better. No one likes a complainer; I didn't even like myself.

Like a cup half-empty or half-full, I needed to celebrate what I *did* accomplish, to establish a pattern of success for myself. Baby steps count! So I counted the days when I sat down to work (even when nothing productive happened). I counted the days when I wrote only one sentence. When I wrote only two sentences, three, then four sentences. And you know what? After a few weeks, I had a pattern for sitting down and writing. I also had a growing stack of pages that served as tangible evidence that I was becoming a writer!

A writing professor once said to me, "Write a page a day, and in a year you'll have a book." Well, it's not quite that easy. But note the logic: a page a day gives you 365 pages. Wow! For a time, a "page a day" became my mantra. Some days I didn't get a page; some days I got several pages! But I reasoned that if, on average, I reached the goal of a page a day, like baby steps turning into a confident stride, I would be on my way to completing a book. It is amazing how the thought—a page a day—comforted me during dark times.

You, too, dear writer, could and should be on your way. Establish a pattern of success by celebrating what you *do* accomplish each day! Don't bemoan what you don't accomplish. Think: *What I don't accomplish today is tomorrow's opportunity for success.*

This sounds so simple, doesn't it? Yet I can honestly say that I became more productive when I broke the cycle of scolding myself and, instead, celebrated what I *did* accomplish (no matter how small or seemingly insignificant). Like a penny saved, a single well-written sentence can be as important as a paragraph or a page filled with words.

Strike a bargain with yourself:

1) Write only what you feel passionate about writing.

2) Be disciplined. Establish a set time and place for writing. Inspiration can carry you far, but a steady pace of writing can be just as (sometimes more) productive.

3) If, after two hours, your writing is going poorly, get up, go out, read a book, visit the library. Do not lock yourself into a negative writing cycle. Sometimes ideas need to incubate, and there is always tomorrow for a newly energized start.

Most people who choose to write want to write well. However, high expectations don't justify self-flagellation. Compassion for yourself is extremely important. You won't continue writing if you lock yourself in a cycle of self-abuse. You'll write more and better if you find ways to soothe your stress.

Music, art, a vase of flowers, a bright room to work in, your favorite cup of tea; all these can enhance the mood for writing. Discover what works best for you.

When words seem locked inside you, try "free writing." For ten to fifteen minutes, write in your journal without censoring or editing, just letting the pen flow and shape words. Not only does this release stress, but most often you'll find a turn of phrase or an idea that will steer you toward productive writing. If not, then take a walk, play with your children, find some joy. Bake bread, visit the library, listen to spirituals, celebrate your life and labors.

A good writer writes. When the writing doesn't go well, have the courage to come back, later that day or the next day, with a full commitment to try again to write well and strong.

Relish dealing with the hard parts of writing because that's when you're learning the most. You're learning discipline; you're learning new skills. If writing was always easy, you wouldn't feel such wonderful satisfaction when you've done it right.

Writing should be your daily priority.

But what about my day job? Child care? Grocery shopping? Spending time with my husband? My children? Balancing the checkbook? Comparison shopping at Costco?

Ironically, many of us have too much that fills our time, yet many of us, nonetheless, are expert at wasting our time. Time is finite. We *will* die. We *will* grow older. But of the minutes, hours, and days allotted to us—how many do we fill with things that don't enrich, stimulate, or entertain us?

Think more consciously about the time you "waste." By "waste," I mean, spending time on things that don't inspire you spiritually, intellectually, or emotionally. Certainly, some waste is unavoidable. For example, I HATE laundry, HATE unloading the dishwasher, and HATE attending mandatory meetings that take an hour when ten minutes would have served. Life isn't always perfect, but time still remains an ally if you're conscientious about how you use it.

Think about what you can do to change your use of time. Reading a good book and keeping a writing journal, for example, can productively fill time while you're waiting for a dentist, a client, a bank teller. Even a lunch hour can be time enough to review your research ideas on index cards. Books on tape can enhance a commute. For myself, I have learned to live with less orderliness at home; socks, in particular, have a hard time getting sorted, and paper plates are often used at meals. I never attend a meeting without my journal, and more than once I've tuned out a repetitious speech and scribbled notes for my next project.

When my kids are at school and when I'm not teaching, I DO try to write as much as possible. I unplug the phone, stop checking e-mail, and IGNORE all house chores. Frankly, though, cleaning bathrooms is preferable to writer's block!

During days long past, I used to get up at four o'clock each morning to ensure I had writing time. Eventually, this took a physical toll, and I've now learned I can write—breathe—exist better, if I get a good night's sleep.

You may have a day job, a growing family, a demanding travel schedule, unavoidable responsibilities—who doesn't? Cut or condense your wasteful time when and where you can. But love yourself enough to devote at least an hour or two each day to writing. Your career relies on *you* to fulfill your dreams. Once you find an hour or two to write, you'll be surprised by how much easier it becomes to find even more time. Like a self-fulfilling prophecy, success at finding writing time often breeds more time for good writing.

A visit to an artists' colony can be helpful, as well. *Artists and Writers Colonies: Retreats, Residencies, and Respite for the Creative Mind* by Gail Hellund Bowler, 1995, has an inclusive listing of colonies that can provide respite from the real world for a week or several weeks. There are also fellowships from Associated Writing Programs, community-based art councils, the Mary Roberts Rinehart Foundation, and others. These can help you gain crucial recognition and financial support. However, even if you aren't awarded a fellowship, you'll continue to write. You may want to seek out a writers' group such as the Carolina African American Writers Collective, the

Harlem Writers Guild, or the Eugene B. Redmond Writers' Club in Illinois. The National Writers' Voice Project, through its affiliation with the YMCA, sponsors both beginning and advanced community-based workshops. Or you may want to create a writers' group as a supportive network, composed of other writers. It may include friends or family members, or it may be one "trusted reader" who will seriously (and honestly) respond to your writing. It is far more valuable to have a reader who is critical of your writing than one who spares your feelings by responding dishonestly. Fellowships, scholarships, writers' retreats make writing easier, but they don't change a basic fact: *"To be a writer, write!"*

If you must slow down and write only two hours a day or one hour a day, okay. Do the best you can. Children will grow. Job demands will lessen. Remain positive. Write on your lunch hour. During breaks. A successful friend of mine manages to write in the pediatrician's waiting room! Amazing, isn't it? But not so amazing if you remember to carry your journal everywhere. In any given day, there are small moments we can all reclaim as our own. The simple truth is: ***If you wait for life to be perfect before committing yourself to a career as a writer, you'll wait forever.***

REMEMBER: Writing consistently for small amounts of time will reward you far more than inconsistent binges.

Whatever your situation, stop and congratulate yourself for the writing that you've done so far. Remember that it was the tortoise, not the hare, which won the race.

GOAL SETTING

If you've come this far, you know you can go farther in your development as a writer. Take ten minutes and write down your goals.

Long-term goals: What do you want to accomplish as a writer? How many books do you dream of writing? What kind of books? Do you have a particular audience you want to reach? Children? Young men? A general nonfiction audience? What do you want to communicate to your audience? What ideas? What themes? What do you want to be remembered for as a writer? Your social consciousness? Your life story? What skills do you want to improve?

Over a lifetime, what accomplishments as a writer would make *you* most proud?

Short-term goals: What are you going to do on a daily basis to help you achieve your long-term goals as a writer? Be specific. "Write," yes, of course. But how much? When? Days when the air conditioning shuts off; your dog gets lost, then found; your children are ill? Do you have a back-up plan for accomplishing your writing goals? Do you stay up late? Add an extra hour of writing to each day for a week?

Be sure to create a realistic schedule for yourself. Writing seven days a week doesn't work for everyone. Even when I'm not teaching, I schedule one day a week for miscellaneous chores. It's also important, of course, to reserve time for rest and relaxation.

Finally, is there any additional reading you want to do? Research? Exercises you should do to succeed in any or all of your short- and long-term goals?

* * *

Once you've written down your long- and short-term goals, type them and paste them on a wall above your desk; also, tape a copy inside your journal. When you're feeling overwhelmed or anxious, look at your goals and remember that *you* selected them, and that without *your dedication,* there is no magic wand to make them come true.

Believe in yourself and your dreams!

EXERCISE 2

CONFRONTING FEARS

What are you afraid of ?

Take some time to think hard about this question. What scares you most about becoming and being a writer?

Write down your fears on paper. Any common themes? Or maybe you have one huge fear? Ask yourself what it is and why it frightens you.

Fears are deeply personal and particular. However, time and again, both fiction and nonfiction writers, both experienced and inexperienced writers, have expressed the following fears:

I'm afraid I won't be a good writer.
You won't become a better writer if you don't try.

I'm afraid I won't get published.
You won't know until you complete an essay and try.

I'm afraid readers won't like my work.
You won't revise and improve your work until you invite readers to respond to your work.

"Try." A powerful word. You *will* fail as a writer if you don't try. Fear can paralyze the best of us. Even being published won't guarantee that your confidence can't be shaken or that you'll never again doubt your writing ability. The best way to stay centered is to focus on what you're trying to say to an audience. Sometimes I imagine I'm writing to my children, telling them what they might need to know to live a better life. Sometimes I flat-out remind myself that life is limited and that if I don't achieve my dreams, then I've cheated myself of living fully. I'd also be a hypocrite, for how can I tell my children to "try" for their dreams if I don't try for mine?

REMEMBER: Courage is doing that which you fear.

If one essay doesn't get published, write another. If respected readers don't like your work, listen to their opinions and consider revisions. Try harder to capture and convey your vision in words. Writing is communication—a powerful social act between yourself and an audience waiting to read your thoughts, your ideas.

Review the fears you've written down—are any of them truly crippling? Use your fears to motivate—say "I can" instead of "I can't." Take your list of fears and scratch them out with a nice thick marker. Then crumple the sheet, tear it into bits, and toss it in the trash. Believe me, these small actions will make you feel wonderful. (If you need to repeat this exercise every month until you turn ninety, then do so! Fears can recur, but so can your strength to overcome them!)

This is your one and only life. Don't cheat yourself on your goals.

EXERCISE 3

SEARCHING FOR INSPIRATION

Select an author you admire and spend an afternoon researching her career. There is often the perception that writers never stumble in their ascent to become "overnight sensations." When we see a finished book, we forget or are unaware of the author's years of effort and anxiety, her discarded pages and struggle to get published. A writer, like anyone else, experiences child-care problems, racism, sexism, professional jealousy, writer's block, and insecurities. No special glow protects her from unfairness, pain, depression, or hostility. The brutal fact remains that, despite hardships, successful writers hold fast to their dreams and create, regardless of the obstacles. This is worth remembering and celebrating! Encourage your own stubbornness and steadfastly pursue your career goals.

Magazines and journals such as *Callaloo, Black Issues Book Review, Poets and Writers,* and the *African American Literature Review* regularly provide author interviews. Local libraries often carry video interviews or documentaries of such celebrated authors as James McBride, Alice Walker, James Baldwin, Langston Hughes, and Zora Neale Hurston. On-line bookstores (Amazon.com, BarnesandNoble.com, Borders.com) promote contemporary author interviews and interactive question-and-answer sessions; also, many of these sites will refer you to an author's home page and e-mail tie-in.

Autobiographies and memoirs, in particular, provide moving glimpses into authors' lives. *Black Boy* is a heart-wrenching glimpse into Richard Wright's development as both a man and writer:

> *Later that day I rummaged through drawers and found Granny's address; I wrote to her, pleading with her to come and help us. The neighbors nursed my mother night and day, fed us and washed our clothes. I went through the days with a stunned consciousness, unable to believe what had happened. Suppose Granny did not come? I tried not to think of it. She had to come. The utter loneliness was now terrifying. I had been suddenly thrown emotionally upon my own. Within an hour the half-friendly world that I had known had turned cold and hostile. I was too frightened to weep. I was glad that my mother was not dead, but there was the fact that she would be sick for a long, long time, perhaps for the balance of her life. I became morose. Though I was a child, I could no longer feel as a child, could no longer react as a child.*

Richard Wright, despite poverty and prejudice, grew up to pen both a best-selling memoir and the highly acclaimed novel *Native Son*. At seventeen, he induced a white co-worker to lend him his public library card. Reading nearly every book in the library, Wright was able to shape his goal to be a writer. Once he found his dream, he never retreated from it.

* * *

After researching the career of an admired author, contemplate how his struggles to be a successful writer may help you to put your fears and self-doubts in perspective. In your journal, write three positive steps you can take to improve your attitude about writing.

Above all, remember that you're already successful, because you're devoting time to becoming a better writer. *Success doesn't come easily.* Success comes from devotion and hard work.

Since you started this book, you've been reading, writing, thinking, observing, and motivating yourself to become a better writer. Bravo! If your journal is more than half full, purchase another. If your index cards and files are starting to bulge, reorganize them to make more room.

The next six chapters are devoted to the writing of nonfiction. You'll plunge deeper into the world of ideas and more challenging writing skills. Don't hurry your learning. Don't berate yourself if your execution as a writer is less advanced than your understanding. Repeat exercises if you need to. Focusing on process, and practice will undoubtedly make you a better writer. Think of each successive chapter in this book as another opportunity to celebrate and enhance your creativity.

REMEMBER: You are a writer.

PART II

AUTOBIOGRAPHY

FIVE

SELF-DEFINITION
AND REBIRTH

Life stories. Life histories. Life memories.

Affirming the self is the root of African American literature.

For centuries, racist practices and laws deemed African Americans as less than people. Even the U.S. Constitution pronounced slaves as 3/5 of a person; thus, seeming to validate and encourage heinous stereotypes of black people. During the eighteenth and nineteenth centuries, many whites considered black people to be subhuman, "apelike," or else stunted, like "perennial children," incapable of growing intellectually and morally.

Rescuing oneself from a white landscape that denigrated your self and encouraged your silence was an extraordinarily heroic, spiritual, and political act of will.

Ever since the European Renaissance, the ability to read

and write was equated with reason. Humans, it was argued, showed themselves superior to animals through their words and literary output. American slave-traders, however, discounted Africans' considerable linguistic talents and made the assumption that their languages were equivalent to communication among subhuman species.

Once slaves demonstrated their facility in learning American English, this did not, ironically and paradoxically, lead to their elevation in white slave-holders' eyes. Whites' unconscious knowledge that slaves were indeed people, and were therefore due legal, social, and moral respect as a people, remained repressed. Blatant prejudice, greed, and the demand for an inexpensive labor force yielded illogical legal sanctions prohibiting the education of the very same slaves who were thought to be incapable of reason. Amazing.

Is it any wonder that slave men and women hungered to change whites' perceptions by giving voice to their inner lives and creating art?

By championing their selfhood in literature and in speeches, slaves helped to propel the abolitionist movement and the end of slavery as an American institution. Appendix A lists several books for further study of slave narratives. I urge you to read as many as you can. These works are the inspiration and foundation of African American autobiography.

Though slavery came to an end, the struggle for civil rights continued, and many authors told their life histories with the subtext of asserting their rights as citizens. The stories became more complex as freedom, interwoven with race, class, and gender as well as social migration (South to North, East to West), demanded new accommodations.

After slavery, Elizabeth Keckley wrote *Behind the Scenes; or, Thirty Years a Slave and Four Years in the White House* (1868):

> *Some of the freedmen and freedwomen had exaggerated ideas of liberty. To them it was a beautiful vision, a land of sunshine, rest, and glorious promise. They flocked to Washington, and since their extravagant hopes were not realized, it was but natural that many of them should bitterly feel the disappointment.*

Keckley went on to relate how, by working hard and eventually becoming seamstress to Mrs. Abraham Lincoln, she was able to provide a life for herself and her son. Hard work, literacy, and opportunity created by emancipation helped her make the transition from slave to independent woman. Racism and sexism were still American ills; nonetheless, Keckley felt proud and confident enough about her journey into selfhood *to write it down.*

Booker T. Washington's *Up from Slavery* (1901) details his journey from slavery to becoming a champion of education, racial integration, and black suffrage:

> *Perhaps the greatest thing that touched and pleased me most in connection with my starting for Hampton was the interest the many older coloured people took in the matter. They had spent the best days of their lives in slavery, and hardly expected to live to see the time when they would see a member of their race leave home to attend a boarding-school. Some of these older people would give me a nickel, others a quarter, or a handkerchief.*
>
> *Finally the great day came, and I started for Hampton.*

Langston Hughes, in his autobiography, *The Big Sea* (1940), focuses on how books opened him to a world of wonder. This respite from real-world struggles encouraged the artistic expression in the boy who would, one day, become one of America's greatest poets:

> When I was in the second grade, my grandmother took me to Lawrence to raise me. And I was unhappy for a long time, and very lonesome, living with my grandmother. Then it was that books began to happen to me, and I began to believe in nothing but books and the wonderful world in books—where if people suffered, they suffered in beautiful language, not in monosyllables, as we did in Kansas. And where almost always the mortgage got paid off, the good knights won, and the Alger boy triumphed.

As an adult, however, Hughes, on a different journey of self-revelation and exploration of his ancestral roots, admits:

> After a while, there came a time when I believed in books more than people—which, of course, was wrong. That was why, when I went to Africa, I threw all the books into the sea.

This impulse toward self-definition never left our people. Even proclaimed writers like Harriet Jacobs in *Our Nig* (1859), James Weldon Johnson in *The Autobiography of an Ex-Colored Man* (1912), Ralph Ellison in *Invisible Man* (1952), and Ernest Gaines in *The Autobiography of Miss Jane Pittman* (1971) created fiction infused with elements of autobiography. The struggle to be visible, to be heard, continues to be a vital theme for our community.

But in each of the examples above, the self is not independent of the community, of the social, political, and historical time in which the writer lived. Keckley, in her autobiography, contrasts her practical attitudes toward freedom with those who had more "extravagant hopes." Washington suggests how his journey to become educated at Hampton Institute reflected the stillborn hopes of ex-slaves. Ultimately, Washington argues his personal journey is a model for the race.

What is autobiography?

Autobiography is the journey of the self up to the present moment. Generally, this journey is filled with the "stuff of life"—conflict, tensions, doubts, triumphs—but often it concludes with a new-found recognition and definition of the self. Wisdom and perspective are gained by overcoming harsh realities, whether they be racism, sexism, or some other soul-repressing abuse. The goal is to live well. One may engage in a struggle but survive and bear witness to how the struggle helped one to develop empathy and understanding of the self and of others.

Why write an autobiography?

Writing about oneself can have a cathartic effect. Old spiritual and emotional wounds can potentially be healed. Putting words on paper encourages self-reflection, encourages an examination of one's memories, thoughts, and feelings. The text itself, then, becomes part of the individual's journey, the struggle to say "I am" in a way that reflects maturity and wisdom, hope and empathy, survival and triumph.

Since writing is an act of communication, autobiography also implies an audience. The journey into self is *written down* so that readers may learn from the "I's" experiences. This notion that any one life may have relevance and meaning for another is quintessentially human. Because autobiography is embedded in a specific time and place, it also resonates as history and social document. Readers learn and, one hopes, are inspired by how the writer lived through such times as slavery, the Harlem Renaissance, or the Black Arts Movement of the 1960s, and journeyed through specific landscapes like Eatonville, Harlem, or St. Louis.

Autobiography is an act of pride, but without boastful arrogance. Indeed, the best autobiography should be intended as a "gift" to readers, a call to action to change society, to alter one's life and reaffirm one's values. Just as the writer gains greater self-definition and understanding through writing, the reader gains self-definition and understanding through reading.

MY BEST ADVICE

Good autobiography should be written like any other good story. The struggle for identity—the rebirth of the self— should be detailed against the landscape of a specific time and place.

Before beginning an autobiography, you should ask yourself:

> How do you think your life speaks to others? What do you want readers to think, feel, and understand? How is your life's journey potentially helpful to others?

≷ Do you have the courage to examine your life, to speak truthfully about your flaws and faults, your failures? (It is always easier to characterize oneself as a hero or heroine, but life and people are infinitely more complicated. Each of us despairs, has doubts, and, at times, acts selfishly and vindictively.)

≷ Can you characterize others in your life not as one-dimensional beings, but as multidimensional people? (An autobiography intended only to complain or settle grudges lacks art; the artist has a responsibility to question her own perceptions.)

≷ Are you capable of connecting how your self is inextricably linked to the time and place in which you were born and raised? Are you comfortable with exploring how social and cultural forces influenced you?

≷ Are you intellectually and emotionally ready to confront the harsh realities as well as to recognize the pleasures of your life's journey? (Autobiography should be emotionally even-handed—not all pain and horror, not all goodness and light. This is not to say that every autobiography has a happy or, conversely, an unhappy ending. Rather, there should be a recognition that experiences are varied in kind and quality.)

≷ Do you recognize how memory is a testament to survival? Are you aware of how remembering helps you to renew and celebrate the self?

Charlayne Hunter-Gault, in her book *In My Place,* writes about her coming-of-age against the backdrop of America's civil rights movement. She was the first black woman to attend the University of Georgia, and her education and experiences fueled her desire to become a journalist.

Following the traditional slave narrative pattern of beginning with one's birth and origins, Hunter-Gault writes:

> *The first of many places that I would call "my place" was a tiny village tucked away in a remote little corner of South Carolina: Due West. There may have been bigger, better known, and happier places on February 27, 1942, but you couldn't have told my mother anything about them. Not even a difficult labor at home, which lasted four days, with the doctor popping in from time to time with encouraging words but little else, could diminish my mother's happiness.*

Contrast Hunter-Gault's opening lines with Douglass's opening in the *Narrative of the Life of Frederick Douglass, An American Slave:*

> *I was born in Tuckahoe, near Hillsborough, and about twelve miles from Easton, in Talbot county, Maryland. I have no accurate knowledge of age, never having seen any authentic record containing it. By far the larger part of the slaves know as little of their ages as horses know of theirs, and it is the wish of most masters within my knowledge to keep their slaves thus ignorant. I do not remember to have ever met a slave who could tell of his birthday. They seldom come nearer to it than planting-time, harvest-time, cherry-time, spring-time, or fall-time. A want of information concerning my own was a source of unhappiness to me even during childhood. The white children could tell their ages.*

For both writers, the journey of the self has begun. However, note the striking differences between the joy surrounding Charlayne's precise birth date and the sorrow surrounding Frederick's imprecise birth date. Hunter-Gault published her autobiography in 1992; Douglass published his in 1845. The span of nearly 150 years between the two autobiographies is reflected in how each author first "sees" and "understands" the self. Hunter-Gault knows that her birth was eagerly anticipated. Douglass knows little about his birth; in fact, he knows only that masters wanted to keep all slaves ignorant of their birthdays. Why?

Being born, having a birthday marks each of us as an individual worth celebrating. Hunter-Gault's parents rejoiced at her birth; Douglass's parents (a white master and a slave mother) probably did not rejoice at his birth. Douglass's mother undoubtedly had mixed feelings about birthing her son into slavery, birthing another "crop" for a master who took as his birthright his right to own slaves and exploit their bodies.

Hunter-Gault gives a personal, intimate glimpse of her birth; whereas slavery caused Douglass to view his birth more impersonally, abstractly. He would have liked to know his birth date less to celebrate it than to have the knowledge as any white child.

Through highly *specific details,* the two autobiographies convey the distinct eras in which each author was born. Their attitudes and views contrast the social and historical climate of the South before and after slavery.

Both autobiographies start the journey of the self but differ in their quest. "The first of many places that I would call 'my place' was a tiny village," states Hunter-Gault. Even as a child, she self-confidently claimed ownership of a place and home. "Tiny village" foreshadows Hunter-Gault's discovery, as an international reporter, of the ever-increasing world of spaces to claim as home. Douglass's birth, on the other hand, foreshadows a journey toward acquiring knowledge withheld from him by whites.

Racism shapes both authors' journeys. Douglass escapes from slavery. Hunter-Gault becomes the first black woman to attend the University of Georgia. During slavery and the civil rights era, each author journeys toward an education to fulfill dreams of redefinition and rebirth. Douglass uses subterfuge to gain an education from white children and his mistress; once educated, he devotes his literary skills to writing a book and speaking out persuasively, in Europe and America, against slavery. Hunter-Gault uses her education to become a renowned author and journalist. By assisting in the desegregation of the University of Georgia, she makes the university "her place" and, in turn, a place for all others of color.

Both Douglass and Hunter-Gault struggle toward self-development. Conflict and tension accompany their journeys. Some of the tension is external, like confronting racism; some is internal, more spiritual and psychological.

Douglass, at times, hated the consequences of his literacy:

> . . . *My learning to read had already come, to torment and sting my soul to unutterable anguish. As I writhed under it, I would at times feel that learning to read had been a curse rather than a blessing. It had given me a view of my wretched condition, without the remedy. It opened my eyes to the horrible pit, but to no ladder upon which to get out. In moments of agony, I envied my fellow-slaves for their stupidity. I often wished myself a*

beast. I preferred the condition of the meanest reptile to my own.
Anything, no matter what, to get rid of thinking!

Whereas Douglass has moments of intense bitterness, Hunter-Gault, when alone in her college dorm room, away from the strife caused by integration, develops ways to soothe and support her interior self:

At the end of the day, that was, finally, what I was—alone—except for the voices, the voices of my grandmother reciting the Twenty-third Psalm: "Yea, though I walk through the valley of the shadow of the death, I will fear no evil; for thou art with me," and of Nina Simone and Her Friends, who soothed and comforted me with "He's Got the Whole World in His Hands" and "Try a Little Tenderness."

Revealing an exterior as well as interior self helps readers better identify with the conflicts and struggles of your life's journey. Both exterior and interior views of the self should be multifaceted. Human nature is inarguably complex. Though Hunter-Gault is able to soothe herself, she shares her feelings of fear and sorrow. Likewise, Douglass reveals himself as bitter, but that doesn't discount his interior moments of triumph and ecstatic joy.

You—the "I"—is the star, the main protagonist of your life. But readers want to know how *being you* affected the outcome of the journey. Presenting yourself in as honest a fashion as possible makes you all the more credible as the narrator of your life. Since we are all imperfect people, presenting yourself as occasionally vulnerable, weak, uncertain about actions or beliefs is likely to evoke empathy in your readers. Additionally, testifying that "I am" and "I am still here" is more powerful if the "I" has had to overcome not only external threats but internal feelings. Everyone knows super heroes are heroic. What readers want to witness is how the so-called ordinary person lights the way to self-growth and development, how each of us has the potential power to become "heroic."

Fine autobiography touches people's lives by showing how an individual overcame emotional, spiritual, and physical conflicts, how one soul struggled, externally and internally, toward a better quality of life, of being.

REMEMBER: The specific life journey of any one person has the power to speak to us all.

Your story is our story. Our people's story. **Write it.** Write it well.

EXERCISE 1

WHO I'VE BEEN, WHO I AM

In autobiography, the *you* becomes the central protagonist, the potential hero or heroine of your life. As you would in writing fiction, you need to take time to reflect on the substance of your character. Who are you? What shaped you? Who were you as a child? Who are you now? How have you changed?

In your journal, write your name. Jewell. George. Diana. Shaneeka. Janet. Alvin. Names have power, and you have had a lifetime of living with your name and your awareness of yourself. Write in your journal what you believe your name signifies, evokes. What emotional response do you have to your name? How did you get your name? Is it a family name, a name your parents made up? Or a name you took as an adult to reflect your changing consciousness? Does your name have any special meanings? "Evan" means strong, warrior. "Khalil" means poet, lover. "Gabriel" means guardian spirit. Does your name's meaning add to your sense of self?

My mother dreamed my name. She claimed a spirit came to her and said, "Name her Jewell." My mother, pregnant, now knowing her second child would be a girl, promptly promised to do as the spirit bid. The name "Jewell" always made me self-conscious. Children made fun of my name; teachers and old aunties, pinching my cheeks, said, "Aren't you a jewel?" It wasn't until I was in my thirties, when my self-esteem was more solid, that I began to love my name and, in turn, love myself better.

Paste photographs of yourself as a child and as an adult into your journal. (You may want to purchase a separate scrapbook, since Exercises 1 through 4 will help you create a pictorial history of your life as a supplement to your journal entries.) Above all, be thoughtful in your photograph selection. Choose pictures that have more resonance than the obligatory infant photos and high school graduation portraits. Maybe the picture of you at eight, fancy-dressed for Easter Sunday, and the one of you at fifty-two, diving in the Bahamas, are most meaningful. Photos should evoke memories, emotions, about the quality of life you're living, have lived, and hope to live.

* * *

Writing about one's life journey invariably involves comparisons and contrasts between **then** and **now.** *Although each of us changes over the course of a lifetime, each of us remains somewhat the same.* The boy-child or the girl-child we once were still peers out of our adult eyes.

In your journal, write about how you looked as a child. What were your physical characteristics—**then?** Were you slight and rail-thin? Was your face filled with wide eyes and bushy brows? Were your tennis shoes untied? Do you remember where and when the photo was taken? What were you thinking? What were you feeling?

Now, study the adult photo of you. How does this face and body reflect you? Do you like what you see? Does the photo suggest success and maturity or impishness and good humor? Study the lines and crevices of your face. What do you think of yourself? Do you remember when and where the picture was taken? How were you feeling? Are your feelings reflected in the photo, or are they hidden? How real is your smile? Are you pensive or joyful in the adult photo? Why?

Then* versus *now. Take twenty minutes to list the obvious as well as the not-so-obvious differences between the two photos. Did you remain petite or gangly? Did you grow a mustache or cut your hair? Are your clothes similar or different? Do you still favor patterns and batiks? Does the child-you appear happy? Discontented? Does the adult-you look foreign and remote? Or contented? Are there other people in your pictures—playmates or a growing family? Which photo best reflects the *essence* of you? The carefree child? The jovial adult? Or neither? Which photo do you find the most appealing?

* * *

Depending on your age or inclination, you may want four or six pictures that highlight key moments in your life. Continue the same exercise, writing in detail and as clearly as you can, what the physical images reveal about you and what moments they inspire you to remember.

What do your photos say about your life's journey so far?

EXERCISE 2

WHERE I'VE BEEN, WHERE I AM

History and environment have helped to shape you. How different is the world you live in now from the world you lived in as a child?

Search for photos of your family's first home, or, if you moved many times, search for photos of the home that meant the most to you when you were growing up. Search, too, for pictures that allow you to "see" again the old neighborhood, your local church, the school playground. What clothes did people wear? What cars did they drive? What social settings and opportunities were available to them? If your family doesn't have photos, go to a library or historical society and search for archival photos and newspaper clippings from the time of your youth.

In your journal, write about how your environment influenced you. Chicago is different from Columbus; Atlanta is different from Austin; Illinois is different from Iowa City. Add in historical time, geography, weather, and the differences multiply. Every community creates a unique landscape and atmosphere for a child's growth and development.

Was your home urban or rural? Did you experience New England seasons or only the hot, arid air of Phoenix? Did you live in a house or a seven-story apartment building? Was your home a welcoming place for a child? Or was it filled with frills and breakables? Did you spend hours in the community center feeling bored or happily playing Ping-Pong? Did your school have a jail-like atmosphere? Did the science lab seem like an oasis?

Contrast your **then** photos with **now** photos of your home and community. If you haven't any "now" photos, grab a camera and take pictures of your home and community. What you select or don't select to photograph can potentially teach you a great deal about how you "see" your environment.

Write for twenty minutes about what "home" means to you. What is essential in your house? Your community? What could you do without? What kind of identity and emotional support do the spaces give you or fail to give you? Do you hate your apartment building, with its maintenance code violations? Yet love your apartment because of the compact window seat and stacked shelves of classical music CDs? Does your street corner scare you? Irritate you? Do you feel soothed by the stained glass images in your church or mosque?

For another twenty minutes, contrast and compare your childhood home and community with the place where you've chosen to lead your life as an adult. Are there any significant differences or similarities? Any yearnings for another kind of space?

THE POWER OF HANDS AND VOICES

It takes a village to raise a child.

—African proverb

A grandmother's hand may have soothed or slapped; a father's hand may have hurt or lovingly held. A teacher's voice may have belittled or encouraged you. A bully may have taunted you; then, grudgingly, after a hard-fought battle, called your name with respect. Hands and voices and what they represent about people's attitudes and feelings can help or hinder a child's growth.

Think about the people in your past. Who helped? Who didn't? Who frightened you? Who consoled you?

In your journal, paste photos of family members, mentors, teachers, friends, and enemies. If you can't find photos, take the time to envision in your mind the people in the past who influenced you, for better or for worse.

Write in your journal about your parents or primary care givers. What were their names? Are they living or dead? What do you remember most about how they treated you? How did their hands feel? What did their voices sound like? Are you the eldest child or the baby of the family? What were your parents' attitudes about raising children? Raising you?

What other people influenced you? Write down specific details about what a mentor or friend, a first love or first enemy, did that strongly influenced your self-image and development.

Now, find or take photos of people presently significant in your life. Write down memories of family members, friends, and colleagues. How do they serve as a support network? Or do they fail to support you emotionally, spiritually? Are the people in the photos necessary to improving your quality of life?

EXERCISE 4

UNFORGETTABLE MOMENTS:
THEN AND NOW

Then, for twenty minutes, write about a memorable event from your pre-adult memories. What details of sight, sound, taste, touch, and smell do you recall? How old were you? Who else was with you? Speaking to you? What made the day unforgettable? What experiences occurred? What were you thinking and feeling?

Now, for twenty minutes, write about a more recent day, a memorable experience within the last three years. What feelings, thoughts do you associate with this memory? Did you share the experience with anyone? Were you at home, at work, at play? Did any ritual or social codes influence your experience? For example, did you marry, "jump the broom"? Did you give birth in a hospital? Organize a healing conference for rape survivors? Did you successfully defend your first client? Or appear in a play? Did you fulfill or not fulfill social and personal obligations?

Reread the information you've written about yourself. Have you left out anything that is relevant? Important?

Using a highlighter, mark those details which might be relevant to the readers of your story. What details need more elaboration? Explanation?

Consider, too, whether there are links between your personality **then** and your personality **now**. Any ties that illuminate who you are. How have you become your self? Have you changed modestly? Or are the experiences dramatically different? Do the **now** experiences make your **then** more meaningful? Or vice versa? Do you think your experiences will seem compelling to a reader? What makes them so?

How has your external world changed? Have your interior thoughts and feelings changed? Which unforgettable moment do you prefer—**then or now?** Did your future bring redemption? Happiness? Or is the past your spiritual Eden, the time when you were most happy?

Finally, revise both *then* and *now* experiences, trying to be more aware of comparisons, contrasts, and emotional links or emotional schisms between the two.

When you've finished, celebrate yourself and the writing you've done so far. Step by step, page by page, you're making great progress.

AUTOBIOGRAPHY STUDY, NO. 1

NATHAN MCCALL'S
MAKES ME WANNA HOLLER

Nathan McCall, in his national bestseller Makes Me Wanna Holler: A Young Black Man in America, *exemplifies beautifully the notion that powerful autobiography is*

*about self-definition and rebirth. With fine and careful prose,
he draws a clear picture of how "self" is rooted within a context of community and environment and how a self can,
through determination, re-create life and make the journey
from violent hopelessness to a life filled with more celebratory
choices and possibilities.*

In Chapters 1 and 2, McCall presents a disturbing picture of
how he responded to racism against black males:

CHAPTER 1

GET–BACK

The fellas and I were hanging out on our corner one afternoon when the strangest thing happened. A white
boy, who appeared to be about eighteen or nineteen years old,
came pedaling a bicycle casually through the neighborhood. I
don't know if he was lost or just confused, but he was definitely in the wrong place to be doing the tourist bit. Somebody
spotted him and pointed him out to the rest of us. "Look!
What's that motherfucka doin' ridin' through here?! Is he
crraaaazy?!"

It was automatic. We all took off after him. We caught him
on Cavalier Boulevard and knocked him off the bike. He fell to
the ground and it was all over. We were on him like white on
rice. Ignoring the passing cars, we stomped him and kicked
him. My stick partners kicked him in the head and face and
watched the blood gush from his mouth. I kicked him in the
stomach and nuts, where I knew it would hurt. Every time I

drove my foot into his balls, I felt better; with each blow delivered, I gritted my teeth as I remembered some recent racial slight:

THIS is for all the times you followed me round in stores . . .

And THIS is for the times you treated me like a nigger . . .

And THIS is for G.P.—General Principle—just 'cause you white.

While we kicked, he lay there, curled up in the fetal position, trying to use his hands to cover his head. We bloodied him so badly that I got a little scared and backed off. The others, seeing how badly he was messed up, moved away too. But one dude kept stomping, like he'd gone berserk. He seemed crazed and consumed in the pleasure of kicking that white boy's ass. When he finished, he reached down and picked up the white dude's bike, lifted it as high as he could above his head, and slammed it down on him hard. The white guy didn't even flinch. He was out cold. I feared he might be dead until I saw him breathing.

We walked away, laughing, boasting, competing for bragging rights about who'd done the most damage. "Man, did you see how red that cracker's face turned when I busted his lip? I almost broke my hand on that ugly motherfucka!"

Fucking up white boys like that made us feel *good* inside. I guess we must have been fourteen or fifteen by then, and it felt so good that we stumbled over each other sometimes trying to get in extra kicks and punches. When we bum-rushed white boys, it made me feel like we were beating all white people on behalf of all blacks. We called it "gettin' some get-back," securing revenge for all the shit they'd heaped on blacks all these years. They were still heaping hell on us, and especially on our parents. The difference was, cats in my generation weren't taking it lying down.

After my older brother Dwight got his driver's license, a group of us would pile into my stepfather's car some evenings and cruise through a nearby white neighborhood, searching for people walking the streets. We'd spot some whites, get out, rush over, and, using sticks and fists, try to beat them to within an inch of their lives.

Sometimes, when I sit back and think about the crazy things the fellas and I did and remember the hate and violence that we unleashed, it's hard to believe I was once part of all that—I feel so removed from it now that I've left the streets. Yet when I consider white America and the way it's treated blacks, our random rage in the old days makes perfect sense to me. Looking back, it's easy to understand how it all got started. . . .

CHAPTER 2

CAVALIER MANOR

For as long as I can remember, it seems that there was no aspect of my family's reality that wasn't affected by whites, right on down to the creation of the neighborhood I grew up in. Known as Cavalier Manor, it was located in Portsmouth, Virginia. Most of Cavalier Manor was built in the early 1960s by a local construction bigwig named George T. McClean. Neighborhood lore had it that he was a white liberal do-gooder who felt blacks in Portsmouth needed a community that would inspire pride and help improve their lot. But just as many people thought McClean was a racist who got alarmed by the civil rights movement and built Cavalier Manor to encourage blacks to move there rather than into white neighborhoods.

McClean started building from the edge of an older, low-income black neighborhood and went southward, making the houses larger and more elegant with each successive phase. He named the streets after U.S. presidents and prominent blacks, particularly entertainers. The streets had names such as Belafonte Drive, Basie Crescent, Eckstine Drive, and Horne Avenue. To add to the sense of optimism that the neighborhood was supposed to reflect, they even named one street Freedom Avenue.

Although some folks there liked to think of themselves as middle-class, Cavalier Manor was a working-class neighborhood. Most of those who moved there were active or retired military personnel. Few had completed high school or gone to college. The retirees usually found blue-collar jobs at one of the massive military installations in the area, which is home to some of the world's largest shipyards. Many others who moved there were uneducated working-class folks who had scrimped and saved enough money to move from public housing.

By the time the bulk of it was finished, Cavalier Manor had come to be one of the largest black neighborhoods in the Southeast. In terms of political power, this meant that our neighborhood emerged as a potentially influential voting bloc. In terms of street power, it meant that Cavalier Manor surfaced as a helluva gang force throughout the Tidewater area, which spans several Virginia cities. The neighborhood was so big that dudes formed distinct gangs in different sections of the community. These gangs fought each other sometimes and united when fighting downtown boys.

But I was unaware of all that street action when we first came to Cavalier Manor. I was only nine years old then, in 1964, the year my family moved to Portsmouth from Key West,

Florida, where my stepfather had served a three-year tour of duty in the Navy. We'd also lived in Morocco and Norfolk, Virginia, and Portsmouth was to be my stepfather's last duty station before he retired after giving Uncle Sam twenty years.

I still remember how excited my brothers and I were about moving into our first real house. When we drove into our new neighborhood, our eyes and mouths flew wide open. We saw impressive homes with freshly sprouted lawns, broad sidewalks, and newly paved streets. On each side of the street that led to our section of the community were two sets of stately white brick pillars with black cast-iron bars flowing regally through their tops. A huge sign printed in Old English lettering was mounted on each set of pillars: "Welcome to Cavalier Manor." My brothers and I thought we had died and gone to heaven.

It wasn't the kind of neighborhood I associated with black people then. We'd always lived in drab apartment buildings that looked like public housing. All the black people we knew had lived that way.

In Cavalier Manor, we pulled into our very own driveway, which led to a garage where we could park our ride. When we walked into the house, the sun shone brightly through the windows, bringing out every wonderful detail of the place. It was a single-story structure with three bedrooms, a living room, a kitchen, and a formal dining room.

I could feel its newness and smell the freshness of the recently painted walls and ceilings. The hardwood floors had been sanded and buffed. Tiny mounds of sawdust remained in corners, as if construction workers had left only hours before we arrived.

My brothers and I ran outside to inspect our front and

back yards. The air was filled with the steady hum of lawn mowers and the sweet smell of freshly cut grass. Pine needles that had fallen from the many tall trees out back were scattered everywhere. We learned to hate raking those pine needles, but our initial reaction to our new home and neighborhood was that we loved everything.

Located in a cul-de-sac named Vaughn Court, ours was one of several streets that the white folks misspelled in their haste. There were twelve homes in the court. We lived in number 6. Several blocks away, a large lake, Crystal Lake, wound through a portion of the neighborhood.

We got that house just in time to accommodate the expansion of our family. Along with my parents, there were my two brothers, Dwight and Billy, who were two and four years older than me respectively. A short time after we arrived, my mother gave birth to another boy, the first child born to her and my stepfather. They named him Bryan Keith Alvin, after Brian Keith, the white actor. As she had in the past, my maternal grandmother, whom we called Bampoose, came to live with us. Then my stepfather took in Junnie, a son of his from a previous marriage who was three years older than me. So within the first year we were living there, our family nearly doubled in size. It was crowded and we were broke as hell, but it felt like we were livin' large.

My harshest introduction to the world of white folks came in September 1966, when my parents sent me to Alford J. Mapp, a white school across town. It was the beginning of my sixth-grade school year, and I was walking down the hall, searching for my new class, when a white boy timed my steps, extended his foot, and tripped me. The boy and his friends nudged each other and laughed as I stumbled into a locker, spilling books and papers everywhere. "Hey, nigger," the boy said. "You dropped something."

The word sounded vile coming from his white mouth. When I regained my footing, I tore into that cat and tried to take his head off. Pinning him against a locker, I punched him in the face and kept on punching him until his two buddies jumped in to help him out. While other white students crowded around and cheered them on, we scuffled there in the hall until the bell rang, signaling the start of the next class period. Like combatants in a prizefight, we automatically stopped throwing punches and separated at the sound of the bell. The white boys went their way down the hall, calling me names along the way and threatening to retaliate. I gathered my papers, straightened my clothes, and reeled toward my next class, dazed, trying to figure out what had just happened to me.

My parents sent me to Mapp in 1966 because that was the first year that blacks in Portsmouth were able to attend school wherever they wanted. The U.S. Supreme Court had long before ruled against the notion of separate but equal schools; still, Virginia, one of the states that had resisted desegregation, was slow in putting together a busing plan. Without a plan to ship black students to schools across town, over the years blacks and whites in Portsmouth had simply remained in separate schools. I could have gone to W. E. Waters, a junior high school that had just been built in our neighborhood, but, like many blacks then, my parents figured I could get a better education at the white school across town.

I was proud of their decision and held it out teasingly to my brothers as proof that I was the smart one in the family, that I held more academic promise than them. Billy had flunked the second grade, and Dwight and Junnie never showed much interest in books. My less studious brothers would attend their regular, all-black high school, but I was going to a *white* school, which made me feel special.

My parents didn't talk with me beforehand about the challenge I would face as one in the first wave of blacks to integrate Mapp. We had all seen TV news footage of police in riot gear escorting black students through hostile, jeering crowds to enroll in all-white high schools and colleges across the country, but for various reasons my parents saw no cause for alarm at Mapp. It was only a junior high school, which seemed far less menacing than the racially torn high schools and college campuses we heard about. Besides, there were no warning signals in Portsmouth to tip off my parents, no public protests by white citizens or high-profile white supremacist politicians like Alabama governor George Wallace threatening to buck the school integration plan.

At Mapp, I was the only African American in most of my classes. When I walked into one room and sat down, the students near me would get up and move away, as if my dark skin were dirty and hideous to them. Nobody talked directly to me. Instead, they shot daggers to each other that were intended for me. "You know, I hate niggers," they would say. "I don't understand why they're always following white people everywhere. We can't seem to get away from them. Why don't they just stay in their own schools?"

It wasn't much better dealing with white teachers. They avoided eye contact with me as much as possible and pretended not to see or hear white student hecklers. It was too much for an eleven-year-old to challenge, and I didn't try. Instead, I tried to become invisible. I kept to myself, remained quiet during class discussions, and never asked questions in or after class. I kept my eyes glued to my desk or looked straight ahead to avoid drawing attention to myself. I staggered, numb and withdrawn, through each school day and hurried from my last class, gym, without showering so that I wouldn't miss the only bus headed home. Students who missed the first school bus had to walk through the white neighborhood to the main street to catch the city bus. Mapp was located in a middle-class section of town called Craddock, where the whites were as hateful as the poor whites in Academy Park.

The daily bus ride home brought its own set of fears. A group of white boys got on our bus regularly for the sole purpose, it seemed, of picking fights. I was scared to death of them. With older brothers to fight at home, I was confident I could whip any white boy my age and size, but many of the white guys who got on that bus were eighth graders, and they looked like giants to me. Others were older, white, leather-jacket-wearing hoods who I was certain were high school dropouts.

When we boarded the bus, blacks automatically moved to the rear, as if Jim Crow laws were still in effect. The white boys would board last, crowd into the aisles, and start making racial slurs when the bus pulled away from school. "I hate the smell of niggers. They sure do stink. Don't you think niggers stink, Larry?"

"They sure do, man. They smell bad."

Before long, fists flew, girls screamed, and people tussled in the aisles. Few of the black guys on the bus were big and bad enough to beat the tough white boys, who outnumbered us seven to one. I never joined in to help the black guys out. I huddled in the far corner at the rear of the bus, tense, scared as hell, hoping the fighting wouldn't reach that far before the driver broke it up.

Children have an enormous capacity to adapt to insanity. I took my lumps in school and tried as much as possible to shrug it off when I went home. Billy, Dwight, and Junnie came home most days full of stories about the fun they were having at pep rallies and football games at their all-black high school. I envied them because I couldn't match their stories with tales of my own about fun times at Mapp. I savored every minute of my weeknights at home and used weekends to gather the heart to face Mapp again. Monday mornings, I rose and dutifully caught the school bus back to hell.

The harassment never let up. Once, when my English teacher left the room, a girl sitting near me drew a picture of a stickman on a piece of paper, colored it black, scribbled my name below it, and passed it around the classroom for others to see. I lost my temper, snatched it from her, and ripped it up. She hit me. I hit her back, then the whole class jumped in. When the teacher returned, I was standing up, punching one guy while another one was riding my back and hitting me in the head. The teacher demanded, "What's going on here?"

The white kids cried out in unison, "That *black* boy started a fight with us!"

Without another word, the teacher sent me to the principal's office and I was dismissed from school. The weeklong suspension alerted my parents that something was wrong. Mama sat me down and tried to talk to me about it. "Why were you fighting in school?"

"It wasn't my fault, Mama. That girl drew a picture of me and colored it black."

"That's no reason to fight. What's the matter with you?

Your grades are falling and now you get into a fight. Don't you like your school?"

I tried to explain, then choked up and broke down in tears. Seeing that, my parents sought and got approval to transfer me to the neighborhood school, W. E. Waters.

But it wasn't over yet. One day, before the transfer went through, I was sitting on the gym floor with the rest of the student body, watching a school assembly program, when a group of rowdy white upperclassmen began plucking my head and ridiculing me. I got confused. *What should I do?* To turn around and say something to them would start another fight. To get up and leave would require me to wade through a sea of hostile white students to reach the nearest exit. With nowhere to go, I sat there and took the humiliation until I broke. Tears welled in my eyes and started running, uncontrollably, down my face. I sat silently through the remainder of the assembly program with my vision blurred and my spirit broken. That was the only time, then or since, that I've been crushed so completely. When it was over, I collected myself, went to the boys' bathroom, and boohooed some more.

There was no greater joy than that last bus ride home from Mapp. I sat near a window and stared out, trying to make sense of those past few months. Everything that had happened to me was so contrary to all I'd been taught about right and wrong. Before Mapp, every grudge I had ever held against a person could be traced to some specific deed. I couldn't understand someone hating me simply for being black and alive. I wondered, *Where did those white people learn to hate so deeply at such a young age?* I didn't know. But, over time, I learned to hate as blindly and viciously as any of them.

McCall gives us vibrant images of his "old self" and shows how even a loving family and community have limits in combating racism and how a young adolescent black male sees himself and his world.

The last chapter of McCall's autobiography is called, appropriately, "Choices." McCall, by the end of his story, has become a successful journalist and writer. He's taken responsibility for his own life choices and reaches out to nurture his stepson and to heal and repair relationships torn asunder by his early rage, carelessness, and alienation. He concludes:

For those who'd like answers, I have no pithy social formulas to end black-on-black violence. But I do know that I see a younger, meaner generation out there now—more lost and alienated than we were, and placing even less value on life. We were at least touched by role models; this new bunch is totally estranged from the black mainstream. Crack has taken the drug game to a more lethal level and given young blacks far more economic incentive to opt for the streets.

I've come to fear that of the many things a black man can die from, the first may be rage—his own or someone else's. For that reason, I seldom stick around when I stop on the block. One day not long ago, I spotted a few familiar faces hanging out at the old haunt, the 7-Eleven. I wheeled into the parking lot, strode over, and high-fived the guys I knew. Within moments, I sensed that I was in danger. I felt hostile stares from those I didn't know.

I was frightened by the younger guys, who now controlled my

> *former turf. I eased back into my car and left, because I knew this: that if they saw the world as I once did, they believed they had nothing to lose, including life itself.*
>
> *It made me wanna holler and throw up both my hands.*

By the end of the book, McCall has changed. No longer devaluing human life, he values it. **Then versus now.** The Nathan of the present is not the Nathan of the past.

McCall revisits old haunts, like the 7-Eleven, but time, drugs, and racism, he finds, have created a "meaner" generation. Growing older and *surviving* have given McCall wisdom and perspective, but he knows he doesn't have all the answers.

Nonetheless, at the heart of McCall's autobiography is the notion that young black males can learn from his life's journey and experiences. McCall "wakes" to himself after a prison term; at the core of his autobiography is the hope that by *reading* about his life, by understanding his example, others may "wake" to themselves and to better choices one day, one month, one year sooner, and thus redeem portions of McCall's life as well as their own. Ultimately, McCall's autobiography is a "loving gift," sent with all its harshness and brutality to undo the violence black men may do to themselves and others.

Reread and rethink the material you've added to your journal. Does your life's journey have the potential to inspire? Have you learned, rebirthed a new you out of the old? Have you written how the world around you helped make you? Have you considered how your self—thoughts, feelings, and actions—helped to validate or change the world and you within it?

* * *

REMEMBER: All of us lead interesting lives. Yet a writer's task is to take the physical, emotional, and spiritual events of her life and try to make sense of them for herself and for readers. Re-experiencing a life's journey becomes art when a writer renders with clarity and honesty the trials and triumphs of being human—of being one's self, of being free, as we all aspire to be—free within ourselves.

SIX

MAPPING THE JOURNEY

How you tell your life story is just as important as
what you tell.

Everything in your life isn't worth writing about. You have to be selective, to weed out dull moments, events, and even people who didn't actively contribute to your transformation. Life continually presents us with choices, different paths, which can lead to celebration, tragedy, or some of both. Life also offers treasured mentors and teachers, as well as victimizers and mean-spirited people. Parents and relatives can play major roles. But sometimes seemingly minor characters are also critical in our lives. Your eighth-grade tormentor may have finally inspired you to fight back. Or your first love affair may have taught you what *not* to want in a relationship. And events may be critical—going to jail, having a child, winning a college scholarship. But even small events, like watching a hummingbird hover or baking a clay pot in a kiln, may have been essential to your development as a field biologist or a sculptor.

Big events or small events, people whom you've known all your life, people you've known only for an hour—all, potentially, influence your journey. Your view of the world as a welcoming or sinister place comes from your emotional responses to your environment, to past events, and to people you've known.

To transform—*to make oneself new*—to grow and continue to develop, is what makes us such complex and wonderful human beings.

When writing autobiography, you have to reflect and discover the patterns that influenced your journey from the "past you" to the "present you."

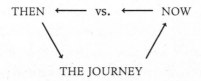

How crooked and demanding was the journey from the development of your "then" self to the person you are today? What were the common pathways in terms of your emotional life, the people who nurtured or failed to nurture you? What uncommon incidents and actions helped you transform your life? Forced you to make new choices?

Reread the excerpt from McCall's *Makes Me Wanna Holler: A Young Black Man in America* in the preceding chapter. Though only a sampling of the book, McCall presents social and environmental influences that dramatically affected the tenor of his life. Violence, the need to establish his identity as a black man, intergenerational and class differences within the black community, and racism all profoundly swayed his life choices.

If you haven't read McCall's book, I suggest you purchase it or borrow it from the library. It is a terrific read and, in its entirety, shows that McCall's life was a pattern of violence that paralleled the estrangement between adults and youths, the affluent and poor, and black and white people. Eventually, McCall chooses to take responsibility for his son by being an involved and caring father. By guiding another young man through the journey of becoming a man—a black man in white America—McCall breaks, at least for his son, the violence of powerlessness and rage.

Autobiography's structure, like a plot in fiction, depends upon establishing the *pattern* of emotions, events, and images that played a major role in your life.

For Nathan McCall, racism, alienation from his father, gang dependence, and violence make up the substance of his life. For Frederick Douglass, his desire to be educated, to be viewed as a man, and to escape slavery constitute much of his life. Charlayne Hunter-Gault seeks an integrated college education to advance civil rights and to further her goal of becoming a journalist, but unlike Douglass's, Hunter-Gault's journey is not one of rugged individualism. Rather, her journey is supported by a loving network of family, friends, and civil rights leaders.

MY BEST ADVICE

Life may seem chaotic, but autobiography systematically reveals the pattern of feelings, ideas, and obstacles to your self-definition and self-respect.

Rosemary L. Bray, in *Unafraid of the Dark,* begins the tale of her life with the keen recognition of how poverty has shaped it:

> *Certain things shape you, change you forever. Years later, long after you think you've escaped, some ordinary experience flings you backward into memory, transports you to a frozen moment, and you freeze. Being poor is like that. Living surrounded by fear and rage is like that. I grew up hating the cold, dreading the approach of night. Thirty years later, a too-cold room at night can trigger a flash of terror, or a wash of ineffable sadness. Voices raised in anger can still make me shrink. Every now and then, a sudden, innocent move by my husband makes me duck to protect myself. It took many years for me to think of night as a time of rest.*

Bray's words clearly demonstrate an awareness of what emotions, circumstances, and events influenced her past life and still haunt her as an adult. Fear of poverty, not being warm enough, and the specter of violence by her father encouraged paralyzing, unhappy memories and feelings of "terror" and "sadness."

Her autobiography, then, is a detailed narrative of how these feelings came to be. She moves from a general statement about what influenced her to showing, one by one, how her feelings were created:

> *I can't remember what awakened me first—my mother's urgent voice, the thick, sooty smoke, or the blasts of icy air through our bedrooms.*

*"Get up, Ro, go sit in the kitchen while I air out this room." I
had bronchitis, and the smoke was already starting to bother me.
I stumbled through the dark into the dim kitchen, lit only by the
burners on the gas stove and the faint flicker from the boiler. The
oven door was open, and though the rest of the room was still
cold, the space near the stove was almost toasty. I coughed a little
as my mother brought my brothers and sister into the kitchen,
then disappeared downstairs.*

*The house's boiler was out again. An ancient coal
contraption, it always seemed to go on the blink in the dead of
winter, pumping thick black smoke through the house. Whenever
this happened, only turning the boiler off until the morning
would alleviate the problem. There was a janitor for our
building, but Mama often knew more about the boiler than he
did . . .*

*It was four A.M. or so; in a couple of hours it would be time
to get up. But Mama wouldn't sleep anymore that night . . . By
morning, the water in the house would be ice-cold. As long as the
stove was on, someone had to stay awake. That someone was
always Mama.*

Bray vividly depicts her childhood memory of being ill, of
being cold and then warm, of how poverty meant living in a
building without a well-maintained boiler. A terrifying experience for a child. But Bray also explains how Mama, like a sen-
tinel, watched over her, protected her and her siblings, and
stayed awake in the dark, to make sure that the stove generated heat, but not fire or poisonous gas. Mama was awake so
that her children could sleep safely, unafraid of the dark.

But what happened when Mama's strength failed? Or
when Mama had other demons to fight?

"You lying, no good whore!"

I lay in my bed in the front room, crying in the dark. Two rooms away, my father continued his tirade against my mostly silent mother. I could tell from the air on my face that the room was ice-cold; the boiler was out again and the whole building was likely most freezing.

"You think I don't know about all your men, you stinking bitch? You think I'm some kind of damn fool?"

Bray's mother was plagued by her husband's ill-founded jealous rages. When her mother was attacked, the child Bray was rendered more helpless, more afraid.

In the autobiography, Bray maps, over and over again, the cycle of fear and poverty and of her mother nurturing and providing for her as best she could between the violent rages of a father with big dreams of success but limited choices.

Bray's life journey chronicles her growth, her development beyond poverty and fear. "I was black, I was a girl, I was smart, I was the oldest of four," Bray states, ready to challenge the world. She moves from the insular world of her family to a larger world of wealth and privilege at Yale. But poverty remains a constant, and not until her father dies does Bray begin to understand that she has her father's stubbornness as well as her mother's caring grace. She holds within herself the ability to shape a life rich with love, with household comforts, and unlimited dreams. Bray becomes a successful writer and television journalist, and creates with her husband a happy, peaceful home in which to raise her children:

Allen is not afraid of the dark, and I am learning not to be. I am learning to love being a black woman in a world that often fears and resents my presence, and using that identity as a passport to my citizenship in the world . . . I am learning to continue in the face of failure, as caring women and men have done before me for generations. Like Allen, I can announce, "It's very dark out there." For the sake of my precious sons, and for the precious children not my own, I can stay unafraid of the dark, and work my way toward morning.

Bray's autobiography follows a basic structure of moving from a **general statement**—being afraid of the dark—to **specific, terrifying incidents** that, one by one, step by step, she overcomes. Consequently, Bray matures, succeeds, and becomes less afraid.

Also, like many autobiographers, Bray begins her story by reflecting in the present. She moves immediately back in time, telling her story with drama and with a sense that the past isn't a flat, dead memory but a vital thing come newly alive.

Paragraph one ends with:

"Every now and then, a sudden, innocent move by my husband makes me duck to protect myself. It took many years for me to think of night as a time of rest."

Paragraph two begins:

"I can't remember what awakened me first—my mother's urgent voice, the thick, sooty smoke, or the blasts of icy air through our bedrooms.

" 'Get up, Ro, go sit in the kitchen while I air out this room.' "

Bray's story is *framed by present time, then goes back in time, and chronologically re-creates certain memories, key incidents, emotions, and obstacles* that she has to overcome. Literally, Bray grows herself up in her autobiography. Readers grow right along with her. The autobiography comes full circle—back to present time—and Bray's final, hard-earned wisdom: "For the sake of my precious sons, and for the precious children not my own, I can stay unafraid of the dark, and work my way toward morning."

If you mapped Bray's "circular" structure, it would look like this:

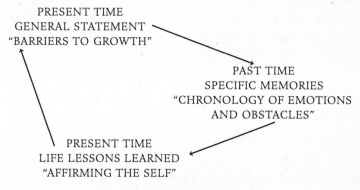

PRESENT TIME
GENERAL STATEMENT
"BARRIERS TO GROWTH"

PAST TIME
SPECIFIC MEMORIES
"CHRONOLOGY OF EMOTIONS
AND OBSTACLES"

PRESENT TIME
LIFE LESSONS LEARNED
"AFFIRMING THE SELF"

*The Journey = Rebirthing her self
through the power of re-memory and writing.*

Nathan McCall's mapping of his life's journey is slightly different from Bray's but fundamentally the same. McCall begins with a **highly specific incident** of violence against whites. The beating of the anonymous white boy is gripping and tightly "hooks" you into the mesmerizing brutality of his youthful world. Nonetheless, McCall ends Chapter One with a **general statement:**

Sometimes, when I sit back and think about the crazy things the fellas and I did and remember the hate and violence that we unleashed, it's hard to believe I was once part of all that—I feel so removed from it now that I've left the streets. Yet when I consider white America and the way it's treated blacks, our random rage in the old days makes perfect sense to me. Looking back, it's easy to understand how it all got started.

Next, McCall structurally begins the process of chronologically rebirthing, growing himself through the power of telling, retelling his story. His story, too, circles from the present into past memories and back into the present of his adult life. Like Bray, he finishes his autobiography with a testament to his new self, his new life's wisdom.

Both Nathan McCall and Rosemary Bray, in their powerful autobiographies, demonstrate their progress toward self-definition and rebirth. Both narratives succeed as literature not only because of their clear, eloquent prose but because Bray and McCall have sifted, sorted through *all* the moments of life and, through honest reflection, discovered the pattern of influences and feelings—good, bad, and mixed—that defined or tried to define their lives. They've made art out of life's chaos and have grown in emotional and moral stature through the process. Readers grow as well. By experiencing other people's journeys, we can learn more about ourselves and our individual road maps toward definition and rebirth.

EXERCISE 1

POSTING SIGNS:
SIFTING THROUGH THE PAST

Take an afternoon and study the "then" exercises and photos in your journal. Allow yourself to indulge in memories, past feelings. What emotions overwhelmed you? Were you generally happy or unhappy? Why? What was your relationship to your parents? Your siblings? How did your community—teachers, mentors, neighbors—support or thwart you?

What events do you remember most? Do you remember constantly moving as an Army brat, feeling alienated, always saying goodbye to just-met friends? Or do you remember the lonely hours of piano practice and the thrilling triumph of winning a recital and a scholarship to college?

How did you feel about yourself? How did others feel about you? Like Richard Wright in *Black Boy*, do you view hours spent in a library as your salvation? Your escape from those who belittled you?

How did you see your self? How did others see you? In your dreams, did you see yourself as beautiful, although others saw you as a pudgy, ill-kempt child?

Reflecting upon your past may make you emotional, dreamy. You may find yourself recalling painful memories. Or you may feel a bittersweet nostalgia for the past. Do not run from these emotions. Strong emotions can open a door to new understanding and growth.

After serious reflection, list for thirty minutes, quickly and without editing, what you believe are your most important memories. (Don't worry about developing each memory; for now, just list the significant markers, the "road signs" of your journey.)

Study your list. At what year in your life does memory begin? Age two? Four? Six? What memories seem most critical? Do these memories cluster around a particular time period, a particular place? Maybe starting kindergarten is your first important memory. You may also discover that you have significant memories of what occurred when you were between the ages of ten and fourteen. Or between six and eight. Or during the summer of 1962, when your family uprooted and moved cross-country to Florida.

What does your list tell you about yourself? What was important to you as you grew? What emotional, social, physical obstacles did you confront?

For now, take one of your memories—a single road sign pointing you toward growth—and write about it for thirty minutes, trying to recall as much sensory detail as you can. Do you remember smells, tastes, sights, a harsh or gentle touch? When you feel as though you have explored the memory as best you can, proceed to Exercise 2.

E X E R C I S E   2

POSTING SIGNS: UNDERSTANDING THE HERE AND NOW

Plan a morning when you can celebrate yourself and indulge in the pleasures of the "now" you. Whether you're twenty-five, thirty-five, forty, or fifty-five, you have made the journey to a self that has survived. You are here. Standing. Holding firm and strong. Though you may have frailties, foibles (we all do), treat yourself to a day of sheer meditative pleasure and enjoyment. Search for activities you enjoy that will engage your senses and still allow time for you to reflect and think about your life—*in the present tense*. The here-and-now. You may want to visit a Buddhist temple, a church, a botanical garden, or take a long, relaxing walk along the beach, in a forest grove, or on your local community trail. Pack a lunch with your favorite and most indulgent foods. Chocolate strawberries. Brie cheese. Grilled chicken and powder biscuits.

When you're feeling the most peaceful, the most satiated with food and sensory experiences, list in your journal the things you wish to celebrate about yourself. For example, emotional resilience, physical strength, a love of hard work and discipline, joy in being a spouse, a cancer survivor—these are all things to admire and write about.

List, too, the fears you've confronted, the challenges you've successfully met. Did you surprise yourself by accomplishing something unexpected? Finishing graduate school? Writing a novel? Giving up alcohol? Overcoming an eating disorder?

What social skills have you developed? Are you a good friend? Have you learned to say *no* to those who might take advantage of you? Have you learned to speak to large groups? Or facilitate conflict resolutions? Have you organized a MADD (Mothers Against Drunk Driving) chapter? Or encouraged grass-roots activism?

How do you want to build on your present strengths?

What are your near- and long-term goals? What new dreams do you have for yourself?

Last, what essential quality or truth would you want people to know and understand about you? Write it down in your journal.

CONNECTING THE DOTS

Compare and contrast your lists. How different are you now from yourself as a child? How do the strengths and survival skills you have now connect with incidents and emotions in your overall life journey? Can you connect aspects of your past with yourself now? How have you transformed and redefined yourself? Have you "broken from your past," or has your development been a logical and emotional extension of your youth?

Spend thirty minutes writing in your journal about how your past and present intertwine. Try to link qualities you have now with specific incidents in your past. Try, too, to show how your present interactions with loved ones and society are a reflection of, or a reaction to, your past self. If you could, what, if anything, would you change about your life's journey?

To tell your life story, where would you begin? *Follow your emotional instinct:* with what idea, what event, what person, what words would you begin your personal history?

For twenty minutes write the opening of your autobiography. Don't edit. Don't feel compelled to begin with "I was born" or even to begin with a picture of yourself at the age of two. Instead, begin where, emotionally, you know you must. Nathan McCall begins his autobiography with a violent image of himself as a young teen; Rosemary Bray begins hers with a description of her emotional state as a young girl awakened from sleep in a cold apartment, ill and afraid.

What you choose to tell and *how you choose to tell it* marks the *significant beginning* of your autobiography.

Next, spend twenty minutes writing the end of your autobiography, the point where you will arrive. Write what you wish to say about yourself, about what you've learned, what you regret, what you take pride in. Write what you want to teach others about life, about being human, about achieving goals, big and small. Write down the wisdom you wish to pass on to another generation, to your family, your children. Write down how you wish to live the rest of your future.

(Later, you may decide to change your opening and conclusion. Often, writing and revising will encourage you to write an improved beginning or ending. But, for now, you have a workable frame for your life story!)

Next, create an outline in your journal for your book. Now that you have a tentative opening and conclusion, try to fill in the important events and developments you listed in Exercise 1. How would you arrange them? Chronologically? This happened, then this happened, and so on? From your opening, will you go deeper into your past history, or does your opening already begin with the appropriate chronology of your life?

* * *

Each major event or development in your life can probably serve as the focus for a chapter. You may want to name these chapters, identifying aspects of your life, or simply number them. Patrice Gaines, in *Laughing in the Dark: From Colored Girl to Woman of Color—A Journey from Prison to Power,* labeled some of her chapters as follows:

Chapter One: Colored Girl
Chapter Two: Turning Black
Chapter Three: Womanish
Chapter Four: Giving Birth
Chapter Five: Riding the Horse
Chapter Six: Locked Up

Eventually, her journey ends with:

Chapter Thirteen: Witnessing
Chapter Fourteen: Joy

Assata Shakur, in *Assata,* on the other hand, simply numbers her chapters 1 through 21. Whether or not you use chapter titles, the central point is to tell your story in the sequence that will best provide readers with a map to follow your journey. Additionally, each major aspect of your outline should have the potential to serve as a single chapter.

Creating any book requires a great deal of hard work. But you should celebrate. You're on your way!

You now have an opening, an ending, and a solid outline to help focus your writing. Bravo! You have the skeleton of an autobiography. Subsequent chapters and exercises will help you add heart, muscle, and flesh!

Maya Angelou's
I Know Why the Caged Bird Sings

It is impossible to talk about contemporary African American autobiography without discussing the great talent and literary brilliance of Maya Angelou. She's written several autobiographies in a steady progression, journeying from childhood to teenage motherhood to acclaim as one of our greatest living writers. Her latest volume is appropriately named Wouldn't Take Nothing for My Journey Now.

"What you looking at me for?
I didn't come to stay . . ."

I hadn't so much forgot as I couldn't bring myself to remember. Other things were more important.

"What you looking at me for?
I didn't come to stay . . ."

Whether I could remember the rest of the poem or not was immaterial. The truth of the statement was like a wadded-up handkerchief, sopping wet in my fists, and the sooner they accepted it the quicker I could let my hands open and the air would cool my palms.

"What you looking at me for . . . ?"

The children's section of the Colored Methodist Episcopal Church was wiggling and giggling over my well-known forgetfulness.

The dress I wore was lavender taffeta, and each time I breathed it rustled, and now that I was sucking in air to breathe out shame, it sounded like crepe paper on the back of hearses.

As I'd watched Momma put ruffles on the hem and cute little tucks around the waist, I knew that once I put it on I'd look like a movie star. (It was silk and that made up for the awful color.) I was going to look like one of the sweet little white girls who were everybody's dream of what was right with the world. Hanging softly over the black Singer sewing machine, it looked like magic, and when people saw me wearing it they were going to run up to me and say, "Marguerite [sometimes it was 'dear Marguerite'], forgive us, please, we didn't know who you were," and I would answer generously, "No, you couldn't have known. Of course I forgive you."

Just thinking about it made me go around with angel's dust sprinkled over my face for days. But Easter's early morning sun had shown the dress to be a plain ugly cut-down from a white woman's once-was-purple throwaway. It was old-lady-long too, but it didn't hide my skinny legs, which had been greased with Blue Seal Vaseline and powdered with the Arkansas red clay. The age-faded color made my skin look dirty like mud, and everyone in church was looking at my skinny legs.

Wouldn't they be surprised when one day I woke out of my black ugly dream, and my real hair, which was long and blond, would take the place of the kinky mass that Momma wouldn't let me straighten? My light-blue eyes were going to hypnotize them, after all the things they said about "my daddy must of been a Chinaman" (I thought they meant made out of china, like a cup) because my eyes were so small and squinty. Then they would understand why I had never picked up a Southern accent, or spoke the common slang, and why I had to be forced to eat pigs' tails and snouts. Because I was really white and because a cruel fairy stepmother, who was understandably jealous of my beauty, had turned me into a too-big Negro girl, with nappy black hair, broad feet and a space between her teeth that would hold a number-two pencil.

"What you looking . . ." The minister's wife leaned toward me, her long yellow face full of sorry. She whispered, "I just come to tell you, it's Easter Day." I repeated, jamming the words together, "Ijustcometotellyouit'sEasterDay," as low as possible. The giggles hung in the air like melting clouds that were waiting to rain on me. I held up two fingers, close to my chest, which meant that I had to go to the toilet, and tiptoed toward the rear of the church. Dimly, somewhere over my head, I heard ladies saying, "Lord bless the child," and "Praise God." My head was up and my eyes were open, but I didn't see anything. Halfway down the aisle, the church exploded with "Were you there when they crucified my Lord?" and I tripped over a foot stuck out from the children's pew. I stumbled and started to say something, or maybe to scream, but a green persimmon, or it could have been a lemon, caught me between the legs and squeezed. I tasted the sour on my tongue and felt it in the back of my mouth. Then before I reached the door, the sting was burning down my legs and into my Sunday socks. I tried to hold, to squeeze it back, to keep it from speeding, but when I reached the church porch I knew I'd have to let it go, or it would probably run right back up to my head and my poor head would burst like a dropped watermelon, and all the brains and spit and tongue and eyes would roll all over the place. So I ran down into the yard and let it go. I ran, peeing and crying, not toward the toilet out back but to our house. I'd get a whipping for it, to be sure, and the nasty children would have something new to tease me about. I laughed anyway, partially for the sweet release; still, the greater joy came not only from being liberated from the silly church but from the knowledge that I wouldn't die from a busted head.

If growing up is painful for the Southern Black girl, being aware of her displacement is the rust on the razor that threatens the throat.

It is an unnecessary insult.

CHAPTER 1

When I was three and Bailey four, we had arrived in the musty little town, wearing tags on our wrists which instructed—"To Whom It May Concern"—that we were Marguerite and Bailey Johnson, Jr., from Long Beach, California, en route to Stamps, Arkansas, c/o Mrs. Annie Henderson.

Our parents had decided to put an end to their calamitous marriage, and Father shipped us home to his mother. A porter had been charged with our welfare—he got off the train the next day in Arizona—and our tickets were pinned to my brother's inside coat pocket.

I don't remember much of the trip, but after we reached the segregated southern part of the journey, things must have looked up. Negro passengers, who always traveled with loaded lunch boxes, felt sorry for "the poor little motherless darlings" and plied us with cold fried chicken and potato salad.

Years later I discovered that the United States had been crossed thousands of times by frightened Black children traveling alone to their newly affluent parents in Northern cities, or back to grandmothers in Southern towns when the urban North reneged on its economic promises.

The town reacted to us as its inhabitants had reacted to all things new before our coming. It regarded us a while without curiosity but with caution, and after we were seen to be harmless (and children) it closed in around us, as a real mother embraces a stranger's child. Warmly, but not too familiarly.

We lived with our grandmother and uncle in the rear of the Store (it was always spoken of with a capital *s)*, which she had owned some twenty-five years.

Early in the century, Momma (we soon stopped calling her Grandmother) sold lunches to the sawmen in the lumberyard (east Stamps) and the seedmen at the cotton gin (west Stamps). Her crisp meat pies and cool lemonade, when joined to her miraculous ability to be in two places at the same time, assured her business success. From being a mobile lunch counter, she set up a stand between the two points of fiscal interest and supplied the workers' needs for a few years. Then she had the Store built in the heart of the Negro area. Over the years it became the lay center of activities in town. On Saturdays, barbers sat their customers in the shade on the porch of the Store, and troubadours on their ceaseless crawlings through the South leaned across its benches and sang their sad songs of the Brazos while they played juice harps and cigar-box guitars.

The formal name of the Store was the Wm. Johnson General Merchandise Store. Customers could find food staples, a good variety of colored thread, mash for hogs, corn for chickens, coal oil for lamps, light bulbs for the wealthy, shoestrings, hair dressing, balloons, and flower seeds. Anything not visible had only to be ordered.

Until we became familiar enough to belong to the Store and it to us, we were locked up in a Fun House of Things where the attendant had gone home for life.

Each year I watched the field across from the Store turn caterpillar green, then gradually frosty white. I knew exactly how long it would be before the big wagons would pull into the front yard and load on the cotton pickers at daybreak to carry them to the remains of slavery's plantations.

During the picking season my grandmother would get out of bed at four o'clock (she never used an alarm clock) and creak down to her knees and chant in a sleep-filled voice, "Our Father, thank you for letting me see this New Day. Thank you that you didn't allow the bed I lay on last night to be my cooling board, nor my blanket my winding sheet. Guide my feet this day along the straight and narrow, and help me to put a bridle on my tongue. Bless this house, and everybody in it. Thank you, in the name of your Son, Jesus Christ, Amen."

Before she had quite arisen, she called our names and

issued orders, and pushed her large feet into homemade slippers and across the bare lye-washed wooden floor to light the coal-oil lamp.

The lamplight in the Store gave a soft make-believe feeling to our world which made me want to whisper and walk about on tiptoe. The odors of onions and oranges and kerosene had been mixing all night and wouldn't be disturbed until the wooded slat was removed from the door and the early morning air forced its way in with the bodies of people who had walked miles to reach the pickup place.

"Sister, I'll have two cans of sardines."

"I'm gonna work so fast today I'm gonna make you look like you standing still."

"Lemme have a hunk uh cheese and some sody crackers."

"Just gimme a coupla them fat peanut paddies." That would be from a picker who was taking his lunch. The greasy brown paper sack was stuck behind the bib of his overalls. He'd use the candy as a snack before the noon sun called the workers to rest.

In those tender mornings the Store was full of laughing, joking, boasting and bragging. One man was going to pick two hundred pounds of cotton, and another three hundred. Even the children were promising to bring home fo' bits and six bits.

The champion picker of the day before was the hero of the dawn. If he prophesied that the cotton in today's field was going to be sparse and stick to the bolls like glue, every listener would grunt a hearty agreement.

The sound of the empty cotton sacks dragging over the floor and the murmurs of waking people were sliced by the cash register as we rang up the five-cent sales.

If the morning sounds and smells were touched with the supernatural, the late afternoon had all the features of the normal Arkansas life. In the dying sunlight the people dragged, rather than their empty cotton sacks.

Brought back to the Store, the pickers would step out of the backs of trucks and fold down, dirt-disappointed, to the ground. No matter how much they had picked, it wasn't enough. Their wages wouldn't even get them out of debt to my grandmother, not to mention the staggering bill that waited on them at the white commissary downtown.

The sounds of the new morning had been replaced with grumbles about cheating houses, weighted scales, snakes, skimpy cotton and dusty rows. In later years I was to confront the stereotyped picture of gay song-singing cotton pickers with such inordinate rage that I was told even by fellow Blacks that my paranoia was embarrassing. But I had seen the fingers cut by the mean little cotton bolls, and I had witnessed the backs and shoulders and arms and legs resisting any further demands.

Some of the workers would leave their sacks at the Store to be picked up the following morning, but a few had to take them home for repairs. I winced to picture them sewing the coarse material under a coal-oil lamp with fingers stiffening from the day's work. In too few hours they would have to walk back to Sister Henderson's Store, get vittles and load, again, onto the trucks. Then they would face another day of trying to earn enough for the whole year with the heavy knowledge that they were going to end the season as they started it. Without the money or credit necessary to sustain a family for three months. In cotton-picking time the late afternoons revealed the harshness of Black Southern life, which in the early morn-

ing had been softened by nature's blessing of grogginess, forgetfulness and the soft lamplight.

CHAPTER 2

When Bailey was six and I a year younger, we used to
rattle off the times tables with the speed I was later to
see Chinese children in San Francisco employ on their aba-
cuses. Our summer-gray pot-bellied stove bloomed rosy red
during winter, and became a severe disciplinarian threat if we
were so foolish as to indulge in making mistakes.

Uncle Willie used to sit, like a giant black Z (he had been
crippled as a child), and hear us testify to the Lafayette County
Training Schools' abilities. His face pulled down on the left
side, as if a pulley had been attached to his lower teeth, and his
left hand was only a mite bigger than Bailey's, but on the second mistake or on the third hesitation his big overgrown right
hand would catch one of us behind the collar, and in the same
moment would thrust the culprit toward the dull red heater,
which throbbed like a devil's toothache. We were never
burned, although once I might have been when I was so terrified I tried to jump onto the stove to remove the possibility of
its remaining a threat. Like most children, I thought if I could
face the worst danger voluntarily, and *triumph,* I would forever
have power over it. But in my case of sacrificial effort I was
thwarted. Uncle Willie held tight to my dress and I only got
close enough to smell the clean dry scent of hot iron. We
learned the times tables without understanding their grand
principle, simply because we had the capacity and no alternative.

The tragedy of lameness seems so unfair to children that

they are embarrassed in its presence. And they, most recently off nature's mold, sense that they have only narrowly missed being another of her jokes. In relief at the narrow escape, they vent their emotions in impatience and criticism of the unlucky cripple.

Momma related times without end, and without any show of emotion, how Uncle Willie had been dropped when he was three years old by a woman who was minding him. She seemed to hold no rancor against the baby-sitter, nor for her just God who allowed the accident. She felt it necessary to explain over and over again to those who knew the story by heart that he wasn't "born that way."

In our society, where two-legged, two-armed strong Black men were able at best to eke out only the necessities of life, Uncle Willie, with his starched shirts, shined shoes and shelves full of food, was the whipping boy and butt of jokes of the underemployed and underpaid. Fate not only disabled him but laid a double-tiered barrier in his path. He was also proud and sensitive. Therefore he couldn't pretend that he wasn't crippled, nor could he deceive himself that people were not repelled by his defect.

Only once in all the years of trying not to watch him, I saw him pretend to himself and others that he wasn't lame.

Coming home from school one day, I saw a dark car in our front yard. I rushed in to find a strange man and woman (Uncle Willie said later they were schoolteachers from Little Rock) drinking Dr Pepper in the cool of the Store. I sensed a wrongness around me, like an alarm clock that had gone off without being set.

I knew it couldn't be the strangers. Not frequently, but often enough, travelers pulled off the main road to buy tobacco or soft drinks in the only Negro store in Stamps. When I looked at Uncle Willie, I knew what was pulling my mind's coattails. He was standing erect behind the counter, not leaning forward or resting on the small shelf that had been built for him. Erect. His eyes seemed to hold me with a mixture of threats and appeal.

I dutifully greeted the strangers and roamed my eyes around for his walking stick. It was nowhere to be seen. He said, "Uh . . . this this . . . this . . . uh, my niece. She's . . . uh . . . just come from school." Then to the couple—"You know . . . how, uh, children are . . . th-th-these days . . . they play all d-d-day at school and c-c-can't wait to get home and pl-play some more."

The people smiled, very friendly.

He added, "Go on out and pl-play, Sister."

The lady laughed in a soft Arkansas voice and said, "Well, you know, Mr. Johnson, they say, you're only a child once. Have you children of your own?"

Uncle Willie looked at me with an impatience I hadn't seen in his face even when he took thirty minutes to loop the laces over his high-topped shoes. "I . . . I thought I told you to go . . . go outside and play."

Before I left I saw him lean back on the shelves of Garret Snuff, Prince Albert and Spark Plug chewing tobacco.

"No, ma'am . . . no ch-children and no wife." He tried a laugh. "I have an old m-m-mother and my brother's t-two children to l-look after."

I didn't mind his using us to make himself look good. In fact, I would have pretended to be his daughter if he wanted me to. Not only did I not feel any loyalty to my own father, I figured that if I had been Uncle Willie's child I would have received much better treatment.

The couple left after a few minutes, and from the back of the house I watched the red car scare chickens, raise dust and disappear toward Magnolia.

Uncle Willie was making his way down the long shadowed aisle between the shelves and the counter—hand over hand, like a man climbing out of a dream. I stayed quiet and watched him lurch from one side, bumping to the other, until he reached the coal-oil tank. He put his hand behind that dark recess and took his cane in the strong fist and shifted his weight on the wooden support. He thought he had pulled it off.

I'll never know why it was important to him that the couple (he said later that he'd never seen them before) would take a picture of a whole Mr. Johnson back to Little Rock.

He must have tired of being crippled, as prisoners tire of penitentiary bars and the guilty tire of blame. The high-topped shoes and the cane, his uncontrollable muscles and thick tongue, and the looks he suffered of either contempt or pity had simply worn him out, and for one afternoon, one part of an afternoon, he wanted no part of them.

I understood and felt closer to him at that moment than ever before or since.

During these years in Stamps, I met and fell in love with William Shakespeare. He was my first white love. Although I enjoyed and respected Kipling, Poe, Butler, Thackeray and Henley, I saved my young and loyal passion for Paul Lawrence

Dunbar, Langston Hughes, James Weldon Johnson and W.E.B. Du Bois' "Litany at Atlanta." But it was Shakespeare who said, "When in disgrace with fortune and men's eyes." It was a state with which I felt myself most familiar. I pacified myself about his whiteness by saying that after all he had been dead so long it couldn't matter to anyone any more.

Bailey and I decided to memorize a scene from *The Merchant of Venice,* but we realized that Momma would question us about the author and that we'd have to tell her that Shakespeare was white, and it wouldn't matter to her whether he was dead or not. So we chose "The Creation" by James Weldon Johnson instead.

These excerpts demonstrate Angelou's storytelling art. She begins with a concrete memory of utmost importance to her as a child. Dressed in Easter finery, the child Angelou believes others will see her magic, see that she is a white, blond, and blue-eyed dream child of privilege. This incident is telling and it keenly reflects the insidious power that white standards of beauty had over black girls before the 1960s. This inner vision of whiteness contrasts sharply with reality, with the "displacement" of Southern black girls in a racially charged America. Angelou doesn't just "tell" us about this conflict; she "shows" it with details of fallibility. The wishful dreaming of a child hoping her dress will work magic and make her and her life more "beautiful," the embarrassment of forgetting her Easter lines, and the added insult of urine stinging down her leg, all add dimension to the image of a Southern black girl's pain.

In the second chapter, Angelou moves back in time to "when [she] was three" and her conscious life in Stamps, Arkansas, began. Thus, she begins mapping her journey—detailing the literal and emotional landscape of a time and place and of the people and events that shaped her.

In order to write the journey, you must appreciate who you are and how the very core of you was created in your travels from childhood to adulthood.

Reread your "then" and "now" exercises. Have you added enough detail to your remembrances? Have you drawn a strong portrait of landscape and people?

Reread the beginning of your autobiography. Does it still seem the right place to begin? If so, why? If not, why not?

Revise your opening. Add, change, or delete anything you're not satisfied with. (Don't be afraid to start over. The first step of your journey is often the most important.)

Like Angelou and McCall, ask yourself whether you're creating pictures of the community and time in which your story takes place. Are you giving enough specific details? Are you sharing, re-creating events and people *with* your readers, or are you talking *at* them? In fiction, the adage is "show, don't tell"; so, too, for nonfiction. Show as much as possible. In other words, use events and actions as Angelou does *to show* a child's embarrassment and as McCall does *to show* the violence of his world.

Finally, study the proposed outline for your autobiography. Are there any events you want to add? Or cut? Does your journey seem clear?

If you're reasonably satisfied with your progress, then move on to the next chapter.

Now that you've outlined a map of your life's journey so far, you need to consider the turning points, the bumps and curves in the road.

SEVEN

TURNING POINTS
AND REVELATIONS

Time heals. Perspective teaches.

Enlightenment, empathy, and understanding often arise from conflicts, obstacles, and heartache.

Life never runs smoothly all the time. But sometimes hurt can be a blessing that affirms what is good in life, and also teaches us how to live more meaningfully. No one should wish pain on another, but in an autobiography, it is *your pain, your hardships,* that readers experience vicariously so that they can better understand your life and its relevance to them.

Confronting past hurts and past pain is never easy. The mind can bury troubling incidents, but the writer's task is to dig deep, to re-experience seemingly hopeless and unbearable incidents in order to transform them into art. "You've got to go there, to know there," says Janie in Zora Neale Hurston's *Their*

Eyes Were Watching God. If you're not ready to examine all aspects of your life, your readers may misunderstand parts of your journey. Hard knocks can be as important as praise, especially if your hardships illuminate positive turning points in your life—opportunities with the potential to change the course of your life from sorrow to joy, from weakness to strength, from victim to heroine.

MY BEST ADVICE

Re-experiencing pain for its own sake is meaningless. Always write with the intention of transforming your pain, of exploring how your choices enabled you to reclaim your life. Write by focusing on understanding, on lessons learned.

Critical junctures, turning points, are akin to dramatic scenes in fiction. Circumstances and choices reveal the state of a character, the condition of her life. As in life, an autobiography may have more than one turning point. Life can be flying joyously by—and wham! something goes awry, like health problems, loss of a job, a divorce—things that hurl you into despair. Or you can experience horrors and then, one day, unexpectedly, experience a chance to heal. A beautiful day or a kind word from a stranger may inspire you. You may decide to finish school, reconcile with your child's father, or stop abusing alcohol.

But while there may be many opportunities for change, a turning point can have force of a climatic moment. Something significant and dramatic happens because *of you . . . to you . . . or by you.* The action, even if external, has the power to shift your life internally toward either positive or negative change.

For example, Jill Nelson, in her 1994 American Book

Award winner, *Volunteer Slavery*, writes about accepting a job, despite severe misgivings, at the *Washington Post:*

> *My fate is sealed. We will move to Washington. I will go to work for the* Washington Post. *We will live the life of the Cosbys, sans Daddy. I feel I owe my daughter stability, bourgeoisdom, charge accounts at Woodies, a chance to join the mainstream. I will be the Cosmo mom, the queen of having it all, and my daughter a Cosby clone. For $50,000 smackeroos, how bad could it be?*

For Nelson, the answer is very bad indeed, given her social and political consciousness. Nelson's decision alters her life immeasurably, but not until another turning point, attended by an *interior revelation* is she able to pair her actions with her inner self. She retreats to her family home in Oak Bluffs on Martha's Vineyard and admits to her mother:

> *"I think I had a nervous breakdown and I think I'm going to quit my job."*

Nelson, later, becomes more decisive and quits her job. But she could not have changed without an interior revelation. She needed to understand herself emotionally and spiritually before she could take a new path.

REVELATION—*(noun)* 1. *a surprising thing revealed;*
2. *admission, confession, declaration, disclosure, leak.*

For African Americans, "revelation" also has the sweet promise of salvation. Whether in secular or Christian terms, the emphasis is on making oneself literally and spiritually "free," on becoming emotionally and physically whole.

Hemmed in by racism, the legacy of slavery, and sexism and sexual stereotypes, black people strive to fly free, to sing even when caged, and to bear witness to their continual survival.

John Edgar Wideman, in his autobiography, *Brothers and Keepers,* manages to tell two life stories—his own and that of his brother, Robby. Robby's external turning point is clear. He participates in a robbery in which a man is murdered; thus, his path becomes one of life imprisonment. But Robby's journey toward *revelation, an interior turning point,* occurs when he shares himself with his brother, John:

> *I ain't never told nobody all of it cause I didn't think I could. Fraid it would make you or Mommy or anybody think I was really bad, that I belonged in here with criminals. Cause I did it all. Your brother was a stone gangster and that's what he wanted to be. I had things figured out. Needed a stake to start me on the way to the top. Robbing people was the only way, so that's what we did. Made up my mind to do whatever it took. Never thought I'd really hurt nobody. Never thought I'd get hurt. We was cool. We could bullshit our way out of anything.*
>
> *Well, that's who I was. I needed to tell you that. I come this far I don't want to hold nothing back.*

Robby's choice to use words to reveal himself to his brother sets the stage for his interior healing. Literally, both Robby's speech and his silences (what he chooses to say or not say) serve as powerful indicators of Robby's estrangement from himself and his family. Ultimately, it is his speech that moves him toward healing his inner self.

John's revelation is "to listen":

Silences troubled me—where was Robby, what was he thinking, why didn't he say something, why didn't—until I learned to accept the quiet interludes as breathing spaces, necessary reminders of the medium—time—in which we were working. Because when we talked, we did lose track of time. And time was all we had. Time ticked or circled or dryly extinguished itself. Time was the sound of one hand clapping, a moving stillness, a roaring silence always there beneath our voices. When we stopped talking, we heard it. We needed to hear it, although it contained no message except the infinite, irreducible hum of its presence.

There are many steps along life's road. What are the turning points in your life? The external actions that made a significant difference? The interior revelation that altered the course of your life?

For example, a critical turning point for me was discovering that black women wrote books. When I was a college junior, I entered the library one twilight evening and saw Gayle Jones's novel *Corregidora*. I was inspired by the world Jones had created and almost immediately switched my major from theater to English.

While I had often written poetry, stories, essays throughout my school days, no one—not a teacher, a parent, a friend—ever mentioned the possibility of a career as a writer.

After switching majors, I taught myself about my African American literary heritage, and I vowed to write stories that moved my heart. Sometimes, I think that finding my true calling as a writer was sheer luck. I suspect that once I had graduated from college, I might have found it harder to study writing or to enroll in creative writing courses. Perhaps, too, I would have been absorbed in another career that left little time for writing. But, for me, my life as a writer stretches back to that moment in the library when I discovered my first role model of a black woman author.

Although discovering my writer's calling was significant, my interior revelation didn't occur until over a decade later. While I struggled to write, I had deep wounds related to my mother's abandonment of me when I was an infant. My parents resumed their marriage when I was eight, but by the time I was eleven, they divorced again. Like many children of divorce, I thought I was unlovable and somehow responsible for my parents' failed marriage.

Becoming a wife and mother did a great deal to heal my childhood hurt. Writing my first novel, *Voodoo Dreams,* was also positive and sustaining. I remember writing through the early morning hours, when the sky was still black and the stars still visible. As I was finishing the final chapter of my novel, I wrote, "Being a woman is just fine," and "Life be a celebration." For the first time, I believed, deeply and personally, that those words were true. Having my own family, having completed my goal of writing a novel, I had become a grown-up black woman. I remember waking my husband so that he could witness my completing *Voodoo Dreams* and share my joy at having achieved the goals of writer, teacher, mother, wife.

Celebrate your turning points and revelations. They are part of your journey, part of what makes you unique and interesting. In an autobiography, your transformation may point someone else toward a needed path.

JUMP BACK, TURN AROUND

Quite likely, you've had several turning points in your life—some predictable and expected, others utterly unpredictable and unexpected. In your journal, list what you think were your significant turning points. You may have had only one or two or three junctures in which your life veered onto another path. The experiences may have been happy or unhappy, wondrous or bitter. What matters, however, is that your life changed fundamentally and dramatically.

Once you've listed the turning points, rank them in the order of their effect on your life. Someone's list might look like this:

1. Loss of spouse

2. Parenthood

3. Crime Victim

4. Finished a law degree

Write for thirty minutes, quickly and without editing, about your most significant turning point, your number one event. Give the details about what happened, why it happened, and how you felt about it. How did your life change? Was the change positive or negative? What do you remember most about this event? What are your sensory memories—taste, smell, touch, sight, and sound? Would you want to re-experience this turning point? If not, why not? If so, why?

Over time, repeat this exercise for each of your turning points. Later, you will use the writing in your journal as a foundation for the first draft of your autobiography.

E X E R C I S E   2

DRAMATIZING THE TURNING POINT

Just as you relive memories, so, too, readers will relive your story with you. The best way to help them achieve this is to dramatize the events as though they were happening again, right before your eyes. But this time, rather than being *in* the scene, you are *outside* it, watching yourself move, live, and breathe. You are like a theatergoer, watching the play and interplay of your life:

> *There were lights and sirens. Zayd was dead. My mind knew that Zayd was dead. The air was like cold glass. Huge bubbles rose and burst. Each one felt like an explosion in my chest. My mouth tasted like blood and dirt. The car spun around me and then something like sleep overtook me. In the background i could hear what sounded like gunfire. But i was fading and dreaming.*
>
> *Suddenly, the door flew open and i felt myself being dragged out onto the pavement. Pushed and punched, a foot upside my head, a kick in the stomach. Police were everywhere. One had a gun to my head.*

"Which way did they go?" he was shouting. "Bitch, you'd better open your mouth or I'll blow your goddamn head off!"

Assata Shakur, in her autobiography, *Assata,* re-creates her turning point—being captured by the police. This capture results in six years of imprisonment until she escapes and seeks political asylum in Cuba.

Shakur *shows* rather than merely *tells* her story. She recreates the scene through:

- **Sensory details** that conjure up the time and place;

- **Thoughts and feelings** that allow the reader to identify with her interior life and experience;

- **Strong verbs** that emphasize action, events happening *now;*

- **Dialogue** that makes the police seem alive, acting in the present rather than in the past.

Review your earlier turning point exercise. How can you use dialogue? How can you better express your thoughts and feelings? How can you describe the event so that readers see, feel, and hear it? Are tastes and smells significant? Is anyone else in the scene with you? Do they speak? Do they act in particular ways? What do they look like?

Using your turning point exercise as a foundation, write for thirty minutes, describing the event as if it were taking place or being performed on a stage. Remember to develop a sense of place, time, and emotional atmosphere through the use of strong verbs and concrete descriptions; link your thoughts and feelings to the event as it happens, and use dialogue when necessary.

When you've finished, compare your revised turning point with the original draft. What are the significant differences between Exercise 1 and Exercise 2? Which version is more vital and alive? Which version do you prefer?

Ideally, Exercise 2 should be the more interesting version of your "turning point." It should be more effective at drawing readers into your world by identifying with you and your experience. If readers "relive" your history via language that *shows rather than tells,* they will more likely be enriched and enthralled by your story.

E X E R C I S E   3

REVELATIONS—BETTER LATE

THAN NEVER

A revelation may be your interior, intellectual, and emotional awakening. It is, in a way, a thoughtful summation of your experiences, your paths, and, most important, the turning points in your life.

In Exercise 1, you listed several turning points. Go back and review that list, but this time write down what you *learned* from each event.

For example, if you listed "divorce," you may have learned that you can endure grief beyond what you thought you were capable of withstanding. You may have learned, too, that you

have the inner strength to carry on; that you have more resilience and valor than you expected of yourself. You may also
begin to cherish life in a new way and to realize that love's en-
durance comes from the equal commitment of two people to
a relationship. To say "I'll never get married again" is a superficial reaction to divorce's pain. Wrestling with what divorce
means in the larger context of your life, your spiritual growth
and maturation, will *encourage revelations that can enhance the
quality of your living and help you to* **construct** *rather than* **destroy**
ways of being.

Select one of your turning points (if you feel emotionally
ready, select the most significant one) and write about your
revelation—your thoughts and feelings about the experience,
what it meant to you, and the lessons you learned. Be as honest and as frank as you can. The tendency will be to write *what
you think you know* in as few minutes as possible. But take at
least thirty minutes to contemplate your feelings and what you
now know about life. Then take another thirty minutes to
write down your revelation. Be expansive yet clear and precise
in what you say. Pretend you're trying to explain to your dear-
est friend the meaning you've found so far in life. Pretend that
someone somewhere vitally needs to know what you've
learned. So write your revelation with beauty, emotion, and
thoughtfulness; say it as well as you can.

When you've finished writing, close your journal and
don't look at what you've written for at least a day.

When you return to your revelation, read it silently, then
read it aloud. Does anything sound false? Do your words seem
powerful and direct or weak and vague? Have you left some-

thing unsaid? Have you been honest enough? Were you self-critical when you needed to be? Did you consider what you still have to learn about life? Or did you artificially make yourself the heroine, who, having learned one lesson, can do no wrong?

Revise your revelation in whatever way you feel you must. It may be a paragraph or several paragraphs or several pages. Length doesn't matter. When the words ring true to you, when they stir emotions within you, then and only then you'll know that you've succeeded as an honest writer. You'll have captured with clarity an aspect of your life's emotional and intellectual truth. As a writer, you'll have caught magic!

And you'll have begun the process of truly sharing your humanity with others.

Bravo!

TURNING POINTS AND REVELATIONS, STUDY ONE

PATRICE GAINES'S
LAUGHING IN THE DARK

Gaines writes passionately about her journey from being a victim of violent and abusive men to becoming a journalist and a woman with healthy self-respect and self-esteem. During her journey, she had setbacks as well as successes. Turning points and revelations.

I was still in love with drugs, but it was hallucinogenics now, including speed, my favorite. I knew the Austins were taking good care of Andrea, so I didn't have to worry about her; I was free to go out and get high with friends. Sometimes I went home and found I couldn't sleep, so I lay awake in bed, tripping while I played Marvin Gaye's "What's Going On," over and over, softly, so I wouldn't wake anyone; then I got up early, and since Mrs. Austin was baby-sitting Andrea during the day now, I dressed, took more speed, and left for work.

In this souped-up state of mind, dressed in my favorite bright pink hot pants, I met a young man named John Harmon at a nightclub one evening. He was high, too, so the night had a bizarre air to it, as if neither of us were meeting a real person or, for that matter, being a real person. This would become a theme for our relationship until I was feeding myself barbiturates, dropping acid, and popping all kinds of pills just to be able to live with John. I had fallen into my lonely well again— and was drowning. Once I had sex with John, there was no rising to the surface. I could not separate sex from love. When his calloused hands touched me, loneliness stood back—at least for a while, staring just out of reach but smiling, too, because it was just a matter of time before it embraced me again.

John was not handsome and I was not sexually attracted to him; he appealed to that hollow part of me that was always open and empty. His hair was black and beady, except for an odd shock of white at the front, which grew curly. He was round like a panda and bounced on the balls of his feet when he walked. John embodied the absence of grace, bumping into the corners of tables, stumbling over his own feet, dropping everything his stubby fingers touched.

He was a low-level civil service worker, wasting the taxpayer's money every chance he got, sneaking off work early. I found him sitting at the bar drinking one beer after another. Everyone who walked in knew him, and he kept them laughing with his jokes and banter. He bought a lot of people drinks, and one day, much later, I would think that what people really wanted from John was not friendship, but whatever he was giving away free that day. Still, that night in the bar, he became my friend, too.

We dated for a year, spending most of our nights high on pills and smoke and our days working and recovering from our nights. John sold marijuana and stolen goods as a side hustle to his legitimate government job. He wasn't a big-time hustler, selling just enough marijuana and "hot" goods to keep enough money to satisfy his longings for material goods. He wasn't a flashy guy, his most lavish habits being purchasing a new car each year, staying in good hotels, and eating at expensive restaurants. For all his flimflams and drugs and late bar nights, what he yearned for most was respectability—that he and his family, his mother and four siblings, be permanent members of the middle class.

Six months after we started dating, I began imagining him as my husband. This was a bad habit of mine. I imagined myself married to men I should never have even looked at once. Still, after somewhere between three and six months I would look into their faces and see H-U-S-B-A-N-D written across their foreheads; then before I went to sleep that night I saw a house and me cooking and this guy, who wasn't ready to be anyone's husband, coming home from work, running to the kitchen, and kissing me.

John's family was similar to Andrea's father's family, which should have been a major red flag. John, like Ben, had replaced his father as man of the house. John's father lived with the family, but he drank a lot and sometimes spent a night or two away from home. He had little education, which meant he worked in low-paying jobs while his oldest child, John, earned a good salary. John supplemented the financial support his father provided to the family and each year, when John bought a new car, he gave his mother the old one. While his father was a shadow of a man who moved through the house hardly noticed, John was worshiped and adored, the reigning king of the household.

I sympathized with John's father and wondered what it felt like to be replaced by your son in your wife's heart. From where I watched I saw the toll Mrs. Harmon's affection took on everyone, particularly John. She had raised her boy to be a stand-in for her husband, which meant manipulating John to make sure he possessed the proper amount of sympathy to make him provide for her. Yet all the time Mrs. Harmon hated John, too, because she didn't really like needing him. What she would have preferred was a husband; it was just plain easier to make a boy be a man than to make a man be a man—even if the boy wasn't ready to grow up. Mrs. Harmon was high-strung and nervous around me, the person who threatened to take away her man-son, and John was cheated out of the experiences in life that teach you that love is worth too much to be bought. In some ways, John was very similar to my own father, in their insistence on providing, financially, for the women in their lives.

Unlike my father, who loved very young children, John wasn't comfortable around them. There would come a time when I believed his discomfort existed because children are the most honest human beings—that, before adults ruin them, children have vision that extends beyond what they see with their eyes. They saw John's real self and reacted with stiff bodies and pouts. He was uneasy playing with Andrea and more comfortable buying her things, so he gave her more clothes than she needed, more toys than one child could ever play with. I, a person who had once shouted to her father that love was more than material things, now interpreted John's actions as love. Andrea did not; she saw the truth.

Mrs. Harmon knew John could not head up two households, so she tried to wish me away by ignoring me, just as she did her husband. She was kind to Andrea, though I was suspicious of her affection. Despite her grumblings, John and I forged ahead with plans to marry. A couple of months before the wedding, we moved our things into a rented duplex. John purchased most of the furniture, heavy, expensive, traditional pieces. I bought a bed and chest for Andrea, a wrought-iron dinette set for the kitchen, draperies, and curtains. John and I agreed that until we were married he would stay at his cousin's and Andrea and I would live in the duplex, a place that represented all the comfort and security I longed for, and wanted for my daughter.

About this time, John began to act as if I belonged to him, as if I were just another piece of furniture in the duplex. He pouted and threw tantrums when I didn't do what he demanded and when I disagreed with him in public. I donned my curly dark brown wig one day when he was driving me and one of my sisters, who was visiting from Maryland, to the store. He stopped the car and ordered me to take off the wig. I refused. He opened the door and pushed me out. My sister—in shock—got out with me, and we caught the bus. I tried to laugh it off, but I was angry and humiliated. Yet after John came downtown, found us, and gave us a ride home, I forgave him.

I had second thoughts about marriage, but I let the fact that I had already sent out wedding invitations tilt the scale in favor of proceeding. One day I would look back and laugh at that, that I allowed a life-altering decision to be influenced by seventy-five dollars' worth of pink paper squares.

My girlfriends planned a bachelorette party for me at the duplex a couple of days before the wedding. On the eve of the party, a friend jokingly told John we were going to have a male dancer. John stormed into the apartment, ranting to me about how we couldn't have the party at our duplex and declaring that no matter where it was held, I couldn't attend if there was going to be a male dancer. I laughed because I knew there was no male dancer and because I thought John was feigning rage, since I couldn't imagine someone getting so upset over something so insignificant. But John rushed into the kitchen and pulled from the cabinets the black wine glasses I adored, and had paid eight dollars apiece for. He threw every one of them against the kitchen wall, while I screamed at him and cursed and cried.

I called people to announce that the wedding was canceled. My mother and a girlfriend, in town for the blessed event, were pleased. From what she heard in rumors and saw for herself, my mother knew John was short-tempered, selfish, and childish. She and my girlfriend quickly packed my things, pulling down curtains, hastily wrapping dishes in newspaper, and emptying the clothes from my drawers into a trunk.

"We prayed John would stay away until we finished," my mother told me months later. "We knew if you saw him and he started crying and begging you'd give in. You were always a sucker for a sad story."

It happened just as my mother feared: John came to the house. We went into the bedroom to talk. He started crying and begging and promising, and I relented. The wedding was on again. I insisted against the odds in my head that this was the marriage that would bring the happy home with the bedroom, the yard, and the doting daddy for Andrea.

My mother, who thought John was mean to Andrea and that I had chosen a man over my child, cried through the entire wedding. We held the reception in a dimly lit nightclub that was normally packed with young black professionals and the older black bourgeoisie. Mama and several friends of mine sat on one side of the cool, expansive room while John's parents and friends crowded together on the other side. We couldn't get our parents close enough to take the traditional photo with the entire bridal party. Anyway, the picture would have been incomplete without my father, who did not come and had told Mama, "She doesn't know the boy well enough. I don't want no part of it." I have wondered over the years if my life would have been different if my father had spoken these words to me, personally. But that gulf between us was widened by secondhand messages.

After the reception, as John and I were headed to the mountains for our honeymoon, we stopped at Mrs. Harmon's because I wanted to take the cake with us. "I hope you're satisfied now," my new mother-in-law said to me as I walked into the house.

"What do you mean?" I asked.

"I guess you're satisfied you got him," she said.

"John?"

"Who the hell you think I'm talking about, hussy."

I laughed, a tired, nervous titter.

"Yeah, laugh," she said.

I reached for the cake and she picked it up. She walked through the living room, out the front door, and onto the porch, with me following close behind. John was walking up the steps.

"I want you to take her out of here and don't bring her back!" Mrs. Harmon screamed.

"Give me my cake!" I hollered. I tugged at the box, then gave up.

"Here's your damn cake." She dropped the box.

The bride and groom figures toppled over; the top layer of the cake now had a jagged split through the middle.

"Your mother is a fucking maniac!" I screamed as I passed John. At the car, I turned and yelled out the window, "And I didn't take your son! He gave himself to me!"

John picked up the cake and followed his mother into the house. He came out a couple of minutes later, still carrying the cake in the box.

"I don't want that thing! Give it to your damn mama!" I screamed.

Later, Mrs. Harmon told my mother the cake had slipped accidentally from her hands. I didn't believe her, nor did my mother.

Over the next year, John provided for my material needs, just as he had been taught. But he was difficult to live with, verbally abusive and prone to severe mood swings. He was a scared little boy in a man's body, afraid to grow up to be a father or a husband. When we were high, our house was peaceful; he laughed and joked and I relaxed. When we were sober, considering what we had gotten ourselves into drove him to temper tantrums and me to the brink of depression and starvation. I lost twenty pounds.

John's meanness fed my insecurity. I wondered why he told me Andrea preferred staying at his mother's house. It hadn't occurred to me, though, that she stayed there because John had turned our house into a maze of chaos and confusion. He played with Andrea one minute and the next he teased her until she cried.

He picked her up from the day-care center one evening, and when they came into the house my daughter was hysterical.

"John said you were dead!" she cried, running to me.

"You told her what?" I snapped.

"She just kept asking me, 'Where is Mommy? Where is Mommy?' I was teasing her. I told her you were dead," he said, as if it were a natural answer.

John stayed out late most nights. I suspected he had girlfriends, though I didn't fret over the issue. Before long, I'd decided that if someone else wanted him, she could have him. He told me he was taking care of business, selling drugs or the trunkful of stolen goods he kept in his car. Soon our rantings woke up Andrea in the middle of the night and, scared, she'd run to me, crying. Instead of letting me comfort her, John made her go back to bed.

"You'll never be the cook my mother is," he said to me after dinner one evening.

He had said this before, and generally, I sulked over it and let it go. But this evening I answered, "If the bitch is so perfect, why are you so fucked up?"

I was closing the refrigerator when he slapped me so hard I fell against the refrigerator door. Before the sting left my cheek, I was planning my departure. A few days later, I sat in a free legal clinic getting information on filing for a divorce.

"If you leave the house your husband provides for you, under North Carolina law you get nothing," the lawyer said. "Nothing."

His words brought tears to my eyes, then down my cheeks. He passed me a box of tissue, his hands shaking worse than mine. He rattled on, delivering one piece of bad news after another, advising me to remain in the house with John while I filed for a legal separation.

"Are you kidding? He'd kill me if he knew I was trying to leave him," I said.

The lawyer perked up. "Well, if he hurts you, then we can do something."

I returned home, hoping to see things differently. Maybe John wasn't so bad; maybe I didn't understand him. But the arguments became more frequent, and after each one John bought Andrea toys and me gifts and took us both to dinner. He confessed his love for us, and for a few days we would live a fairly normal life. Then his behavior turned erratic again and Andrea begged to spend nights at his mother's house. I withdrew, not eating, not paying attention to my personal hygiene, half-combing my hair and wearing no makeup, which gave my face a blank look, as close as I could get to being invisible.

The alarm went off one morning, and when I rolled over to turn it off I discovered I couldn't lift myself from the bed: I was paralyzed. Every time I tried to move, a sharp pain shot up my spine. John dressed me and called an ambulance. At the hospital they admitted me for tests.

"Are you under a lot of stress?" a doctor asked me the next day.

"Some," I said.

"We can't find anything physically wrong with you. I believe your illness is caused by your mental state."

"What do you mean, 'mental'?"

"Stress, anxiety. Something has you wound so tight your muscles aren't relaxing. As long as we give you tranquilizers you're fine, but that's not natural. You should be able to live without tranquilizers. I suggest you see a psychiatrist."

I didn't hear the rest of his explanation, because I was mulling over the idea that a twenty-three-year-old woman could worry herself into a state of paralysis. Could I kill myself with my mind? I was intrigued and frightened by such power.

The paralysis of my body set me into action—I had to get out of my marriage. But I didn't have any money. John always paid the major bills, since he made more money, while I paid Andrea's day-care center and took care of my personal expenses. Subconsciously, I used my money to try to buy happiness, splurging on expensive clothes for Andrea and me and taking trips to see my family as often as possible. Everything I owned could be used up or would be outdated within a year; there was no savings account. Also, John and I were shopping around for a car for me. My plan was to save money and get a car first, then leave. But my plan was shortsighted and rooted in concerns about material items, when what I needed to think about was the mental health of myself and my child.

A therapist at the mental health center agreed to see me— at no cost—twice a week on my lunch hour. Meanwhile, I was having a recurring dream: I was alive in a grave. I looked up and saw an opening in the ground, a circle of light. John was standing at the top of the hole looking down at me. I didn't see him; I felt him. The light got smaller and smaller, as someone threw dirt on the hole. I always woke up, sweating and choking, before the opening closed totally.

In addition to my dream, there was my daughter, who through her innocence and honesty nudged me to leave John in a hurry. She and one of her friends were playing in Andrea's bedroom one afternoon, growling loud like beasts.

I walked into the bedroom. "What are you doing?"

"We're playing monster," Andrea's friend, Regina, said.

"Yeah. The monster's name is John, and we're running from him," Andrea said.

I meant to tell them to keep down the noise, but instead I shut the door and left the room. "They named their monster John," I repeated to myself.

A half hour later my daughter ran into the living room with a toy camera. I was watching television.

"Smile, Mommy," she said as she pointed her camera at me.

I flashed a phony smile.

"No, Mommy. Smile the way you smile when John isn't here," she said.

I looked at my child, her big eyes full of love and pity for me. Had I heard her right? Was my sadness so obvious that my daughter, who was not yet four, could see it on my face? Could she pinpoint when I smiled and know why my smiles disappeared?

"I'm leaving you," I told John when he came home.

"You can't do that," he said.

He pleaded with me to reconsider, and though I knew I wouldn't, my concession to him was to take Andrea to his mother's house so we could go out to dinner that evening and talk. It was a bad idea from the beginning. By the time we got home, my head was throbbing from too much listening and explaining. We were both so exhausted we fell asleep immediately.

A loud noise woke me up around eleven. John was standing next to the bed holding the phone, which he had yanked out of the wall. Now he threw the phone out of the bedroom and locked the bedroom door.

"What the hell are you doing?" I asked.

"I want us to talk. I don't want anybody disturbing us," he said.

He had gone off the deep end, I thought, but I wasn't scared, because he looked like a worried, weary baby. I stretched out across the bed, and he sat down next to me. He talked for nearly two hours, his sentences pouring out until he sobbed. I was so tired that my body ached. The phone in the living room rang. My girlfriend, I found out later, called the police when I didn't answer. She knew this was the night I was announcing to John that I was leaving, and she was afraid he had hurt me. Eventually, two police officers banged on the front door and yelled our names for about five minutes, then left.

John held me in the bedroom while they were at the door. "Don't say a word," he ordered, his big hand pinning my shoulder to the bed. I didn't fight, but I was getting scared now. I thought of the rifle John kept in the closet.

After the police left, John opened the bedroom door and

went into the kitchen. I tried to open the bedroom window to escape, but I couldn't get it up. By now it was 2:00 A.M. Trembling, I opened the closet door; the rifle was still in the corner. I went into the kitchen.

John stood at the sink, his face contorted, beads of sweat dripping from his forehead to his wet undershirt. He held up a shaking hand, clutching an empty bottle normally filled with tabs of mescaline.

"What's wrong with you?"

"I took an overdose," he said.

I forgot about being angry. "John, why?" I cried, hugging him.

"I can't live without you," he sobbed.

"I'm calling help," I said.

"Not the police."

I called a drug rehab program that had counselors on call twenty-four hours a day to deal with overdoses. I patted and hugged and stroked John until a young white woman knocked at our door. She talked to him, gently, then forced him to throw up. We dressed and she accompanied us to the hospital.

Neither John nor I could see what was coming. We both thought he'd get a checkup and then they'd release him. But shortly after our arrival at the hospital, a counselor whispered to me that people who try to commit suicide are kept in the psychiatric ward for observation for a few days. I was shocked, and I knew if John discovered their intentions he would run. I kept quiet.

They put him in a wheelchair and rolled him upstairs. I looked at him and saw the fat, boyish face I had seen the night we met. He acted bewildered and frightened. They rolled him into a padded room, and I followed. John squirmed. Now a nurse explained that he would be treated for the drug overdose and also counseled in the psychiatric ward over the next few days.

John's disposition changed. He grew visibly angry, instantly possessed, and his body appeared to swell to twice its normal size.

"I'm not gonna stay in here. You got the wrong guy. There's nothing wrong with me," he snapped. As he stood, several men in white coats grabbed his arm.

The nurse spoke to him gently: "Please lie down."

One of the men held a syringe. They were just starting to wrestle with John, to make him lie on a cot, when I stared into his eyes and saw hate and fear, but mostly hate. I backed away.

"I didn't really take those damn pills!" he hollered. "I was faking!"

"Faking?" I screamed, my concern for him turning instantly to a hate I was sure matched what I saw in his eyes. "You put me through all this shit and you're playing? You selfish muthafucka!"

I was crying. John flailed his arms wildly, but the men subdued him, pinning him down.

He screamed his last order: "Call them off, Pat!"

I backed away and wiped my tears.

"Fuck you, John!" I ran from the room, headed home to pack my clothes.

Gaines's need for drugs, her inability to separate sex from love, and her pursuit of inappropriate marriage partners all set the stage for the dramatic events in her life. There are at least two critical turning points: 1) her decision to marry John; 2) her decision to leave him. These opposing decisions create external change in Gaines's life. But these external changes cause interior revelations.

Review Gaines's story again. With a highlighter, mark all thoughts that reveal Gaines's inner self, the hard and hurtful knowledge she's acquiring because of her turning points. In your journal, compare and contrast Gaines's revelations.

What revelations does Gaines have *after* she decides to marry John? How do these revelations contribute to her next turning point, her decision to leave her marriage? What revelation or revelations does she have once she decides to leave? How does she come to know that John hates her? How does this knowledge further fuel her flight?

Gaines brilliantly shows how mental agony can be reflected in the body. She wakes up one morning, paralyzed. "Could I kill myself with my mind?" she wonders. Her dreams, too, reflect her pain. She dreams she's "alive in a grave . . . John standing at the top of the hole looking down at [her]."

How do you think paralysis and dreams contribute to Gaines's decision to leave her marriage? Why aren't paralysis and dreams enough? How is her daughter the final trigger for Gaines to take action?

LORENE CARY'S *BLACK ICE*

Black Ice *is Lorene Cary's coming-of-age tale, detailing her ambitious hopes to leave Philadelphia to attend the elite, predominantly white Saint Paul's School in New Hampshire. The transition heightens cultural, social, and racial tensions precisely at the time of Cary's unsettling transition from girlhood to womanhood. Her life's journey is complex and resonant of young African American womanhood.*

Mike Russell appeared to take us for a tour of the grounds and buildings. They were little more to me than a backdrop to our own improbable drama. Russell could have been leading me through the Land of the Sweets, I was so dreamy. He'd be gone by the time I got in, *if* I got in, I kept reminding myself, trying not to lose control. Like a tourist in a foreign country, I felt that it might be possible to come to this school and be free of my past, free to re-create myself. I smiled at Russell as he guided us into the New Chapel. He did not know that on a bet I'd eaten half a worm in fifth grade, and up here there'd be nobody to tell him or anyone else.

From the antechapel we looked down a long aisle flanked on either side by three rows of graduated pews for students and high-backed seats carved into the walls for teachers. The floors were laid with brick-colored quarry tile. At the end of the center aisle, the altar rose distant and ornate. Slants of sunbeams were colored by tall stained-glass windows overhead.

To our left a bright white marble angel cradled an equally white nude in muscular tribute to the school's war dead.

My head filled with the words and melodies of familiar prayers: the doxology, the Lord's Prayer, snippets of music:

> My soul be on thy guard
> Ten thousand foes arise:
> And hosts of sin are pressing hard
> To drive thee from the skies.

In the African Methodist Episcopal church, the minister would continue: "Honor thy father and thy mother that thy days may be long upon the land that the Lord thy God giveth thee." I heard the music, punctuated by the creaking pews, in my head. I heard the floor of Ward A.M.E. groan under its red carpet as the parishioners lined up in the aisle to take their burdens to the Lord. We touched hands and hugged each other as we made our slow progress toward the altar.

In the Chapel of St. Peter and St. Paul the heels of our shoes clicked on the stone floors. The aisle was wide enough for a mummers' procession. My music would not fit here. Neither would my God, He whom I had held onto, just barely, through the music that spoke comfort and retribution, and the community, the perfumed and bosomy women who approved of me, and the old men who nodded at me each Sunday. I could not conjure my God in this place, and it seemed His failure. Surprise, as cold as the electric blanket had been warm, overwhelmed me. We left the chapel. It was time for my interview.

* * *

Inside the Schoolhouse, at the top of a slate staircase, was a waiting room where Russell handed us over to Mr. Price. I smelled coffee brewing, and I heard classroom sounds— discussion, laughter, lecturing, but no shouts or threats, no yardsticks banging for silence, no words of shame or derision. My father, who taught in a public junior high school, looked away from Mr. Price and my mother for a moment and smilingly shook his head.

Our admissions officer, Mr. Dick, came into the waiting room. After a general greeting, he ushered us into an office and closed the door. This was what we had come for, and it was nothing like I had imagined.

For one thing, I had not expected my parents to be invited into my interview. Once they were in, I could not keep my eyes off them. They filled the room with their presence. Mr. Dick, I could see, was impressed by them. They were altogether natural, and yet larger than I'd ever seen them. My mother engaging and shiny-eyed, my father, thoughtful and imposing. They wanted St. Paul's, too—I saw that for the first time—or else they could not have created this portrayal of themselves: the ambitious couple in their thirties, grateful for an opportunity for their daughter, eager to help, reluctant to let her go. Why, St. Paul's, they said, was a dream come true, and I agreed. I loved to look at them like this. It was almost too good.

And yet it was true. I knew it. It was as true as the estrangement that had settled between them like chill damp in our basement. It was as true as our weekdays, morning after chaotic morning, when I looked in vain for the correct time on the faces of our several too-fast clocks, as my mother shouted up the stairs at approximately seven-forty-five that it was eight o'clock and we were late. Late! Always late. Always rushing, hobbled, baffled by the confusion that came our way. Whose fault? Whose?

And it was as true as our barely acknowledged disappointment in the big Yeadon house, which had not made us happier together, as I'd expected it would. Why else had we bought it? Why else the scrimping and saving, the thrift-shop furniture, the careful hand-washing of delicates, the parade of used, rather than new, auto parts?

I made a freeze-frame of my parents in my mind: big, expansive, generous, unhurried. It was what I had done as a child when I had felt in danger of getting too happy. I'd make a picture in my mind to go back to later and enjoy in bits. My mother was wearing her best lipstick, and my father sat content, wanting to be nowhere else but right there, with us. I made a picture of them like that—I can still see it—and I held my new gorgeous reverence for them way deep inside where it made me warm and giddy like brandy.

Then, Mr. Dick asked my parents to leave. Their interview was over. They had passed; how could they not? It was my turn, but I felt guilty that they should go. How could I sit alone in the office, discussing my worthiness for an education they'd never had? It was quiet after he'd shown them out. Quiet. It was hard to pull myself back, to stop watching others and start promoting myself. I wanted to watch some more. I wanted to look at Mr. Dick, his mannerisms, his eyes. I wanted to read his files and eavesdrop on his phone calls so I'd know who I was dealing with.

"Tell me, Lorene, what most attracts you to St. Paul's School?"

"I guess what I would look forward to most is being somewhere where all the students *want* to learn. In my school, if you get a really good report card, you feel like you better hide it on the way home."

It was partially true. Afraid of becoming an egghead and of appearing to be one, I smoked in the bathrooms, cursed regularly, and participated in mild pranks. But Yeadon High had plenty of ambitious kids of ambitious parents, and was hardly so tough a place as I insinuated. Mr. Dick did not seem to know that. I wondered what he thought it was like.

"It's not considered cool to do well?"

"Not really."

"And do you like school?"

"Most of the time, yes." A bald-faced lie. I disliked school, always had—the clanking institutional sounds in cavernous old buildings, the cheap dropped ceilings and multipurpose cafeteria-gymnasium-auditorium rooms in new ones. I hated fights. I was offended by standing in lines ("We're not moving until everybody is standing ab-so-lute-ly still"); insulted by teachers' condescension ("If you can't pronounce Mrs. *Rakour,* you just call me Mrs. *Rock-over*"); I was numbed by busywork ("Copy pages five hundred and fifty-five through five hundred and fifty-eight from your dictionaries, and see if *that* can keep your traps shut"). I dreaded gym. Mr. Dick could tell that I was lying; he smiled.

When we got around to books, I was finally set, as our minister would say, on solid ground. I gorged on books. I sneaked them at night. I rubbed their spines and sniffed in the musty smell of them in the library. I sped through my grandfather's paperbacks that lined the wall of their mint-green sun parlor and read and reread the dirty parts until I was damp. I memorized black poetry—stately sonnets, skittering bebop rhymes, any celebration of black women—and I drank in the fury of my contemporaries. I did not tell Mr. Dick that I'd been reading *The Spook Who Sat by the Door,* or that I was attracted to the murderous rage of the protagonist, a token black like me.

When my interview ended, Mr. Dick opened the door for me. He held it while I stepped through. "I hope you're ready for homework," he said. "Because there's plenty of it here."

Was he assuming that a black girl from public school might not be up to it? I wondered. Or was I too sensitive? I'd been told that before, and I knew it was true, but I couldn't always tell when. Sometimes "sensitive" was what kids called each other when they wanted license for cruelty, or what white people said when they did not want to bother to change.

"Really," he said as we walked toward the waiting room. "If you would not look forward to three hours—and sometimes more—of homework a day, then St. Paul's is the wrong school."

"I do my homework," I said. It was too quick and too sharp. I smiled to soften the defiance I'd let slip.

Mr. Dick reunited me with my parents. Once again we stood in a group chatting. We had been chatting all weekend. Chat. Chat. Chat. I could not think of one more thing to say. Not one. I smiled. My temples were sore.

A buzzer sounded the change of period. Doors banged open, and students swarmed the halls. A few girls walked by, but for the most part the Schoolhouse teemed with boys. They were tall and short, wiry, stocky, fat, skinny, loud, groomed, unkempt, babyish, manly—and they were white.

Then a group of black boys passed by. They stopped on the second-floor landing. A couple of boys smiled. A couple looked elsewhere. A couple looked me over. One boy, who was wearing a black leather jacket and cap, stepped forward.

"Well, hello there," he said. "Are you here to apply to St. Paul's?"

I nodded. "Yes."

"Oh, wow! That's great. Where're you from?"

"Philadelphia."

"How about that? What's your name?"

"Aw, come on, Wood." The boys had been amused to watch their buddy in action for a while. Now they wanted to move on.

"You'll be gone next year, anyway."

"You'll have to excuse him," one of the boys said to me.

They laughed together and bounced in a group down the steps. I was annoyed. I smiled again at the adults. My temples were rigid with exertion.

Mr. Price appeared to take us to lunch. On the way we stopped at his dorm. His modern apartment had tall windows and bright white walls. He told my parents that the school paid for faculty members to do graduate work in the summers and, after a few years' teaching, to go to Europe. He showed us a red-and-white china bowl depicting scenes from the grounds that he was given after five years' service. My mother said that my father should think about teaching at St. Paul's. I was appalled to hear it.

"It doesn't look like your daughter thinks that's a good idea," Mr. Price said. He enjoyed the joke and kept it going.

"We could use you," he said to my father, looking to me for a reaction. "I'm sure we could arrange to have you put in his class. Would you like that?"

I was relieved when, on the way to lunch, Mr. Price found another student to tease. "Alma Jean! Alma Jean!" Mr. Price mimicked a Southern accent and laughed at a girl at the top of the path. "Alma, come meet a visiting family."

The path sloped steeply. Underneath the sawdust, a thick crust of ice gave off the dull gray sheen of moonstone. Students going to and from lunch stepped around us. They slipped off the shoulder of the icy path and made giant steps into the surrounding snow. Two or three of them fell. They laughed at each other and slid away. I felt my toes curl under in my boots, even though I knew that nothing short of grappling hooks could save me if I began to fall. And, of course, my mother was holding onto my arm, smiling a blaze of new lipstick. Her fingers dug into my sleeve. God forbid one of us should slip. We'd both go down, brown behinds right up in the air for Mr. Price and all these white people to see, my father grabbing for both of us with some wild, involuntary cry from ancient Japan, my mother screaming, and everybody rushing to help us, their solicitude, the shrieks of hysterical laughter once they were out of earshot.

Alma Jean reached us alive. The door she'd come out of at the top of the path might as well have been cradled in the clouds. I'd never make it.

"Welcome to St. Paul's," Alma said. She was a short Southern girl with acne on her round cheeks, glasses, and a big, fluffy Afro the color of old honey. "I hope you had a good trip." She'd already taken in the knee socks, I could see that, and was now processing my "classic" getup in all its devoutly-wished-for understatement.

"This is Alma's first year," said Mr. Price. "She came here

from Memphis, Tennessee, and she's in the Fourth Form." He looked down at her.

"Oh, you must miss home," my mother said.

"Yes, ma'am, I do."

"And it's a lot colder than you must be used to," Mama said. "Is that all you wear?"

Like the other students, Alma sported a jacket. We, of course, were swaddled in everything but buffalo hide.

"Yes, ma'am. They told me it was going to be cold up here, but nobody told me it would be *this* cold!"

I could see that Alma was a little feisty for my mother's taste in teenagers, but Mama couldn't help but go for that "ma'am" stuff. Mr. Price tried to steer Alma back to a proper discussion. "Now, Alma, aside from climate considerations, are you enjoying your first year here? Your classes, sports, activities?"

Alma giggled and rolled her eyes. Nope, she did not dig this place. She'd signified it, OK, and now I waited to hear the words that would disavow her look.

"Well, naw, not really, Mr. Price." She burst into quick laughter, but she stuck to her story. "I mean, this is an *excellent* education. The best. But 'like it'? I don't know if those would be my exact words."

I watched her leave, jealous of the cool disdain with which she looked up at Mr. Price and the way she bounded over the ice when she left, careless and confident as a cat.

We waved gingerly in Alma's direction. Then we turned, arms still locked, to begin our ascent. By the time we made it safely into the building, I had begun to sweat into my layers of wool.

We walked through a cold, bright cloister. On black iron hooks along the windows, jackets were hung to chill while their owners ate. We folded our coats—these were our good coats we were wearing—and laid them on benches by a wall that was covered with oak panels carved, like the panels in the Schoolhouse, with the names of graduates. Heaps of textbooks and paperbacks lay scattered on benches and the floor. Like toppling cairns they led us to the dining room.

The lunch line snaked through the Upper Common Room, past the formal dining hall with its dark, high-backed chairs and forbidding portraits, and into the kitchen. We collected trays and battered silver-plate utensils. In our turn we stepped up to be served. Behind a long steam table stood the poorest-looking white people I'd ever seen. These were residents of a state training school for the mentally retarded, Mr. Price explained. During the school terms they worked with the food-service staff and boarded in rooms above the kitchen. Students, for some reason, referred to them as wombats.

"But aside from that rather predictable teenage cruelty," said Mr. Price, "the kids, on the whole, treat the staff with at least a modicum of respect."

"Nice hot soup," said one of the women. Her teeth were rotten, and she showed them when she smiled.

It seemed wrong for these people to stand there, separated from us by chrome and glass and crusted-over sheet pans. It seemed wrong for them to remain stunted in the presence of growing, budding, blooming talent, able only to feed the young aristocrats who would go away and forget them. I took the bowl from the woman with the medieval mouth. There seemed nothing else I could do. Soup, thick with cornstarch,

sloshed onto my thumb, and the woman apologized fast, like a
child who has been beaten.

"Lost your appetite, eh?" Lee Bouton sat across from me at the
lunch table. She was a year or two older than I, long and lean
and unhurried. Her beige face was framed with nearly black
hair, thick and wiry, pulled back into a big, Africanized bun. I
would never have guessed—almost no one did—that Lee's
mother was white, as were her older brother and her stepfather,
a college professor. Years later Bouton called her urban black
image a literary creation, one she'd absorbed from her peers
and fashioned from books her stepfather had recommended.

A few other students sat with us. They were friendly, welcoming, quirky. I wondered if I'd displayed enough character
in my interview. Perhaps the Yeadon High booklist I bragged
that I'd read was as tacky as those fishnet stockings I had
wanted to wear and insisted on packing. There was no solid
ground up here for me, but neither was there any going back.

My parents and I repeated, as if it were just the right thing
to say, that St. Paul's was a dream come true. During our stay
the dream began to take on an aura of inevitability. I cradled
my desire gingerly, as if I could keep it secret even from myself,
but the visit had given me a feeling of necessity. I had to go to
St. Paul's. I had been raised for it.

Why else had my mother personally petitioned the principal of Lea School so that I could attend the integrated showcase public grade school at the edge of the University of
Pennsylvania's reach—out of our West Philly district? Why
else would she have dragged me across the street on my knees
when I balked on the morning before the big I.Q. test, the one

that could get me into the top first-grade class, the class on which free instrument and French lessons, advanced Saturday-morning classes, and a special, individualized reading series were bestowed? I remembered the bandages, white and meticulous, covering the suppurating red flesh underneath. Why else had I learned to hold myself to standards that were always just beyond my reach, if not to learn early and indelibly that we'd have to do twice the work to get half the credit? Why the thrift-shop Dickens volumes, stiff and stinking with mildew, the Berlitz records, *Weekly Readers,* and Spanish flashcards? Why the phone call that night from Mrs. Evans? Hadn't I been told, hadn't they said all along, that each of us had work to do? Wasn't it time for me to play my part in that mammoth enterprise—the integration, the moral transformation, no less, of America?

I had been waiting for this the way a fairy princess waits for a man. But I'd never suspected that my fate would be revealed so handsomely or so soon.

By the time we arrived in New Jersey to pick up my sister, the events of my life had rearranged themselves in perfect anticipation of my beckoning academic career. I entered my grandparents' familiar home yearning to soak it in, as if part of me had already left.

We crowded into the cool aroma of the vestibule, where Nana kept her fruit in the winter, and then into the house. The cold air we brought in disturbed the quiet pale green rooms; pointed crystals that hung from pink-and-white lusters on the dining-room bureau swayed in the draft. They were antique glass lusters, older than I was, Nana had told me, made from opaque white glass over cranberry glass over crystal, the last of the fine cameo glass to come out of Czechoslovakia before the

Communists took over. The lusters did not require candles in their cylindrical crystal centers. They needed only the light from elsewhere in the room, which reflected off their many surfaces. They were elegantly efficient, purely feminine, the most unnecessary objects in my universe. They caught my eye when we walked in. This time I was delighted to wonder how such a rich cranberry color could emanate from such fragile glass. They were as beautiful as anything I'd seen at St. Paul's, a gratifying thought.

In fact, something about St. Paul's reminded me of my grandparents. They belonged to clubs whose members were the old, genteel black Philadelphia, alternately called "dicty" or "blue-vein" years ago. My grandmother had inherited from her father a real-estate business whose profits provided scholarships for black college students. My grandfather had played semipro baseball in the Negro leagues. He worked in a corporate sales job where he earned, he said, not as much as he would have had he been white, but more than he would had he looked black. He was the only person I knew who loved to go to work. That's how I wanted to feel about school.

Carole ran down the stairs and hugged me. We had missed each other, and we laughed at her throaty chuckle. I wondered why our family was so seldom happy enough to stand together embracing, and why I could not absorb the encircling sweetness but only anticipate the estrangement to come. I felt certain that my going away to school would pull the family further apart. With unutterable shame I realized that I wanted to go anyway. No matter what, I wanted to go.

In February I completed my application. I copied my essays onto the elegant red-and-white form in my best Palmer-method handwriting. My hobbies included water colors and "dramatics," I wrote. ("Hiding behind another personality is a fun carryover from my childhood make-pretend.") I played violin and cello. The most important thing in my life was my family, who supported my decision. One recent experience that was important to me was going out at midnight on Christmas Eve with my father to select a tree. The vendors had closed early on account of the snow, I wrote, so my father had had to climb the fence and throw trees over to me. One year he heaved a dozen before I found one acceptable. Another year the harvest was so plentiful that we packed the car and made deliveries to family and friends. What I didn't say was that we purposely went out after midnight to make sure that the tree-sellers had gone home. Still, it was clearly a case of bald-faced stealing. I wrote as prettily as I could and dared them not to like it.

Desiring to attend Saint Paul's is a significant turning point for Cary's academic, social, and family life. Yet she suggests that her wish and ultimate decision to attend Saint Paul's was inevitable. She says "I had been raised for it." What do you think she means by this? If Cary was "raised" to attend a school like Saint Paul's, does it lessen the impact of her decision? Of her desire?

With a highlighter, mark the social and familial details Cary gives to demonstrate that she was raised for academic excellence. In your journal, write what these details convey about Cary and her family. How dependent and independent are any child's decisions from family, social, and cultural background?

Cary's journey begins to suggest the metaphorical weight of "racial uplift."

Although not officially accepted to Saint Paul's at the end of the second chapter, Cary has written her application essay as "prettily as [she] could and dared [Saint Paul's] not to like it." If Cary wants to go, why does she risk telling the admissions office about the Christmas tree theft? Like Gaines's dream, what is Cary trying to tell her inner self? That she'll still be black? Still be part of the Cary family? Still be an outsider, fighting literally, to get over racial barriers? Still trying to remain true to her cultural and familial traditions?

Review the story. What is young Cary's revelation?

While Cary's decision may not be as dramatic as Gaines's choice to lose an abusive husband, for a young teenager her desire to live apart from her family leaves her guilt-stricken. "With unutterable shame, I realized that I wanted to go. . . ." As much as she loves her family, she's appalled that she wants to leave them. While adults may recognize this familiar rite-of-passage of teenagers rushing headlong to be independent, to become adults, Cary shows the youthful angst such decisions bring. While Cary may have been raised to go to a school like Saint Paul's, clearly, it is *her choice, her revelation* that she's ready and eager to journey such an unfamiliar path. She, too, is willing to pay the price of possible estrangement from her home and family.

Your life story will be filled with many turning points and revelations. Some choices may be more dramatic than others; some revelations may be more painful than others. Events like marriage, divorce, parenthood, career decisions, can exert powerful influence, but, ultimately, what you feel, believe, and know about your self drives the direction of your life. Maturity and self-definition help you to make wiser decisions as you move along life's journey. Revelations should become more life-affirming, not less so.

REMEMBER: You are the hero or heroine of your own life.

PART III

MEMOIR

EIGHT

SWEET, BITTERSWEET, AND JOYFUL MEMORIES

Who are we if not our memories?

As years pass, memories compile, shaping, shading, and helping to construct our evolving self. Unlike autobiography, memoir doesn't seek to retell an entire life's journey; rather, it excerpts moments in time that are compelling, memorable.

MEMOIR—n. historical account written from personal knowledge
Memorable—adj. 1) worth remembering; 2) easy to remember

Memoirs speak to the heart of our selves, and often serve as a testament to an era, a life passage, an event, or a relationship that influenced the self. In memoir, the impulse is not necessarily to *tell it all* but rather, to tell those memories which dominate, which rise repeatedly to the surface of one's consciousness. Time isn't necessarily sequenced chronologically. Rather, in memoir, the attempt is to use language *to evoke the feeling of a time, place, and self.*

Choosing what to remember is a powerful assertion of the self and one's point of view. bell hooks, in her powerful memoir, *Bone Black: Memories of Girlhood,* states in her foreword:

> *Writing imagistically, I seek to conjure a rich magical world of southern black culture that was sometimes paradisical and at other times terrifying.*

Good writing always relies on fine *images—word pictures* as powerful as a painted picture, capable of evoking strong emotions and responses. Both autobiography and memoir might use images to "connect the dots," to explore and explain the fulfillment of one's self. But a memoir, freed from narrating an entire life, relies perhaps even more so on images to evoke the heart, soul, and spirit of a moment in time and space of a particular life.

"Bone Black"—What does that mean? Suggest? Evoke emotionally?

In *Bone Black,* bell hooks conjures a time and space, a memory:

> *I have discovered paint. Mixing the water with the powder makes color bright and primary. I imagine that I have returned to the cave of my childhood dreams, to the paintings on the wall. The art teacher, Mr. Harold, watches me stirring. He tells me he has been watching me since class began, that he enjoys the sight of a student falling in love with color again and again. He brings me a stack of paper. I always wait before I begin*

painting. He says that I take too long, that such intense concentration may block the creativity. I want him to leave me alone. I am silent. He understands. He will come back later. I am trying to remember the pictures in the cave, the animals. If I can paint them all I am sure I can discover again the secret of living, what it was I left in the cave. I start with the color black. In a book on the history of pigments I come across a new phrase, bone black, *Bone black is a black carbonaceous substance obtained by calcifying bones in closed vessels. Burning bones, that's what it makes me think about—flesh on fire, turning black, turning into ash.*

bell hooks, like an autobiographer, is writing about her life and her self-definition as a young woman. Yet from her experiences, her memories, she has caught the image, the picture of being *bone black*. This color, in time, becomes linked to her own body: 1) as a black girl; and 2) as a comment on her process of defining the self. She is on a quest to "discover again the secret of living." Because she is experiencing a moment in her life when she feels vulnerable and lost, she thinks of her flesh and bone burning into ash.

Images become symbols when they accrue meanings beyond the actual definition of the tangible object. Black is merely a color. Its pigment comes from "calcifying bones in closed vessels." In African American culture, however, black has a racial, social, and cultural context. "Black to the bone" as a cultural saying can resonate with post-black power pride, but it also can resonate (for the pre-1960s unenlightened) with a more problematic "color-complex," self-hatred. Black, too, in Anglo-Western culture, has been linked with death and negative racial stereotypes.

However, the young girl bell hooks is trying to make art on paper; she is trying to remake herself by exploring color. On another level, the grown woman bell hooks is now using words in a memoir to paint her mental image of herself as a developing girl.

"Calcifying," "fire," "ash," imply destruction, the undoing of the self. But the writer also explores the constructive, regenerative power of calcified, burning flesh turned into ash. She is engaged in her own resurrection. Bone black is both an **image**—a mental picture—and a **symbol** of hooks's rebirth.

Reread the above excerpt again. Note: the young artist wants, needs to paint her way from her own silence and inner self. "I am trying to remember the pictures in the cave, the animals" becomes another interesting and symbolic image. hooks is talking about **prehistory,** talking of a time when stories about the self were drawn by early people on cave walls. A cave was *home,* and *walls were a space for making art, for writing the self, writing a historical record of the self* in the earliest known form of autobiography and memoir. Civilization implies learning, but it also entails cultural conditioning and societal restraints. Given this, how does a person rebirth themselves anew? One way, suggests hooks, is to begin again in the home space—the cave—inside our selves, in a metaphorical womb where we can symbolically rebirth our identity.

MY BEST ADVICE

Memoirs are less about the chronology of events and more about the spiritual and emotional quality of life. As with real memories, emotional images dominate. The emphasis is not on logical truths, but on interior needs, dreams, and desires.

Images—word pictures—aren't exclusive to memoir. In fact, most fine writing relies not only on concrete descriptions but on more evocative, imagistic renderings as well. Both Gaines's autobiography, *Laughing in the Dark,* and Bray's autobiography, *Unafraid of the Dark,* use the color of darkness as an image of something to be overcome. Nightmares, demons, fears, lack of social- and self-awareness (as in "being in the dark"), suggest both women's struggle to overcome barriers toward selfhood. Because the color of darkness is also associated with blackness in racial divisions, both women emphatically celebrate their ethnicity while deploring racist connotations.

For Lorene Cary, the image of "black ice" becomes a powerful image of growth. "I have never skated on black ice, but perhaps my children will." Ice—slippery, dangerous, frozen, and cold—can become a triumph, a state of grace. And ice can uniquely reflect the blackness of an ancient earth. Maya Angelou, too, plays on the way racism inhibits growth with her image of the "caged bird." But this image also evokes limits of gender, geography, experiences, and much, much more. Angelou the young child, once silenced, learns to sing songs of herself despite societal limitations; in doing so, she becomes internally and eternally free.

Well-formed images capture the essence of memories, the essence of interior feelings and yearnings. Each of us, I believe, is swayed by powerful images that shape us at least as much as, if not more than, actual events.

For example, anyone can report, "In 1985, I was fired from my job." But if someone asks, "What do you remember of the day you were fired?" chances are the response would be in "word pictures," images of bleakness on a bright, sun-filled day. Perhaps you pictured yourself growing smaller and smaller as giant-sized guards cleaned out your desk and escorted you out the door. Images may have flitted through your mind—pictures of a mouth clamped shut when you wanted to scream; hands shut tight when you wanted to flail and hit. You may even have fantasized about hitting a smirking co-worker.

What images shape your most potent memories? Darkness? Silence? Music? Jail? A euphoric high? A nurturing touch?

What images shape your most potent dreams? Sometimes what we dream is a reflection of our conscious life. Dreams of an ancestor visiting from the dead, an endless walk toward the horizon, even a dream of hitting a "lucky seven," can signify the tenor of our waking life and of our past memories.

Images—word pictures—are reflective of your theme. *Theme is what your story means,* what you're trying to express as an author, what you're trying to say to readers.

In African American autobiography, the thematic message is often a testament to survival. As in the song "We Shall Overcome," autobiographers tend to write about the social, economic, and cultural barriers they've broken in order to succeed. Memoir, too, may cover this terrain, but the writer has greater freedom in selecting which portions of his or her life to reveal. Henry Louis Gates, Jr., in his memoir, *Colored People,* speaks lovingly of a community that nurtured its children. Veronica Chambers, in her award-winning *Mama's Girl,* focuses on her bittersweet relationship with her mother. Bebe Moore Campbell, in *Sweet Summer: Growing Up With and Without My Dad,* focuses on the summer months she went South to live with her father.

Writing a memoir offers a multitude of advantages primarily because, as an author, you have a range of choice regarding what to tell or not to tell. Autobiography demands explanations of how a life journeyed from point A to point B. A memoir may focus on only one significant summer spent backpacking after you finished college. Or you may write about the year you spent training for the New York marathon or attending culinary school or preparing for an amateur piano competition. You may even want to write about your role as care-giver to aging parents or your quest to adopt a child.

Memoir's scope can be narrower and deeper than autobiography. But even though you're writing more selectively, don't sacrifice the sense that you're sharing a special story with significance for you and perhaps for others. As with autobiography, the reader wants to feel pulled into the essence of your life.

Before beginning a memoir, you should ask yourself:

- What unifies your memoir? Is there a particular image associated with a special time of your life? An overwhelming event, such as new parenthood, midlife renewal, or living in a foreign land?

- What is important about your memories? What do you hope to communicate about them? How do you think they will be useful, entertaining, meaningful to others?

- Are you intellectually and emotionally ready to confront the totality of your memories—the pleasant as well as not-so-pleasant aspects? Are you ready to recognize the complexity of events, time, space, and distance that influenced experiences as they were **then,** as well as the experience of recovering memories **now?**

§ Do you recognize how remembering is an act of re-
covery, of retrieving vital information about your life
and your survival?

History and memory are intertwined. When choosing a
subject to write about, you should let your passions be your
guide. Write only about those memories that are most essential to who you are, your quality of living, and of being in this
world. Memories are the essence of the self.

E X E R C I S E   1

SETTING LIMITS IN TIME

You were once a newborn. Now you are what? Twenty-two?
Thirty? Sixty-eight? What do you remember most about the
chronology of your life? Are there memories that sparkle with
vitality? Moments that helped define you? Years that influenced your attitudes toward life, your development as an
adult? Of all the times in your life, what period was most crucial? The years following the Depression? The 1960s' black
power revolution? Your residency training in the early 1980s?
Or the winter you became pastor of your own church?

In your journal, write down the time period that holds a
well-spring of memories for you. For twenty minutes, list some
of the special moments you recall. (Remember, to be interesting, you don't have to write just about sad things. Memories
can be joyful, too. Nor do you have to write only about big
events, like being hit by a car or losing a parent. Small events—
admiring the flight of a bird or spending a year becoming a

gardener—can be as interesting and momentous as acts of high drama.)

Review your list of special events and select one to write about in your journal. Writing quickly for twenty minutes, without editing, try to recall as much as you can about the event. For example, it may have been a school talent contest that convinced you to become a singer. Write about the contest with as much detail as possible: the time, the place, the atmosphere. What did you wear? Sing? Was there a band, or did you sing *a capella?* What were your feelings? What did you see? Hear? Smell?

What marked the beginning of the event for you? Was it at home, undoing your curlers and applying make-up, that made the forthcoming talent show seem real?

What marked the end of the event? The applause of your friends and family? Or your quiet acknowledgment that as you sang the last note, you knew you had sung your best?

EXERCISE 2

SIGNIFICANT RELATIONSHIPS

Relationships can either help or hamper your development. They can make any event a celebration or a disaster. Relationships with parents are often cited for their profound influence, but a host of other people can play supporting as well as critical roles in your life too.

Review the list of events you just completed in Exercise 1. For each event, list in your journal the people who were pivotal in influencing that particular event and your participation in it. Don't worry if you repeat names. A favorite aunt or a mentor's name may appear over and over again. That's okay. It's even possible that the person who most influenced your special event wasn't present. For example, your music teacher may have been touring Europe with a well-respected singer. Or an absent father may have fueled your ambition but never witnessed your accomplishments. Sometimes it is the people missing from our life who haunt and influence us the most.

Focus on one person who influenced your life. For twenty minutes, write in your journal the qualities this person nurtured in you. How specifically did they change or alter your behavior? How did this person make you feel? Did they nurture and sustain you or pose obstacles for you to overcome?

What do you remember best about this person? Their eyes? Or strong will? What habits, mannerisms do you best recall? Is the person you're writing about alive or dead? If dead, do you think you're still influenced by them? What do you miss most about their presence?

How did your relationship with this person begin? (If you're writing about someone you've known all your life—then write about the first time you felt a strong and abiding attachment for them. For instance, as a child, you may have taken your sister's love for granted, but as an adult, commiserating with her about everything from dieting to dating to finances, your relationship has deepened.)

Is there anything that could threaten or end your relationship with this special person? If so, what and why?

* * *

Repeat Exercise 2, but this time choose a different example of an influential person linked to a particular event. The aim is for you to acknowledge how others participate in your life and how they contribute to what has happened and is happening in your life.

EXERCISE 3

THE POWER OF IMAGES

Memories are like a scrapbook of Polaroids in our minds. It isn't necessarily language that we hear during the act of remembering; rather, we *see* pictures that hold a wealth of meanings and memories. These pictures—visual images—show us how we think about, shape, and respond to our memories.

Even if you aren't a visual artist, you may want to pick up some colored pencils and, for fifteen minutes, try to sketch the event you wrote about in Exercise 1.

Be attuned to the colors you use and the scene you draw. Is it a garden? A stage, bathed in bright light? Or is it a somber drawing of a hospital scene? How have you sketched yourself into the scene? What does your pose suggest about your feelings and behavior?

Next, sketch the person you wrote about in Exercise 2. If possible, draw yourself into the picture. Don't worry if you're drawing stick figures. The point is to tease out visual pictures that you can write about in your memoir. For now, spend fifteen minutes coloring and adding as much detail as possible.

Study your two drawings and consider what they tell you about yourself and your attitudes toward your memories.

What are the similarities and differences between the pictures? Do the drawings convey more information than your words? If so, how can you capture the visual impact with words? Do you need to add more description? More specificity?

Finally, consider whether your drawings suggest different images that could reflect the emotional tone of your memoir. In other words, beyond literal meaning, do your drawings suggest more connotative *symbolic imagery?*

For example, Maya Angelou's "caged bird" is a symbolic picture of her hopes and rite of passage. So, too, Gaines's "laughing in the dark" is symbolic of her inner strength and bravery. Clifton Taulbert, in his fine memoir *The Last Train North,* literally means he boarded the last train north. But the newly canceled rail service from his Delta home also symbolizes the ending of massive black migration to the North and serves as a harbinger of social unrest in the North. "Filled with hope, fear and anticipation as I boarded the last train north from the Delta," Taulbert writes, "I hardly envisioned my dreams being interrupted by war, riots, and racism."

The train, for Taulbert and for readers, unifies the story of a young man's coming of age. The train, symbolically and literally, is the cultural bridge between two geographical and social worlds. The image of the "last train" also emphasizes how the technology of the 1960s altered transportation. Taulbert's memoir ends with another journey, this time by plane, to begin a career in the 89th Presidential Wing of the United States Air Force.

If you haven't yet discovered any unifying, symbolic images, don't worry. Give yourself more time for thoughtful remembering, writing, and revising. The images and patterns are certain to appear.

If you wish, repeat Exercise 3, using any photographs you have to encourage your memory. Like language, photos have both literal and symbolic meanings. As you review old photos, you may discover images that make you recall vital instances in your life. For example, a photo of a mentor, his head resting on a well-worn piano, may suggest true weariness, but it may also hint at a musical career gone stale. Ironically, this mentor, teaching music from an old piano, may have been the stimulus for your own success. The picture of a "well-worn piano" may have multiple connotations that you can use to define and unify your memoir.

Poets are often masters of symbolic imagery. Langston Hughes is perhaps most famous for his image of a "dream deferred" that "dries up like a raisin in the sun." But in his memoir, *The Big Sea,* he uses the image of water to suggest how bountiful his life has been as a poet and how joyful his trek across the sea to rediscover his African homeland. Traveling throughout Africa, hiking beside dynamic bodies of water, Hughes refreshes and rebirths his emotional and spiritual self.

As you write your memoir, always be attuned to how images can help to communicate your world to your readers. "Word pictures" enrich any work. Sometimes, too, it is these pictures that unify memories and symbolize the complexity of what you feel, how you have lived and continue to live in both the past and in the ever-changing present.

EXERCISE 4

STRINGING MEMORY BEADS

During the week, review (and repeat, if you wish) Exercises 1, 2, and 3. Identify what you think are the important life lessons you've learned. Next, in your journal, begin to outline the scope of your memoir. What time period do you want to remember? Which events? How did these events affect you emotionally, spiritually, and psychologically?

Who influenced you? What issues and ideas confronted you? How did you grow as a person? What did you learn about the world and about yourself?

Once you establish the time frame for your memoir, the key events and people, the significant issues and emotions you experienced, you'll be ready to create a chapter outline for more extensive writing. Don't forget that not all memoirs need to be book length. Short essays can be emotionally powerful. Strategically, you may even choose to write your memoir in separate essays, each one dealing with a significant memory of a particular time of your life. After a few essays, you may decide that the essays are really chapters of your new book-in-progress! Whatever your pleasure, give yourself time to develop and to write your remembrances well!

Using this book as a guide, along with the critical study of other writers' work and thoughtful writing of your own, you're well on your way to developing your talents and becoming a better, stronger writer!

MEMOIR STUDY, NO. 1

HOUSTON A. BAKER, JR.'S
"ON THE DISTINCTION OF 'JR.'"

*Renowned African American scholar Houston A. Baker, Jr.,
retrieves a memory of his father—"the man at the furnace"—
and displays, compellingly, how a parent's actions can remain
in one's memory for decades. In struggling to find the meaning behind his father's behavior, Baker pieces together images
of his younger self and his father and explores how limited
notions of gender can alienate and harm a growing son.*

I am eleven years old, giddy with the joy of fire and awed by
the seeming invulnerability of my father. He is removing
dead coals from the glowing bed of the furnace. He is risking
the peril of flames. We are sharing, I think, the heroism of taking care of the family. We are together. He is intense, sweating
slightly across the brow. He still wears the shirt and tie from
another long day's work. For some reason I am prompted to
move with the pure spirit of being. I begin dancing around the
furnace room with light abandon. My voice slides up the scale
to a high falsetto. I am possessed by some primitive god of fire;
I feel joyful and secure. I am supremely happy, high-voiced,
fluid.

Then I am suddenly flattened against a limestone wall,
bolts of lightning and bright stars flashing in my head. I have
been hard and viciously slapped in the mouth as a thunderous
voice shouts, "Damnit! Houston, Jr.! Stop acting like a sissy!"

(sissy, *n*. 1. an effeminate boy or man; a milksop 2. a timid or cowardly person 3 [informal]. sister). Having heard my falsetto chant, my father had turned from the furnace with the quick instinct of an exorcist. He had hit me with the fury of a man seeing a ghost. The smell of woodsmoke is what I recall as I ran up the basement stairs and out into the Louisville night, astonished at how much I had angered my sacred and invulnerable father, whose moods of manhood were as predictable as the San Andreas Fault.

My name contains the sign of ownership and descent appropriate to the bourgeoisie. I am not a "second" or "II." I am a "junior" (junior, *adj*. I. younger: used to distinguish the son from the father of the same name, and written, *Jr.* after the full name). The inheritance that passes to me from "Sr."—the man at the furnace—remains a mystery seasoned by small details.

He was born in Louisville, Kentucky, to a mother whose entire life was spent as a domestic for white families. His great-grandmother had escaped, or so the story was told, from a Mississippi slaveholder. She made her way to Kentucky with her owner in hot pursuit. His father, my paternal grandfather, was so light-complexioned that he might easily have been mistaken for the white slaveholder from whom my great-great-grandmother escaped. Harry was my paternal grandfather's name, and his greatest talent, or so I was led to believe, was fishing.

The cryptic unreadability of my father's life appears before me with the strange attraction and repulsion of a keloid (keloid, *n*. a mass of hyperplastic, fibrous connective tissue, usually at the site of a scar). I want to turn away from his wounds, the scars, the disorder that I believe ripped his consciousness and shredded his boyhood days. But I cannot turn away. With each new revelation or addition detail supplied by my mother, who is in her mid-eighties, or by my older brother, in his mid-fifties, my attention is more firmly riveted. My head and gaze are fixed like Winston's in Orwell's *1984*. I see the pain coming, but am never certain where it will fall.

Prostitutes were a successful and shame-free business for my father's grandmother. From my father's boyhood perspective, his grandmother's "girls" must have seemed like uncanny citizens of a bizarre extended family. I vaguely remember his telling me one day, in a faraway voice, that his first sexual encounter was with one of his grandmother's girls, who in effect "raped" him.

So much is difficult to turn away from in what I perceive to be the scarring of my father's life. There is his mother urging him to stay forever her own "good Negro Christian boy," yet regaling, tempting, titillating him with tales of the glory of white success. Tales of the spartanly clean windows, shining cars, and infinite spaces of white opportunity in America. His boozy father, hunkered down in an old leather chair with the radio playing schmaltzy popular songs, dozing in the middle of some urgent question his son was trying to ask. Reverend Shepherd, a white Anglo-Saxon messiah of a boxing coach, urging those black Presbyterian boys of Grace Church to self-extermination for the glory of God and the good health of a "Negro race" that white American insurance companies would not even consider as clients.

Houston, Sr.'s, answer to the aching incoherence of his boyhood was summed up in an exhortation that he barked at my brothers and me whenever we came close to tears or were on the brink of a child's response to pain. This exhortation—an admonishment that was his Rosetta stone for surviving chaos—was "Be a man!" There was nothing, mind you, ethnic or racial in this injunction. Just "Be a man!"

Since I remember no stories from my father's lips about being comforted by the arms of his mother or told fuzzy bedtime stories by Harry, I have to assume Houston, Sr., was like the children of the Dickens character Mrs. Jelleby, who just "tumbled up." This process translates in Afro-American terms as "jes' grew."

Houston, Sr., was left on his own to formulate commandments for his life. There were no tender revelations from his parents or burning-bush epiphanies from the mountaintop. "Be a man!" was therefore his resonant admission that only the most tightly self-controlled and unbelievably balanced postures could ensure a journey from *can't* to *can* in America. There was no time or space for sentimentality, tears, flabby biceps, fear, or illness in the stark image of American conquest my father set before himself. His notion of success was as deadpan and puritanical as the resolutions scripted by F. Scott Fitzgerald's Great Gatsby. Houston, Sr.'s, manhood code was every bit as full as Gatsby's of cowboy morality, gutsy goodwill, and trembling guilt about treating one's parents better. Mental control was like sexual control in my father's vision; it was kind of *coitus interruptus* expressed in maxims like "illness and pain are all in the mind," "a woman should never make a man lose control," "race has nothing to do with merit in the United States," "the successful man keeps himself mentally, physically, and spiritually fit." Manhood was a fearless, controlled, purposeful, responsible achievement. And its stoutest testimony was a redoubtably athletic body combined with a basso profundo for speaking one's name—especially to white folks. "Hello," he would growl in his deepest bass, "my name is

Baker—Houston A. Baker!" I often step back and watch, and hear myself in the presence of whites—especially those who overpopulate the American academy—growling like my father: "Hello, I'm Houston A. Baker, Jr.!"

If Houston, Sr., had a notion of heaven, I suspect he saw it as a brightly modern building where his own well-lit and comfortably furnished office was situated right next to the executive suite of Booker T. Washington. Washington's manly singleness of purpose and institutional achievements were taught to my father. He absorbed them into his very bones while putting himself through West Virginia State College under the mentorship of the great John W. Davis. Houston, Sr., and Booker T., building a world of American manhood, service, progress, and control; Houston, Sr., and Booker T., in their lives of service becoming swarthy replicas of ideal white businessmen like Carnegie or Vanderbilt the Elder.

And, like Booker T.'s paradise at Tuskegee, Houston, Sr.'s, ideal heaven would surely have housed wives tending children who if they were male would be vigorously instructed to "Be a man!" When not tending children, these wives would be satellites of manly Negro enterprise, raising funds and devoting themselves to the institutional growth of a world designed by and pleasing principally to men. In my father's heaven there would certainly be no confusion between love and sex, race and achievement, adults and children, men and not-men.

With the household furnace billowing smoke and ash on that evening long ago, my father must have suffered the fright of his life when he heard my falsetto and turned to see my lithe dance, accentuated by the whitewashed walls and the glow of the fire. Houston, Sr., could only, I think, have grasped this scene as a perverse return of his arduously repressed boyhood. His boyhood had been marked by a Louisville East End of commercial sexuality and muscular Christianity. The West End had been colored by a mother's ambivalent love for her light-skinned prodigy. He struck out in a flash against what he must have heard and seen as my demonic possession by the haunting fiends of unmanliness. What, after all, could God be thinking if he had somehow bequeathed to Houston, Sr., a sissy instead of a son? And so he hit me very hard. Walking in the woodsmoke air that autumn evening (actually just around the block and through the back alley, since I didn't dare stay out too long), I could not get a handle on what precisely I had done to make Houston, Sr., so angry.

Many years after the event, I learned the term "homophobia" and labelled my father's actions accordingly. As I think now about that moment long ago, I realize that my father was indeed afraid, yet his fear was not nearly so simple or clearly defined as an aversion to physical, emotional, intense and romantic love between men. There is a strong part of me that knows my father was fascinated by and even attracted at a level of deep admiration to what he believed, with great earnestness, to be the intellectual superiority and discipline of what he called the homosexual lifestyle. I think what terrified him on that evening years ago was not homosexuality as he ideally conceived it. Rather, he was afraid on that autumn evening that I was fast approaching adolescence and had not found what he deemed to be the controlling voice of American manhood. Clearly, then, it was time for Houston, Sr.—he knew this with both fierce dismay and instinctive terror—to busy himself with the disciplining of Jr.

The tragic emotional shortcoming of that evening was that

my father did not realize that the letters at the end of my name were not meant to confirm his ownership or responsibility with respect to my name. "Jr."—as its formal definition makes abundantly clear—is meant to distinguish a younger self from the woundings of "Sr." It is sad that my father failed to realize that it was precisely those feelings of assurance, security, and protection which he had bestowed on me that overwhelmed me, that made me want somehow to dance for him.

It has required many hours of painful thought since that violent moment in which my father branded me a sissy to extract and shape for myself a reasonable definition of my life in relation to my father's. For decades I have sought patterns to fulfill a Jr.'s life. Mercifully, I have found some. They include much that my father was forced to ignore, deny, reject, or misunderstand. He could never, for example, have given approving voice to the informal definition of "sissy" that is sisterhood. Tragically, he never envisioned a successful man's life as one measured and defined by its intimate, if always incomplete, understanding and sharing of a woman's joys, dangers, voice, and solacing touch—shaped definitively, that is to say, by sisterhood.

Unlike the "Sr." produced by ordeals I have yet fully to comprehend, it is impossible for me to imagine "Jr." without a strong woman's touch. I am now the middle-aged father of a quite remarkable son. And at this moment I imagine that with God's grace I shall be able to live up to the standard of distinction the concluding marks of my name are meant to signify. If I do achieve such distinction, perhaps in some far-off fall twilight my son will dance for me. Speaking through rhythmic motion and with the very voice of possession, he will pronounce his own name in the world.

With a highlighter, review Baker's essay, marking his visual pictures. What images seem frozen in his memory? How do these images make the essay more complex and memorable?

Compare Baker's opening paragraph with his conclusion. How are the visual images related? How does "voice" relate to "pronouncing [one's] own name"? How does the designation "Jr." contrast with Baker's wish for his son to have "his own name in the world"?

By opening with a portrait of himself at eleven and closing with reference to his own son, Baker adds a timelessness to his essay. A single painful memory affects the ties between father and son, son and grandson.

"[My father] had hit me with the fury of a man seeing a ghost." Though Houston Baker, Sr., isn't always present, nonetheless, his attitudes about manliness resonate over the course of a lifetime. As with a turning point in autobiography, the father's vicious slap serves as the stimulus for the son to transform himself, to make himself "new." The visual image of a father hitting his son unifies Baker's essay and introduces his enlightenment regarding gender roles and parenthood.

Then, too, the father's words—"Damnit! Houston, Jr.! Stop acting like a sissy!"—are weighted with symbolic meaning. Part of Baker's task is to explore what his father meant by the word "sissy," versus the meaning the words have for him as a wiser man now grown.

* * *

While structurally, Baker returns again and again to the "violent moment" of his father's slap and curse, he also writes about his father's background and upbringing. How does knowing more about the father increase your compassion for both Houston, Sr., and Houston, Jr.?

Does Baker's willingness to explore his father's life strengthen his own credibility? I think it does. For beyond remembering the harm done to him, Baker has pursued, with courageous empathy, the harm that may have been inflicted on his father. By trying to understand his father's action, Baker in his memoir rises above mere tale-bearing and explores the terrain of the human heart and the power of pain to alter behavior and self-image for the worse as well as for the better.

MEMOIR STUDY, NO. 2

JEWELL PARKER RHODES'S "GEORGIA ON HER MIND"

My grandmother was the center of my childhood. She raised me with spiritual and family values that sustain me to this day. Grandmother-figures often appear in my fiction—Grandmere in Voodoo Dreams, *Miss Wright in* Magic City. *These portraits are my praise-song to my grandmother and all the wondrous black women who nurtured, taught, fed, and kept clean a host of needy children. This memoir essay is the first time I allowed myself to explore more fully the edges between celebration and sorrow, between unabated joy and everlasting pain.*

Grandmother Ernestine was born in Georgia, raised in a rural backwater ("way down the road from Athens," she would say), in a huge house with a screened-in porch, on a half-acre with pecan trees in the backyard.

"We didn't live in these nasty brick houses with cement for backyards. Many black folks held land in the South; come North, we rent, struggle, trying to make a fair dollar. We go to stores to buy our greens."

Grandmother always told me stories about this Southern heritage I had. Telling me, passing down tales, was her way of making it real for me, and maybe for herself as well. It wasn't until Grandmother died that I realized how out of place she must have felt in Pittsburgh. What lure was there in steep hills covered with brick and trolley rails? What ease in a land of more rain and snow than was good for her arthritis-stricken hands and knees? What pleasure in soot cascading from the steel mills' furnaces? Even for Easter services Grandmother never wore white anymore.

"What sense," she'd ask, "when it'll only turn gray? Now, in Georgia—"

I'd groan, "Not another Georgia story."

"—white stayed white. White shoes. White gloves. White pearls."

It didn't matter where you were: in the basement shoveling coal, in the kitchen making designs in your breakfast grits, or outside on the front steps trying to suck salt sprinkled on ice cubes. Grandmother told stories. Didn't matter if she'd told you before. Didn't matter if you didn't want to hear it. Telling tales seemed to be Grandmother's mission in life. Sometimes I wondered whether they were all true, whether she'd made them up, imagined more than she knew, or whether memory and time had created a South more glimmering than any reality.

This is true. Grandmother raised me, my sister, and my cousin. She fed, clothed, and cleaned us—three little girls—in a battered and broken-down three-story house. Both my father and aunt were single parents, and Grandmother did the cooking, cleaning, and laundry. She'd boil Argo starch and then trudge down to the dank basement to add it to the rinse water. She didn't trust the washing machine or dryer that my father had given her. She still did laundry on the wooden and metal washboard and used a manual wringer. Then she'd hang the clothes to dry in the basement.

"Georgia has clean air, clean water. Nothing like sheets flapping on the line, flapping in the wind." She persisted in washing by hand, hanging our clothes indoors, though it must have made her tired and sore.

It would take me years to understand that as surely as us grandkids could jump double Dutch and play a mean turn of jacks, we were keeping Grandmother from her beloved "down South."

"Down South—" she'd whisper, especially on summer nights when we would watch fireflies blink as we waved to neighbors sitting on their front stoops.

"Down South, in Georgia—"

"I know Georgia's down South. You've done told me."

Grandmother would stare at my sassy young self then start again: "Down South, *in Georgia*—"

I'd roll my eyes.

"—everybody in the family was a nice chocolate brown

with lots of fine, black hair. Chocolate and silky-haired 'cause a handsome Seminole left his seed in my great-grandmother Ruthie. Sure did. As I witness. Ruthie's parents were newly freed slaves. They went to church nearly every day to testify about how their 'brighter day' had done come.

"One Sunday in August, Ruthie pleaded sick to stay home from church. Nine months later Grandfather was born. Birthing, Ruthie told the story about her Indian. Said they didn't need words. Some folks said she was crazy, out of her mind. Knocked up by a local boy. Her baby was beautiful. Ruthie raised her son. When he was grown, folks say, Ruthie took to her room like a ghost. She never married. No one knows why. I suspect the men who came courting talked too much. The Indian just got busy with his hands and mouth." (I was thirteen when I finally understood her comment enough to blush.) "Her son became my grandfather Wade. Your great-great-grandfather."

I've seen pictures of Grandmother Ernestine when she was young, her lips pulled into a wide smile and her eyes black and sparkling. She was gorgeous, more legs than trunk. Her bosom was just the right size for a baby or a man to rest his head upon.

I remember, as a child, loving the feel of her smooth skin, high cheekbones, and black hair. I'd climb onto the toilet seat to comb her hair and to see myself, in the mirror, rising out of my grandmother's head.

"Grandma, can I do it? Please? Pretty please?"

"No," said Grandmother, taking the tufts of hair from my cupped hand.

I remember standing beside the sturdy, grease-splattered range. "Tell me why you do it."

"I've done said it before."

"Tell me again. And say it like you said the first time."

Grandmother turned the flame on high. She spun around, opened her eyes wide, and said, "Jewell, child, what if I didn't? Why if I didn't burn my hair, some tweety bird might catch hold of it and use it for some nest, and as soon as the mother bird's speckled eggs started hatching and the little birds squeaking for meat, my hair would fall right out."

I giggled as the singed hair stank up the air.

I would also cry at night because my hair was quite kinky next to Grandmother's silk. Even when her hair grew white, it stayed smooth, looking like strands of crystal. My hair always had a million nappy braids. I always felt that I was less beautiful than my sister, who took after Grandmother Ernestine, Wade, Ruthie, and that Seminole Indian. I seemed to take after no one.

On nights when Grandmother tucked me in, she'd sometimes say, "Down South, the peach is rock hard, then fine weather comes: Summer heat makes it bloom. You'll bloom. See if you don't."

Grandmother also talked about education. "Read," she'd say. "Read," though I'd figured out long before then that she couldn't read well.

"Down South my folks felt eight grades of schooling was enough. After all, I was already pledged to be a clerk's wife. I knew how to cook and clean. I served in the church, passing out fans with portraits of Jesus to folks who cried and shivered with the Holy Spirit."

Ernestine: Obedient. Dutiful. Clean. Earnest.

"I was supposed to be just the right gal to help uplift the

race. But one summer I met a sailor so light he could pass for white. Like great-grandmother Ruthie's beau, he didn't talk much. But I had visions of moving North for better opportunities, for more freedom.

"The South had its race problems, but so does the North. I should've known better. I shouldn't have listened to a man who passed for white so the Navy could make him a lieutenant. What's the sense of pretending who you're not?"

In Pittsburgh Ernestine had had two babies in quick succession whom she'd struggled to keep dressed and fed while Grandfather James sailed out (or so he said) and forgot to mail his pay. Later it was discovered that Grandfather James was a bigamist: He'd married a white woman just across Pittsburgh's three rivers and had raised five kids.

Grandmother Ernestine never talked much about Grandfather James. The one time she did, she'd brought a care package of food to my college dorm.

"Don't let a man lead you astray from your roots."

I wondered what roots I had.

" 'A bee gets busy even when the flower's still young.' 'One mistake today mean sorrow tomorrow.' 'Don't do as I did, just do as I say.' "

Then, before she left, she reminded me to take my cod-liver oil so I wouldn't catch cold.

After she'd gone from my dorm I realized she'd been advising me not to get pregnant. I suspected then that she had another tale about Grandfather James that she would never tell.

Just as she'd never tell me further details about race. Except to say, "Be careful"; "Be self-respecting"; "Wear clean underpants and socks." I never understood the latter until the day I flew over the top of my bike, breaking a rib and collarbone. White policemen three feet away saw me slam hard onto concrete, the bike crashing on top of me. A middle-aged black man pleaded with me to allow him to take me to a hospital. I was wary of strangers but finally consented because the pain was too much. He took me to Allegheny General, not Divine Providence, known for the nuns' care of the poor and brown, and also as the only hospital where colored doctors could work on staff. Allegheny was closer, he said.

Grandmother came to see me, all dressed up like she was going to church. When she was satisfied I'd live, she whispered low, "Clean underwear?" I nodded. "Good. Don't let them think you ignorant. Poor or dirty."

For the most part our North was just as segregated as Grandmother's South. Except for the occasional teacher or policeman, we lived in a black working-class world with peeling linoleum and plastic-covered sofas. If violence shattered our neighborhood, I never knew it. Like a sentry, Grandmother kept ill tidings at bay—"Hurt and harm stay outside our door."

But issues of *Ebony* and *Jet* were always scattered about our house, never hidden. Their photographers didn't flinch at racism's bitter harvest. And Grandmother, who wouldn't let me see a fistfight on the street, did allow me to see pictures of violence from down in her beloved South. I'd sit on the porch steps, studying grainy black-and-white photos of men hanging from trees, of men, tarred and feathered, splayed on the road, hands knotted to a car. I still remember one naked soul, dead, his chin resting on his chest, his body marked with holes from a screwdriver.

When I asked, "Why?" Grandmother would sing, "Were

You There When They Crucified My Lord?" The song was heartbreaking, but Grandmother would sing it, at first low and deep in her throat, then it would soar to upper registers and she would start to clap her hands, and before I knew it, my sister and cousin and I would holler and clap and sing, and what had been sorrow would turn into a strengthening joy. Words by themselves were of little use, but music soothed, and with Grandmother, now long dead, I still hum and sing when hurt seems too much to bear.

"How'd your mother die?" I once asked, a brave eight.

"She died while I was here, up North, 1962. I had just gotten you kids off to school. I was hanging laundry outside when a ladybug crawled along the wire line to my arm. As kids we sang, 'Ladybug, ladybug, fly away home. Your house is on fire, your children are gone.' And I felt something, someone, clutch my heart, and I knew my mama was gone."

Grandmother looked up quickly, then whispered, "Did I ever tell you that folks can call the dead?"

I shrieked. "Really? Truly? Can you call your mother?"

"I could. She wouldn't appreciate it. 'Sides, she's with me everyday. That's how I know she forgave me. But that ain't the tale."

I leaned closer.

"My aunt—on my father's side—played the numbers and relied on dreams to tell her what to bet. Five dollars on 462. Ten on 765. Eleven on 891. One whole summer, when I was eight like you, no dreams came to her. Down South everybody cherishes dreams. In dreams this world and the next mix like sugar and grits. So Aunt Hattie called the dead. Put a glass of water under her bed, right beneath her pillow, quoted from the Bible, and chanted some slave prayer. She took a slip of paper and wrote, 'Give me a number,' then she slipped it on top of the water glass and slept."

"Did you see?"

"My mother told me. Told me too that the spirit was so angry she slapped Aunt Hattie's face, leaving a black, hand-shaped mark, and gave her the number 337. The number hit, and Aunt Hattie gave our town a party with marshmallow yams, watermelon, barbeque, and smoked corn. She never played the numbers again, and her mark never faded."

"Scratch a wall, somebody die." "Do good and it'll fly right back to you." "Walk the right side of the street, memories stay sweet." "Never go backward, only forward." "Curse an enemy, curse yourself too." "When I die, I'll be with you. Standing two steps behind."

I always wanted to know who said such things, who taught Grandmother to believe them.

"Down South, in Georgia, everybody knows what I say is true. Miracles abound."

Grandmother toiled raising us kids, and some nights she'd fall asleep in the chair watching late-night movies—*Carmen Jones, Imitation of Life, All God's Chillun Got Wings*—and us kids would laugh and play until we got too rowdy and she'd wake and scoot us off to bed. Climbing the stairs, favoring her sore left side, I'd hear her mutter softly, "Down South, women don't leave kids." I knew the complaint was directed at my mother, and though I didn't know where my mother was, I knew she wasn't down South.

"Good night," Grandmother would whisper. "Say your prayers. Remember: The world is alive. Everything has a living spirit."

Animate, inanimate, it didn't matter. Grandmother believed that a sensibility, a soul, existed in everything. Many a night I suspected the rocking horse near my bedroom window was alive and watching me, daring me to ride it past dark.

In all the years Grandmother lived up North, she only returned to Georgia once.

I hated every minute of that drive. We drove fourteen hours straight and went to the bathroom on the side of the road. I didn't understand then that there were few places for "coloreds" to stay. We drove and drove (three adults up front, three kids in the backseat), and with each mile Grandmother seemed more fidgety, nervous.

Today, long grown, I barely remember that humid July in Georgia, the rope swing in the yard, running barefoot through grass, chasing chickens and catching lightning bugs in washed-out jars. I hardly remember relatives who pinched my cheek, patted my hair, and offered me platters of bright, pepper-spiced food. But I do remember Grandmother growing more languid, moving with a grace I'd never seen. It was as though the wet heat had soothed the aches in her bones, smoothed the lines that creased her brow.

Grandmother was the prodigal child come home, and our relatives waited on her, fed her, and kissed her a thousand times. An old suitor, now a carpenter with blunt and scarred hands, came to call. At church the preacher praised Grandmother's return. The sewing circle made her a quilt. All the while, the Georgia sun shone bright, making the dampened air shiver with rainbows.

While I know Grandmother loved sitting on the wide, bright white porch, rocking in a wicker chair, staring at the point where the grass gave way to groves of trees, she also spent many hours in a back room, tending her elderly father. He looked shriveled, his eyes nearly blind with cataracts. Grandmother stayed beside him each moment he was awake. She straightened his pillows, washed his body, changed his soiled sheets, and fed him mashed peaches. Us kids never went farther into Great-granddaddy's room than the threshold. The room was too dark; it smelled of camphor and sweat. But at night, when we were camped out on the porch, we could hear Grandmother inside murmuring stories to him. Never about Pittsburgh but always about her childhood down South.

"Do you remember, Daddy, teaching me to fish? I caught my finger in the line and nearly lost my thumb.

"Do you remember baptismal day—me crying, water? You promised me pie if I wiped my tears.

"Do you remember Christmas, our money low, you hunted squirrel for Mama? Whenever Mama looked sad, you tickled her, making her laugh.

"Do you remember carrying me on your shoulders when I turned five? You bounced, twirled me till I was dizzy.

"You remember teaching me to harvest? Working before dawn and well into night?"

One morning it was "time to go. I got to go." Grandmother made us pack our clothes box, our newfound toys of pecan shells, our dried snakeskin, and marbles. We left with a wicker basket of chicken, biscuits, peach cobbler, and plastic cups and spoons. Kool-Aid was in a jug. Grandmother made everyone kiss her father, and after her last kiss she said again quietly, "I got to go."

The drive home was a killer—us kids bored, squabbling, and the adults in the front seat speaking nary a word.

I was thrilled to be home. The North Side of Pittsburgh, with its hardened poverty and sun-starved weeds, nonetheless seemed magical to me. I raced up our front steps, barely conscious of the grown-ups unpacking, of Grandmother gingerly stepping down the basement stairs to start the first of many load of laundry.

In truth, if Pittsburgh ever had any magic, it was because of my grandmother. All the children in the neighborhood were her children. She scolded us and doled out sugar cookies and meringue, peach, pumpkin, or apple pie. No person was ever turned away from her door. If you needed something, Grandmother, who really had so little, found a way to provide. She was funny, generous, the very glue that kept our ragged family rich in love rather than bitterness.

We in turn teased her about her Southern ways, laughed when she simmered black-eyed peas and greens on the first of January to bring our family luck and money.

On chitlin days everyone complained about the skunky smell. "Slave food isn't always bad food," she'd say. After Grandmother fried the chitlins and smothered them in hot sauce, she'd eat her fill, then carry pounds of leftovers to the neighbors.

Grandmother's father died. Parentless, she kept parenting us, her second set of children. And like all children, I hurried to grow up. Each of us grew older, though usually not wiser. And like a blink in time, Grandmother was caring for my cousin's children. She helped to raise three generations of kids.

I called Grandmother on a Sunday from the phone in my college dorm. I said, "I'll visit next week." Grandmother sounded tired but happy. Another Christmas had passed, but winter was still holding on, and Good Friday was weeks off.

"In Georgia I'd be planning my garden. Pole beans, sweet peas, and early tomatoes. I'm too old to be raising kids. One day, down South, I'm going to put my feet up and watch my garden grow."

"Next week, when I see you, will you tell me about cauls?"

"Why you want to know about that?"

"Research. I'm writing a novel."

"Cauls are special. In Georgia Mama's midwife would talk about cauls. Meant the baby had the gift, the sight. None of Mama's babies were born with it, but the midwife kept hoping. Midwife told her just what to do with it."

"What's that?"

"I'm not sure I remember. Bury it. Light some candles. Save a piece and boil it with tea. I don't know what all else. Down South folks can be funny."

"Are you funny?"

"I was always funny. So were you." Grandmother laughed, and her voice sounded years younger. In my mind's eye I could see her in the hallway, just beyond the vestibule, sitting in the telephone chair, her arms draped on the small table. Flowery house dress. Pink terry-cloth slippers. Her hair squeezed tight in curlers.

That Tuesday, walking from the store with her new children (my second cousins: two boys, ages seven and ten),

Grandmother collapsed onto the sidewalk, clutching at her heart.

This is what I was told: A kind man stopped his car and offered a ride to the hospital. Ernestine was still conscious. She asked for Divine Providence hospital.

When they got there the nurses made her wait. Ernestine was having trouble breathing. The eldest boy answered questions: "Yes, she has pressure problems. Diabetes. Pains in her chest."

Ernestine was taken upstairs for heart monitoring. They rolled her wheelchair into the elevator. By the time they got to the right floor, she was dead.

I have been to Georgia. I stayed in the Peachtree Atlanta Hyatt and stared out the windows on the twenty-first floor, looking at a skyline of concrete, steel, glass, and a light blue sky.

I did not rent a car. I did not visit the ancestral home. I was afraid Grandmother's house would be a will-o'-the-wisp, a mirage cloaked by humid heat. I was afraid that the soil that nurtured Grandmother's love would appear only barren and dry as a desert.

Older, I understand better the complex weave of how generations of children chained Grandmother like steel. I understand, too, that Grandmother would not, could not, have behaved any other way. She would mother us all as long as she believed we needed her. I know I needed her. I need her still.

Weaving memories about myself as well as my grandmother, I tried to explore the texture of both our lives. I tried to recall not only what I *saw* about grandmother but what I could *sense*—see, touch, taste, and smell—about our family's life in Pennsylvania in contrast to the promise of Georgia. I wanted, through visual images and dialogue, to do nothing less than resurrect my grandmother so that all the world could feel her enormous, big-hearted humanity and understand the cultural and family life surrounding her.

Using a highlighter, mark sentences and passages that create images in your mind. How does dialogue enhance these images?

"Now in Georgia—"
I'd groan, "Not another Georgia story."
"—white stayed white. White shoes. White gloves. White pearls."

Can you see and hear my grandmother and me? Do you think my memories would be less powerful if I had deleted the dialogue?

Like Baker, I begin my essay with a pivotal incident: Grandmother telling stories, "passing down tales" about our Southern heritage. However, I try to reveal how storytelling was "Grandmother's mission in life." Through the repetition of "down south . . . down south, in Georgia . . ." my grandmother's tales build suspense for the actual visit "down south." I write, "Grandmother was the prodigal child come home, and our relatives waited on her, fed her, and kissed her a thousand times."

Once again, dialogue helps me convey the essence of my grandmother, who, while watching over her dying father, murmurs stories, repeating the phrase: "Do you remember? . . . Do you remember? . . . Do you remember?" Grandmother's voice passes down the stories and memories of her childhood with her father just as my voice, the writer's, passes on the stories and memories about my childhood with her. Stories crossing generations support my theme that memories and stories never fade, never die.

The power of stories to outlast life is made evident by my grandmother's death. Although I didn't witness her death, I report it, based on "what I was told." I wanted the seemingly flat telling of Grandmother's death to contrast sharply with the vivid image of Grandmother telling her tales.

Review my essay again and count how many stories, pieces of stories, you hear. How do these stories trace almost the entire course of Grandmother's life?

Though the focus of the essay is on Grandmother, what other people populate her tales and her life? How do these individuals reflect Grandmother's character, values, and upbringing?

In my conclusion, I show how my adult sensibility was affected by my grandmother's life (rather than by her death); how her life was a turning point for me. Older and wiser, I understood some of the sacrifices Grandmother had made to nurture her children and her children's children.

Baker, *elaborating on one memory,* builds his essay by analyzing the meaning of his father's rage. His analysis compassionately explores how the pressures of one man can influence his son, and his son, and so on, down through the generations.

Using memories and stories, I *compare and contrast Grandmother's Southern stories with her Northern life.* At its core, my essay is the tale of the way a young woman sustained generations, at the expense of her dreams. Like Baker, I try to explore how family and societal influences can encourage constructive as well as destructive behaviors from one generation to the next. Like Grandmother, I tell stories. Like Grandmother, I have my own complex weave of family responsibilities and relationships. But, fundamentally, Grandmother's life, her storytelling, and my storytelling are about love. And love has its price as well as its heavenly and never-ending rewards.

These discrete chapters on autobiography and memoir, may make the two genres seem unrelated. But, in fact, they are "kissing cousins"—close, intimate, and reflective of each other. Be sure to study both. Whether you are reading a good memoir or a good autobiography, you can learn invaluable lessons about being a writer.

Keep the faith, keep writing in your journal, and keep hold of your memories!

PART IV

BEYOND MEMOIR
AND
AUTOBIOGRAPHY:
WITNESSING
AND THE
PERSONAL ESSAY

NINE

CELEBRATING OUR
PERSONAL STORIES

I can tell you what I witness and experience.
I can testify to our people's triumph and survival.

African Americans have always been deeply spiritual people. While questions about which faith to practice may
bother some, many African Americans who are true to their
"mixed blood roots" find cause to celebrate—in song, in story,
in music and dance, arts and crafts, and holistic healing—the
notion that a spirit moves and sustains us. This spirit is both
inside and outside our bodies.

In addition to church membership, many African Americans also find faith and hope in African-based rituals, Christian and Muslim prayer groups, family gatherings, sisterhood
and brotherhood groups, storytelling and book club circles,
family reunions, and in cultural celebrations like Kwanzaa and
Juneteenth. To survive slavery, our people nurtured the strong
belief that the human soul existed, as did spirits in the heav-

ens, and spirits who worked through the loving support of family, friends, and community to encourage continued growth of our people, with heads upright and unbowed.

Telling tales is celebrating culture and passing along traditions, modes of survival, to remind new generations that "wrongs" can be made "better" and sometimes "right" through faith, self-love, community, and family. Searching for a *griot* to survive in the New World, African Americans turned to folk songs, oral storytellers, preachers, and, ultimately, essays, letters, and diaries, which conveyed the importance of "witnessing" and "testifying" to the spirit of our people.

"Witnessing" an event through any and all avenues of perception (sight, taste, sound, hearing) and giving voice, "testimony," to one's experiences is fundamentally good for both individual and collective identity.

Personal-development and testimonial books, such as Stephanie Stokes Oliver's *Daily Cornbread;* the *African American Book of Values,* edited by Steven Barboza; the *Autobiography of a People: Three Centuries of African American History Told by Those Who Lived It,* edited by Herb Boyd; *This Far By Faith,* by Linnie Frank Bailey and Andria Hall; and many others, all combine a "gumbo blend" of African American heritage and culture, an emphasis on affirming the self, and a belief that the individual struggle toward spiritual growth and maturity is of benefit to an entire community.

Other nonfiction works, among them June Jordan's *Affirmative Acts,* Randall Robinson's *Defending the Spirit: A Black Life in America,* Tavis Smiley's *Doing What's Right: How to Fight for What You Believe and Make a Difference,* Katie Cannon's *Katie's Canon: Womanism and the Soul of the Black Community,* Darlene Clark Hine's *A Shining Thread of Hope,* and Alice Walker's *In*

Search of Our Mothers' Gardens, combine political, social, and religious or spiritual commentary on African American life. These books are of extensive scholarly range (sociology, literature, history) and research and journalism methods, but they have in common the use of personal ("I") stories and the healthy implication that the personal *is* political.

The "I," the first-person voice, is not dismissed for its lack of statistical or quantitative weight. Rather, the "I," the voice speaking, is given due respect precisely because, as African Americans, we refuse to silence voices, and we emphatically believe that a single voice can be extraordinarily powerful and can serve as a spiritual and moral guide. Personal witnessing is essential for people who have sometimes had to rely on one voice in the wilderness to encourage and affirm the next generation's survival.

In particular, the preacher's sermon—both oral and written—has enhanced personal witnessing as a strategy for communication. Henry Louis Gates, Jr., and Nellie Y. McKay, general editors of *The Norton Anthology of African American Literature,* devote a section to sermons, noting that the best preachers render personal testimonies of human nature and God's presence. Thus, a well-preached sermon becomes part of our cultural witnessing, a bedrock of African American literature, both fiction and nonfiction.

The preacher-man or preacher-woman, fictional or real, more often than not carries a spiritual authority that demands an audience: *To Listen up! Hear the story . . . hear the testament and celebration of self.* Whether it is Baby Suggs in Toni Morrison's *Beloved* saying, "Love your hands! . . . love your neck . . . and all your inside parts . . . love your heart" or Martin Luther King, Jr., preaching love and nonviolence, it is the cultural sign that spiritual affirmation and spiritual witnessing have *persuasive force.*

In his sermon "I've Been to the Mountaintop," Dr. Martin Luther King, Jr., preaches:

> *Somewhere I read of the freedom of speech. Somewhere I read of the freedom of the press. Somewhere I read that the greatness of America is the right to protest for right. And so just as I say, we aren't going to let the injunction turn us around. We are going on. We need all of you. And, you know, what's beautiful to me is to see all these ministers of the Gospel. It's a marvelous picture. Who is it that is supposed to articulate the longings and aspirations of the people more than the preacher? Somehow the preacher must be an Amos, and say, "Let justice roll down like waters and righteousness like a mighty stream." Somehow the preacher must say with Jesus, "The spirit of the Lord is upon me, because he hath anointed me to deal with the problems of the poor."*

The "I" is foremost. With "I read . . . I read . . . I read . . . so just as I say . . ." Dr. King uses **repetition** to reinforce the authority he assumes as an individual and as a preacher. This repetition reinforces the ***orality*** of Dr. King's sermon—he is witnessing, talking aloud to his peers and African American community. *"We need all of you."* He is affirming everyone's importance, individually and collectively. Dr. King is also encouraging a course of action: "I say, we aren't going to let the injunction turn us around." Persuasion is the core of why Dr. King testifies and affirms. He is encouraging continued protests for civil rights, despite civil injunctions.

Everyone knows that Dr. Martin Luther King, Jr., was a

powerful persuader for social justice. But the strategy of witnessing—*"I have seen"*—affirming his own and the community's worth, of testifying, preaching to his peers and community, follows traditions. And in the retelling or the rereading, the affirmation becomes exponential, for each listener can echo the tale and pass along to others the story orally or as literary text.

Ellis Cose, in his 1993 best-seller, *The Rage of a Privileged Class,* blends personal accounts with history, sociology, economic, educational, and professional career studies to answer the questions: "Why are middle-class blacks angry? Why should America care?"

While Cose brings considerable research skills and investigative journalism to his topic, he also relies on interweaving personal testimonies with his reporting and analyses:

> *Youtha Hardman-Cromwell, a Methodist minister, mother of four, and university professor and administrator in Washington, D.C., says she would never encourage a black child to believe that America is color-blind. "I wouldn't . . . because there's too much racism that they have to face. And if they have no idea that that's what it is, then it looks crazy. Because they . . . can't understand why this [discrimination] is happening to them."*
>
> *How does one teach a child about prejudice? "First of all," says Hardman-Cromwell, "you can tell your story . . . And they need to have a sense that you value them."*

The words *"tell your story"* and *"value them"* underscore the African American tradition of testimony and affirmation. The mother's story is told to sustain and hearten the next generation.

Cose titled his book's introduction "Shouts and Whispers," emphasizing, again, the importance of personal voices telling of their experiences. *But why bother?* Because in Cose's view (and in African American testimonial tradition), the "I" voice is a powerful persuader not to be discounted. Cose wants us to answer knowledgeably about the rage of middle-class blacks and why America should care. Personal recounting doesn't subtract but adds weight to his statistical arguments and sociological analyses.

MY BEST ADVICE

Never discount the power of the personal voice and personal experiences in nonfiction. An "I" voice—motivated by a desire to celebrate, inform, or lovingly criticize our people—can have significant persuasive power and moral authority.

Regardless of the scale of your project, you need to *establish that you are an authority, someone worthy of belief.*

Direct experience, in-depth knowledge, and a willingness to commit yourself intellectually and emotionally to your subject—all help to convince readers that your prose is worth reading and potentially valuable to their lives.

As a "witness," you need to make clear that you are writing from *inside,* not outside, your subject.

Charlotte Pierce-Baker, in *Surviving the Silence: Black Women's Stories of Rape,* establishes her authority through her tale of rape survival. But Pierce-Baker's supreme accomplishment is how she creates a loving network with a dozen other women who shared their survival stories; and how, in turn, this network expands to include the voices and stories of men who love these women who are rape survivors.

Pierce-Baker is herself a witness to rape and a witness to the sisterhood among black women who have a long history of sharing stories to provide strength to their sisters. By speaking with men, Pierce-Baker expands her readers' knowledge of the harm rape does to an entire community. The personal becomes political and bears significance for an entire world.

Pierce-Baker's testimony is direct and eloquent: "On September 6, 1981, the evening of a gorgeous late summer— early fall day, the kind with winds that catch ceiling-high curtains and whip them gently against window sills, I was raped."

Pierce-Baker's "voice" reflects the sensibility of a remarkable woman—observant, sensitive, attuned to seasons, senses, and the marvels of nature. There is honesty and openness in her language. There is intimacy, too. Reread the paragraph, and then close your eyes. I suspect you'll conjure an image of a strong, special, and vulnerable woman sitting across from you, talking to you in a voice imbued with simplicity, power, and sincerity.

Her language is not filled with fifty-cent words from a thesaurus. Nor are there convoluted sentence structures. The voice's power comes from concrete details and from fury kept in check so that the writer can best tell the tale. Like all fine communication, you sense the writer is enveloping you, sharing intimacies in the widest sense of that word. She is credible, articulate, and persuasive. Her voice is forceful, not strained. **When a tale needs to be told, it is best told simply and**

directly. Language should reveal, not obscure, meaning. Because of her clarity of voice, Pierce-Baker's testimony is not only credible but unusually moving.

Without a doubt, **emotions add weight to an author's persuasiveness.** However, Pierce-Baker is not manipulating readers' emotions with a heart-rending subject; rather, by keeping her focus as a writer on telling her tale (and on letting others tell their tales truly, honestly, and openly), she allows the emotions to come flooding out, like a dam unbanked.

Finally, Pierce-Baker's affirmation of self and her community makes the book exceptional. Readers can hear the pain, the silencing of women that accompanies rape, but by courageously lifting her own voice, Pierce-Baker creates a book that is an odyssey, encompassing other voices, within and outside her text:

> *I am now able to articulate without fear, guilt, or shame that I am a black woman who has survived rape. I have survived my own silences. I am forever changed, and this realization no longer paralyzes me. Each day brings new revelations. Finding my place in a chorus of sound, I mean to knock pods off chestnut trees and bring the guilty to justice, the indifferent to attention, and the needful to safe harbor . . .*
>
> *The way out is to tell: speak the acts perpetrated upon us, speak the atrocities, speak the injustices, speak the personal violations of the soul. Someone will listen, someone will believe our stories, someone will join us. And until there are more who will bear witness to our truths as black women, we will do it for one another.*

* * *

Surviving the Silence succeeds as a glorious celebration of the spiritual power of black women and men in America. Pierce-Baker's book explores wounds, but her prose also heals.

Basic keys to writing strong, personal essays:

- *Assert your "I" voice; establish yourself as an authority, someone worthy of belief.* Reveal how direct experience, in-depth knowledge, and an intellectual and emotional commitment make the story important to you.

- *Tell the tale simply and directly.* Don't strain for language or overinflate the significance of your story; rather, tell the tale as though you were speaking to a close friend, as though you were sharing intimately a story that needs to be told.

- *Use specific details and examples.* Never be vague or write generally; use specific settings, details, and examples to add credibility and to illuminate your meaning.

- *Persuasiveness enhances content.* Essays aren't written in a vacuum. A good essay seeks to move an audience emotionally and intellectually. Keep focused on *why* you're telling your story. Whether as a call to action, compassion for another human being, a new perspective on life, an essay written *honestly, openly, and with feeling* engages readers to understand your point of view.

- *Make events active, rather than passive.* Avoid the trap of just relating boring events; i.e., "This happened . . . then this happened . . . then this happened." Just like a storyteller, the essayist should, whenever possible, re-create characters, use concrete details, set the scene for their events, and use strong action verbs. A good personal essay can engage readers' imaginations as completely as fiction does.

When I was a young assistant professor, I wrote the following essay for *Ms.* magazine:

WHEN YOUR SENSE OF HUMOR IS YOUR BEST TRAVELING COMPANION

Jewell Parker Rhodes

Business travel can be treacherous when you're female and black. Sooner or later, in neon script, the double whammy of racism and sexism hits.

One morning in Saratoga, I was nibbling a cantaloupe for breakfast when a white colleague cracked a watermelon joke. "I thought y'all preferred to pick seeds," he said. A white couple at an Ivy League Club in New York mistook me for a maid and asked me to clean their room—despite the fact that my hair was neatly pinned, I carried a briefcase, and wore my "intellectual" glasses and my three-piece pinstripe suit. A fellow professor at a convention in Detroit assumed I was a local black hooker. Why? I wasn't near a bar. On one excursion South, I eschewed a conference cafeteria lunch in favor of a hamburger diner; over relish and onions, an ancient white man offered me five dollars if I took a trip to his house: "Just for an hour." (He must have been recalling pre-inflation days.) Needless to say, my professional performance lacked luster when I delivered my paper during the afternoon conference session.

Like an innocent or a fool, I begin each trip with optimism, still determined that race and sex not impede my performance and acceptance. My pretensions get depressed.

How potent is the subliminal irritation of being the only woman on the businessman's shuttle between New York and Washington? Of being the only minority at a professional meeting? Each trip represents for me a lesson in alienation. Yet because I'm conducting business, "networking," and trying to promote a career, I can't afford feeling alien since it engenders mistrust and withdrawal. So each trip I'm vulnerable anew.

Why *can't* business travel be pleasurable? I've read all the books and articles on "how to dress for success." Wind me up and I conduct myself with adequate charm. But after following all the advice, I find myself still belittled—*and* rendered less effective—due to the emotional and psychological assaults.

Articles and books don't tell you how to deal with the loneliness of being the only visible minority in a Midwestern town, or in an airport, or at a meeting. Once I walked through a community for hours and never saw another face with the slightest hint of brown. I did, however, spend my evenings being interrogated by "well-intentioned" liberals who wanted my opinion on every civil rights issue since the Civil War. Willy-nilly, I am a spokesperson for my race.

Articles and books also don't tell you how to deal with

sexual assaults beyond "carry a book to dinner." My rage gets dissipated only in a Howard Johnson's hotel room, alone, with room service.

It becomes doubly hard to ward off sexual invitation when you feel intense loneliness because nowhere else in the conference, the hotel, or the lounge, is there anyone who in the least resembles your sex or color. One loneliness begets another. Yet ward off sexual invitations you must—since the macho, conquering male abounds at professional meetings and since men compound their sexism with racist awe regarding your color. Any nonwhite characteristics can be viewed as exotic plumes.

Once, in the District of Columbia following a conference dinner, my white male colleague and escort was nearly attacked by three black youths. Only a police officer delayed their action. Do you honestly believe I was at my professional peak the next day? And there also have been predominant black conferences where sexist attitudes angered me so intensely I could barely function. I recall the time in Ohio when an African colleague called me in my hotel room at 1:30 in the morning so we could "discuss" improved relations between his country and mine. The rest of the night I didn't sleep.

In Atlanta, I spent a whole day shunning a black male's advances. The bathroom provided my sole measure of peace. At dinner, I was enjoying my conversation with an author on my right when my ego-bruised pursuer shouted, "I'm a man too!" I groaned. I wanted to hide beneath the table. I'd forgotten that any public conversation between a male and female is seen as sexual.

What are the strategies for negotiating the sexist and racist trails of professional meetings? I honestly don't know. A business suit doesn't necessarily serve as armor. A book doesn't shield one from all sexual encounters. I've tried wearing makeup and no makeup. I've tried dressing up and dressing down. I've tried the schoolmarm's bun and also the thick-rimmed glasses. Still, sexism abounds. Superficial transformations don't negate discrimination. About my color, I can do nothing (nor would I want to if I could).

The best one can do is try to prevail with dignity. When I've been the only woman at a conference, I search for minority colleagues—shared interests and shared culture sometimes bind. When I've been the only black, I search for women—women hug when you're down and encourage you in your work. When I've been the only black *and* the only woman, I call long distance to reach out and touch a friend.

Sometimes humor helps. One year I dressed severely to compensate for my baby face. I wore high heels to compensate for my lack of height. I felt every inch the professional. Yet at the academic convention registration, I was brusquely pulled aside. "Can't you read the signs? Student registration is to the right."

If they don't get you for race and sex, they get you for something else.

In this essay, I voice my personal experiences with racial and sexual discrimination. I wrote the essay as though I were talking to my best girlfriend. But my intent was also to assert my voice, to rail against unfair circumstances that hamper rather than help my professionalism. I remember vividly feeling, too, that unless I used humor, I would break down and cry. Ultimately, I think, humor invites readers to empathize and perhaps to laugh or nod at their remembrance of similar experiences. Shared laughter in the face of strain and conflict has its own persuasive appeal. My "I" becomes joined with a "we," a community, a sisterhood crossing racial and sexual boundaries. The essay affirms and, potentially, may make people rethink how they see professional women of color.

Many other essays have as their theme racism and traveling within the United States. Brent Staples, in his 1987 *Harper's* magazine essay "Black Men and Public Space," focuses his testimony on dampening his rage and becoming less threatening to others:

BLACK MEN AND PUBLIC SPACE

Brent Staples

My first victim was a woman—white, well dressed, probably in her late twenties. I came upon her late one evening on a deserted street in Hyde Park, a relatively affluent neighborhood in an otherwise mean, impoverished section of Chicago. As I swung onto the avenue behind her, there seemed to be a discreet, uninflammatory distance between us. Not so. She cast back a worried glance. To her, the youngish black man—a broad six feet two inches with a beard and billowing hair, both hands shoved into the pockets of a bulky military jacket—seemed menacingly close. After a few more quick glimpses, she picked up her pace and was soon running in earnest. Within seconds she disappeared into a cross street.

That was more than a decade ago. I was twenty-two years old, a graduate student newly arrived at the University of Chicago. It was in the echo of that terrified woman's footfalls that I first began to know the unwieldy inheritance I'd come into—the ability to alter public space in ugly ways. It was clear that she thought herself the quarry of a mugger, a rapist, or worse. Suffering a bout of insomnia, however, I was stalking sleep, not defenseless wayfarers. As a softy who is scarcely able to take a knife to a raw chicken—let alone hold one to a person's throat—I was surprised, embarrassed, and dismayed all at once. Her flight made me feel like an accomplice in tyranny. It also made it clear that I was indistinguishable from the muggers who occasionally seeped into the area from the surrounding ghetto. That first encounter, and those that followed, signified that a vast, unnerving gulf lay between nighttime pedestrians—particularly women—and me. And I soon gathered that being perceived as dangerous is a hazard in itself. I only needed to turn a corner into a dicey situation, or crowd some frightened, armed person in a foyer somewhere, or make an errant move after being pulled over by a policeman. Where fear and weapons meet—and they often do in urban America—there is always the possibility of death.

In that first year, my first away from my hometown, I was to become thoroughly familiar with the language of fear. At dark, shadowy intersections, I could cross in front of a car stopped at a traffic light and elicit the *thunk, thunk, thunk, thunk* of the driver—black, white, male, or female—hammering down the door locks. On less traveled streets after dark, I grew accustomed to but never comfortable with people crossing to the other side of the street rather than pass me. Then there were the standard unpleasantries with policemen, doormen, bouncers, cabdrivers, and others whose business it is to screen out troublesome individuals *before* there is any nastiness.

I moved to New York nearly two years ago and I have remained an avid night walker. In central Manhattan, the near-constant crowd cover minimizes tense one-on-one street encounters. Elsewhere—in SoHo, for example, where sidewalks are narrow and tightly spaced buildings shut out the sky—things can get very taut indeed.

After dark, on the warrenlike streets of Brooklyn where I live, I often see women who fear the worst from me. They seem to have set their faces on neutral, and with their purse straps strung across their chests bandolier-style, they forge ahead as though bracing themselves against being tackled. I understand, of course, that the danger they perceive is not a hallucination. Women are particularly vulnerable to street violence, and young black males are drastically overrepresented among the perpetrators of that violence. Yet these truths are no solace against the kind of alienation that comes of being ever the suspect, a fearsome entity with whom pedestrians avoid making eye contact.

Over the years, I learned to smother the rage I felt at so often being taken for a criminal. Not to do so would surely have led to madness. I now take precautions to make myself less threatening. I move about with care, particularly late in the evening. I give a wide berth to nervous people on subway platforms during the wee hours, particularly when I have exchanged business clothes for jeans. If I happen to be entering a building behind some people who appear skittish, I may walk by, letting them clear the lobby before I return, so as not to seem to be following them. I have been calm and extremely congenial on those rare occasions when I've been pulled over by the police.

And on late-evening constitutionals I employ what has proved to be an excellent tension-reducing measure: I whistle melodies from Beethoven and Vivaldi and the more popular classical composers. Even steely New Yorkers hunching toward nighttime destinations seem to relax, and occasionally they even join in the tune. Virtually everybody seems to sense that a mugger wouldn't be warbling bright, sunny selections from Vivaldi's *Four Seasons*. It is my equivalent of the cowbell that hikers wear when they know they are in bear country.

Compare and contrast my essay with Staples's. We each assert the "I" voice and rely on personal experience to add authority and persuasiveness to the argument that African Americans experience frequent, day-by-day discrimination. Our tales are forthright and re-create specific moments of prejudice. Fundamentally, we are both expunging tension as well as demonstrating how demeaning prejudice can be. We are both "bearing witness" for fellow sufferers as well as "testifying" so that we can heighten the consciousness of people who, consciously or unconsciously, react to African Americans as stereotypes rather than as people.

Yet for all the similarities in our essays, each is different in tone. Staples's testimony (like mine) is colored by who he is, his perceptions, and experiences. Rage is "smother[ed]" in his essay, whereas humor bubbles to the surface in mine. We each have distinct defense mechanisms, which, without a doubt, shape how we tell our personal stories.

When writing a personal essay, remember that your greatest strength is *who you are, what you know, and how you know it*. Your knowledge is deeply felt, deeply personal, and deeply meant. Revealing your experiences with careful descriptive details, forthright language, and emotional honesty will help you shape a message that is clear, resonant, and absorbing.

EXERCISE 1

WITNESSING, TESTIFYING
ABOUT THE SELF

Take twenty minutes and consider what aspect of your life you would most like to write about in a personal essay. Consider what might appeal to readers spiritually, emotionally, or intellectually. For example, overcoming a fear of flying, learning how to manage debt, finding pleasure in cooking nutritious meals, and improving one's health through meditation and yoga are all topics worth considering. Certainly some personal experiences may be more traumatic than others, but you shouldn't feel an obligation to write only about painful issues in your life. Everyone is searching for a pathway to better living; practical testimony about what you've learned and discovered can contribute to a wide and continuing discussion about improving one's quality of life.

Once you've selected a topic to testify about, pretend you're speaking to a dear friend, a support group, or a friendly audience. Write quickly for twenty minutes, recalling your experience with as much detail as you can. Try to write at least two pages. If, at first, you feel hesitant about writing, turn on a tape recorder and pretend you're speaking to an audience. Very often the informality of your speaking voice sets precisely the tone you want to capture in your writing. Remember: your prose voice needn't be formal and studied; instead, it can be relaxed and conversational. You are literally telling a story about your life experiences. *Speak it, if need be, and then write it, as you would to a friend.*

When you've finished writing, evaluate your rough draft. Consider:

- *Have you asserted your "I" voice?* Established why you're an authority on this subject? Have you shared with readers your passion about your subject, your knowledge and research, and your belief in the significance and importance of your subject?

- *Does your writing sound like you?* Can you "hear" yourself speaking? Do you sound inviting? Is your writing honest, direct, and detailed about what happened as well as about how it felt, how it affected your senses and being?

- *Is it clear how your "witnessing" might aid others?* Have you tried to enlighten and inform your readers? Are you encouraging them to consider new perspectives, new ideas, and new emotions? What is the "gift," the essence of the communication you wish to share?

Revise your writing using the above guidelines. Most likely, your writing will double and possibly triple in length. Make sure your writing stays focused on detailing your experience, how this experience benefited you, and why you think it might be of benefit to others.

EXERCISE 2

WITNESSING, TESTIFYING ABOUT OTHERS' LIVES

Take twenty minutes and consider what moment, what aspect of someone else's life, you would like to share with readers. Positive and negative role models help us to consider our own life's choices. A drug abuser may lead you to eschew all drugs. A working mother who fulfills a lifelong dream to graduate from college may inspire you. Sometimes these role models are family members or strangers with whom you've connected through work, school, or volunteering. As a nurse, you may have witnessed an optimist's fight against cancer. As a brother, you may have witnessed a sister's struggle with bulimia. As a child, you may have learned about life through your grandmother's actions and wisdom.

Like opening a curtain or looking through a camera lens, life presents us with *indirect experiences,* which, if understood, can shower us with grace and lead us to opportunities for better and more humane living.

As with personal, direct witnessing, indirect experiences should be retold, because they may be useful to an audience—spiritually, emotionally, or intellectually.

* * *

Once you've selected a person to testify about, write quickly for twenty minutes, recalling not only the person but your experience with them. Write with as much detail as possible. For example, if readers closed their eyes, would they "see" this person? Do readers need to "hear" this person? Can they "hear" you telling the story, inviting them to listen?

When you've finished writing, evaluate your rough draft. Consider:

- *Have you shared how you met this person and what makes them special?* Is it clear why you more than anyone else are best able to "witness" this person's life and experiences?

- *Is your subject "alive" in your writing?* Did you use specific details to describe what is most important about them and their actions?

- *Is it clear how your "witnessing" might aid others?* What can be learned from this person? What have *you* learned? How can the story of this person and your relationship with them enrich readers?

Revise your writing specifically detailing and celebrating your relationship with your subject. Let your readers experience some of the joy and potential challenges of knowing this person too!

Gloria Wade-Gayles, in an introduction to her marvelous anthology, *My Soul Is a Witness: African American Women's Spirituality,* testifies about her mother's life:

239

*Making lists at the end of every day was as necessary to my
mother's awaking the next day as setting the clock to ring at a
designated hour. I can see her now, sitting at the kitchen table, in
her right hand a yellow pencil she had sharpened to an almost
point with a black-handled paring knife. Open before her on the
table is a small spiral notebook, blue, red, or green, depending
upon which one she pulled from the plastic-wrapped package of
three purchased at the five-and-dime, several at a time when
they were on sale. She thinks, as if in meditation, and then she
writes therein her responsibilities for "a new beginning."*

Wade-Gayles has re-created an image of her mother so
that readers may "see" her as clearly as Wade-Gayles sees her
in memory. Note: Wade-Gayles hasn't given details about her
mother's hair or eye color, height or build. Indeed, in this case,
appearance is far less important than her mother's *actions and
her relationship to her yellow pencil and spiral notebook.*

Details should never be written just for details' sake.
Rather, as a writer, you should be selective. Write down only
those details which are essential for readers to appreciate and
experience your ideas and memories. More is not always best.
In this particular essay, Wade-Gayles's mother's habit of "list-
making" is the critical information:

*When I was a child, I thought my mother's daily list-making a
boring routine, a mere habit rooted in her penchant for
organization. But when I became a woman and, as Scripture says,
"put away childish things," I realized that the activity was part of
a spiritual ritual: first the lists, then the meditation, and before
turning off the light, the prayers. It was therefore, with an
unsettling feeling, a dread, really, that I accepted the list my mother*

forced me to take on the night before the morning of her death. I would need it, she said. I remember the small notebook, wired at the top and dark blue in color, and the important information she had written therein with a firm hand: names of doctors and medicines and the numbers of her Blue Cross, life, and burial policies. My mother's spirituality in life and in death started me on a search for my own, giving me a "new beginning." It is that search, I am convinced, that led me humbly to this anthology. I know my responsibilities: I must "do what the Spirit says do" and serve as a conduit for the testimonies included herein.

Wade-Gayles's desire to create her book, *My Soul Is a Witness,* stemmed from her mother's calling to create lists, meditate, and organize each day. In witnessing her mother's life, Wade-Gayles testifies not only about her mother and their relationship, but also about how their relationship served as a catalyst for her to create a testament to the spirituality of all black women. A mother enriched her daughter's life, and, in doing so, planted a seed that was nurtured with love. The fruit of her mother's wisdom lives on in an anthology that is an everlasting gift to all who read it.

E X E R C I S E   3

WITNESSING SMALL, PERSONAL MOMENTS OF AFFIRMATION AND SELF-AWARENESS

Affirmations like meditative moments, prayers, and useful beads of wisdom are designed to help our everyday lives. Popular African American self-development books often com-

241

bine daily meditations, oral chants, prayers, rituals, and "to do" lists in various combinations of prose and poetry.

Marita Golden, in her essay "The Power of Affirmations," says:

> I recite the following affirmation each day as a way of staying centered on the essentials of life and fighting off the onslaught of invasive, dangerous distractions that blind you sometimes to who you really are and what you really do possess.
>
> > Everyday I am blessed
> > Each day brings me joy
> > God, family, friends, work
> > are my network, my saving grace
> > I am a child of God
> > I am where I am supposed to be
> > My life is full and complete.

Golden's sharing is not merely confessional; instead, she is drawing on a cultural belief that personal prayers and loving affirmations of self and a belief in God can work for the individual as well as for a community. Golden's "sharing" is quintessentially within the testimonial tradition of black peoples. *The implicit belief is: "What gives meaning and power to me may help to affirm you."* Charity, generosity, faith are the hallmarks of African American affirmations, and such values dominate many sisterhood and brotherhood groups.

Consider:

How do you affirm your life? What words do you pray, shout, whisper, or sing to yourself when you're in need of spiritual and loving support?

⅀ *How do you honor your own needs during hectic times?* How do you establish inner harmony? (Susan Taylor, editor of *Essence,* suggests in her essay "Your Inner Voice" that people need to continually ask and answer life-supporting questions. *Who am I? What does my happiness require? Am I growing, moving forward with my life?*)

⅀ *Do you have any rituals that may be helpful to others?* (Best-selling author Iyanla Vanzant suggests establishing an altar with water, white flowers, and candles to help invoke African "guardian spirits.")

In your journal, try to respond to the above considerations. You may want to take a day, or several days, to consider what habits and skills you already use to make your life manageable and satisfying. If you are dissatisfied with your life, then consider what actions, thoughts, and feelings might improve it.

If you're truly serious about writing a book filled with daily affirmations, you may want to start a separate journal in which you keep track on a day-to-day basis, your attempts to maintain balance and harmony in your life. After a month of record-keeping, you'll be better able to identify the themes and strategies that you use and that might be helpful to others. You may want to organize your book according to daily or seasonal affirmations or topics, such as love, happiness, or achieving simplicity. Keeping track of all the daily soul-soothing techniques and thoughts you rely on to maintain your self-esteem may lead to even greater personal development, since it encourages more conscious self-awareness.

* * *

Witness, testifying, and affirming the self and others are extremely satisfying expressions of African American culture. Celebrations of our soul and humanity can be woven into an essay, a book, or a companion journal of meditations. The Delany sisters' memoir, *Having Our Say: The Delany Sisters' First Hundred Years,* was brilliant, but the second book by Sarah Louise Delany, *On My Own at 107: Reflections on My Life Without Bessie,* is a touching work of "daily witnessing and celebration." The surviving sister watching the seasons, observing her garden slumber and then thrive, meditates on the meaning of life, her sister's death, and what it means to be a long-lived black woman. She creates a text that shimmers with compassion and shows a possible pathway *to thinking and being more humane* and *living and dying with dignity.*

Personal stories that bear witness to our human condition and spirituality have always been a forceful presence in African American literature. Western cultural traditions have long supported individualism—a celebration of uniqueness. However, embedded in African American cultural tradition is another notion: the importance of the "I" in celebrating, reflecting, and informing the cultural group. The slave's narrative journey becomes a journey all of us seek to make—a journey into selfhood, which celebrates "I am." A political, social, and spiritually sustaining act for peoples.

Even if discrimination lessens and all civil rights are actively enforced, autobiography, memoir, and the personal essay will still have power because of the historical roots of our people. To assert one's voice, and therefore one's identity, is to share oneself with society, essentially an act of grace. *We are all storytellers. We all have stories to tell.*

Keep the faith. Believe in your ability to write. Your journey toward greater self-awareness, your insistence on giving voice to the thoughts, feelings, and dreams inside you, helps to sustain me. Sustain our culture. Sustain the world.

"Tell your story. Let me 'hear' you say it. I want to listen."

"Tell your story. Write it down. I want to read it."

Like mirrors, we reflect one another as we exchange tales and testify to our individual and collective glory:

I can't see you, if I don't hear you. I can't hear you, across time and space, if you don't write it down. If you don't write it down, you may miss the chance to know and understand yourself better. I will miss the chance to know and understand you, to know and understand myself better.

PERSONAL ESSAY, NO. 1

WITNESSING THE SELF:

GLENN TOWNES'S "CONFESSIONS OF A WOUNDED WARRIOR"

Glenn Townes, a prolific nonfiction writer for various magazines and journals and the author of a forthcoming book on depression, uses his personal experience to bear witness and testify about depression's pain and the pathway he found to survival and redemption.

I was The Man: single, thirtysomething and secure in my dream job as a journalist. But night after night, I came back to my Kansas City apartment, sat in the middle of my living room and cried. If somebody stopped by, I pretended I wasn't home. If they called, the phone was off the hook. Later, when I would finally get to bed, I'd lie awake for hours and hours, then be too tired to get up the next morning. My fantasy: to get into my car, drive away and never return.

Depression had cold-cocked me. But this dismal scene, which reached its peak about three years ago, wasn't my first bout. I can remember plenty of times over the years when I despaired for no particular reason. Back in high school, for instance, I'd written a paper for my English class called "Is It Worth It?" Several teachers, friends and family members complimented me on the writing, but I don't think they picked up on the underlying pain.

In college these periods of depression got longer. After college they got worse. And three years ago they became unbearable. That's when I found myself holed up in my apartment sobbing as if there were no tomorrow. The dark cloud would lift for a week or two and then envelop me again.

As I look back now, I remember feeling tremendous pressure. My work days often stretched to 12 hours; my answering machine was crammed with messages from people waiting for me to call them back. My family wanted me to come home for a visit; yet it was hard to get away, which made me feel like a bad son.

My sister and I were raised in an upper-middle-class New Jersey suburb by our parents, who were still happily married after 40 years. I was healthy, with money in the bank and a beautiful woman I thought I would marry. What did I have to be sad about? Guilt only intensified the strain.

It got worse. My relationship hit the skids, and my writing slipped. I began to hate my job. Over and over I asked myself, *Is this all there is? Is this what I'm going to be doing the rest of my life? What contribution am I making by covering a city-council meeting or writing about a woman who opened a plant shop?* It used to be wonderful seeing my name in print, but now I didn't care.

A second job as a medical-billing specialist for a group of Kansas City-area psychiatrists claimed even more of my time. It seemed logical that that would be the first thing to let go. But it turned out to be my saving grace. Initially I had taken the part-time gig only for a couple of months to save up more quickly for a computer and to pay off some bills. But I became fascinated by what I was learning about the human psyche and ended up staying on for nearly three years.

Patients would sometimes call and start talking about their bill, then end up discussing their treatment. Or they would chat with me when their doctor was running behind. It was only through them that I learned that insomnia, irritability, crying spells and mood swings are symptoms of depression. It seemed odd, but in getting to know some of the patients, I began to understand myself. It was like looking into a mirror or listening to a tape recording of my own thoughts.

Up until then I'd written depression off as weakness, something people have to find a way to face so they can get on with their lives. Besides, I figured, my ancestors had it a lot worse than I did. But when I saw all these people—men, women and children—flowing through the ritzy doors of the therapists' posh offices and freeing themselves of their deepest, darkest pain, I had to reevaluate my position. If Black folks traditionally don't undergo therapy, maybe it was time for me to break with tradition.

I finally went to one of the psychiatrists at the office. I told her about all the tension and the stress, and she understood. For about six months I had regular sessions with her. They were informal: She would sit in a chair next to mine and ask me questions about my feelings, helping me see where they came from and understand how to deal with them so they wouldn't cause me so much grief.

During our talks, I became aware that I was trying to do too much and be too many things to too many people. For a while my doctor prescribed Prozac, which also helped me feel more positive about life. (Prozac initially caused me to gain weight, a normal side effect. But after a while that subsided. When I stopped taking it six months later, I had no lingering craving for it and no withdrawal symptoms.) She gave me another medication for those sleepless nights.

The fog of melancholy began to clear. I wasn't nearly as lethargic. And the mood swings and crying jags stopped. People noticed. "You look better and seem happier," they told me. Even my family, calling long distance, told me that I sounded stronger. For a time my relationship with my lover improved as I opened up to her and shared my fears. The pressures of the job? Not nearly as intense. That's partly because I started putting myself first, which meant I no longer routinely worked 12-hour days at my newspaper. And I quit worrying about what other people expected of me. At first, some folks said I was being selfish, but they got over it.

These days, when I get blue, I still give my therapist a call. I did have a relapse recently when my lover decided to end our relationship. She told me that she had some personal problems and didn't want to be involved with anyone. I couldn't understand it, and I got depressed. Both of us are routine-oriented people, and I missed our standing Friday-night date at her house, where we would eat take-out Chinese and watch movies. But with the help of friends and my therapist, I picked up the pieces and moved on.

I still find there's a strong stigma attached to African-Americans' being in therapy, particularly for brothers. Tell someone you're seeing a shrink and they may haul off and hit you with "Man, you must be crazy." But I think it's just the opposite: Sometimes you'd have to be crazy not to seek therapy.

Study Townes's first sentence. How does it disarm readers and make Townes immediately sympathetic? Townes begins with "I was The Man," a boastful announcement; yet he ends his sentence by creating a picture . . . "sat in the middle of my living room and cried." Can you see him? Why is this picture more powerful than the boast: "I Was The Man?"

Townes's voice is part of what makes his essay compelling. Can you hear him speaking to you? How does the use of the "I" make Townes seem informally real and approachable?

What makes Townes most credible? His sharing of his background? His honesty about his relationships, his bills, his second job? His honesty about his depression battle? Or are all these confidences important to Townes's credibility and authority as a spokesperson for those suffering from depression?

Using a highlighter, show which lines make clear that Townes is affirming himself. Next, highlight the line or lines that make clear Townes's wish, in testifying, is to help others.

BEARING WITNESS OF OTHERS

CAROLYN C. DENARD'S
"DEFYING ALZHEIMER'S:
SAVING HER SPIRIT IN SONG"

*Carolyn Denard writes a moving essay about her grand-
mother's mental decline and the fleeting yet momentous
regaining of her "voice" through hymns. While Alzheimer's
ultimately claims Denard's grandmother, the essay is filled
with concrete memories and celebrates an elder in the family.
In so doing, it gives voice to the pain and compassion and the
spiritual strength with which one family met a profound loss.*

During my grandmother's eighty-fifth year, she developed
Alzheimer's disease. We didn't know much about
Alzheimer's disease then—not even enough to call it "Alzheimer's"; we just called it "senility." And, because most of our
older relatives had died early, what we knew even of senility
was second-hand or observed from a distance. Stories told
about a relative we had never met or small moments of participation in the life of the elderly relatives of friends we visited
were all my two sisters and I knew. My father had died three
years earlier at forty-eight. And my mother, now only forty-
eight herself, was nowhere near the challenges of senility and

old age. Grandmother's situation was new to us; and we had no idea of the journey we were about to witness.

Grandmother would forget the days of the week, where she put the mail, where she was going, how to get home, and what she had just said. She confused who was living with who was dead, her house of fifty years as a married woman with the house she grew up in as a child, school with church, sugar with flour, the list of confusions seemed endless. She would get fully dressed at 3:00 A.M. and knock on the door saying she was ready to go to town. She would leave the house—whether in her own in north Mississippi or in mine later in Atlanta, headed for the Delta where she believed her mother and sister would be waiting. She got lost, she forgot to cook her food before eating it, she forgot our names. We were saddened and amazed at the persistence and severity of what was happening to her.

Occasionally, we thought of those words so dreaded in the Black community: THE NURSING HOME. But we didn't think we could do that—"It would break her spirit," I said. We continued to struggle with solutions as we watched her grow worse every day. I had spent much of my young life with her, and since I was not yet raising a family, I volunteered to assume primary care when we realized she could no longer live alone. I brought her to Atlanta, and I read as much as I could about Alzheimer's. We tried everything: inositol, choline, vitamin B and E supplements, naturopathy, long walks, reality orientation. But every day it seemed as if the little connectors that held the spindles of her brain together were gradually unwinding and getting tangled into a new jumbled pattern that was taking her more and more out of the reality of the present and memories of the past that she and I had once known and shared together joyfully. As a woman who did not know my name or where she was or what day it was, she was becoming a shell of her old vibrant self—the woman I knew and laughed with and whom I had sought out for grandmotherly protection. It broke my heart.

After two years with me, we decided in desperation and with conflicting cultural emotions to place Grandmother in a nursing home. Our worst fears were confirmed. Grandmother didn't understand the dormlike atmosphere of the nursing home. She couldn't tell one room from the other, so she often got lost, and the nurses would find her confused and frightened in someone else's room. She didn't understand why other people that she didn't know were staying in the room with her so she was always ready to go when we came to visit, tired of being at "other folks' house." The nurses decided to use medication to restrain her. The medication further disoriented her, and the long hours of restraint caused muscle contractures in her legs. And most regretfully, her spirit seemed bruised by the uncertainty, the wandering, and the restraint. We could not stand to watch what was happening to her. We had to take her out.

We were finally able to find a personal care home with a woman who took care of two other elderly patients, each with individual rooms. After years of denial and hope, of medication and institutions, things stabilized in the atmosphere of the personal care home. We had finally found a place with which we could be comfortable. I began weekly visits, and for a time we were relatively at peace with her situation. The further deterioration of her mind and body, however, began to take its toll. The most noticeable change in her, beyond the contractures which had left her frozen in a sitting position, was her inability to talk clearly. It went from random incoherency to hardly any responses at all. I would ask benign questions or make no-response-needed comments so that we could at least appear to be having a conversation. Occasionally, she would blurt out unconnected sentences: "Light the fires!" "Get the baby in out of the cold." "Daddy's gone to town." But eventually even those sentences—often totally unrelated to what she was being asked—turned into a constant moan. She didn't talk at all. She just moaned, subdued moans mostly with some occasional crescendos—but always a constant and indistinguishable moan. It got more painful with each visit as even her smile of recognition turned into a blank stare that meant no recognition at all. I was devastated. I had always loved her conversations. Although they had been incoherent and repetitive with the onset of Alzheimer's, they had always been lively. Now, in this later stage, there were no conversations at all. We could no longer talk engagingly the way we always had—with her minister's wife jokes and certainty-of-the-right-way-to-live disapproval of people who didn't know how to hang curtains, act in church, or plant flowers. I longed for her to just talk in sentences again, to know me, to have a shared moment with me. But I couldn't figure out what would make her respond in a way that was shared and remembered.

Since I could no longer talk *to* her, I began bringing someone with me on my visits—that way I could at least talk *around* her just so she could hear the conversation. During one summer visit when my sister had come to Atlanta, we sat out in the backyard with Grandmother at the house where she stayed. Brenda and I talked about our times growing up in the church as little girls with our grandparents. Grandmother's moaning had vaguely reminded me of the responses to the old lining hymns we used to sing at devotions in country churches when there was no piano. My sister and I began to recall some of those old songs, and following our own paths of memory, we tried to think of the words. We began with an old standard, "A Charge to Keep I Have . . . ," but neither of us could think of the second line. As we stared off into our individual windows of memory trying to remember the line, I leaned over to Grandmother in a half-hearted gesture to include her in our conversation and asked, "What were those other words, Grandmother?" "A charge to keep I have . . . a charge to keep I have . . ." I repeated searchingly, not expecting a response. And then a miracle happened: as clear as a bell with no stuttering or moaning and from a woman who had not spoken even her name clearly in a year she answered, "A God to Glorify!"

My sister and I were astounded. I couldn't speak. My mouth was open as I looked at my grandmother. She was right! Those were the words! Brenda and I shared shocking glances. I smiled at Grandmother, and as if just as surprised as I was by her burst of clarity, she smiled, too. We hugged each other tightly. And for one moment, one grace-filled moment, it seemed the awful monster of Alzheimer's that was daily taking her away from me was held at bay. She had not said "Good morning" or even my name or hers clearly in over a year, but here she had spoken those words from an old country song sung so often in the Black church devotions of her past. A flood of hopeful thoughts raced through my mind. "Did the ravages of Alzheimer's leave something intact after all?" "Was there something in the soul immune from its destruction?" "Was the song so deep in her memory as to be invincible, not wiped out by Alzheimer's, and its accompanying odyssey of medication, nursing homes, strange doctors, and new places?" I held Grandmother for a long time. And with tears in my eyes repeated those words over and over, "A Charge to Keep I have, A God to Glorify. A Charge to Keep I Have, A God to Glorify, A God to Glorify."

I couldn't get what had happened out of my mind for several days. It gave me a new burst of energy and sense of possibility. I didn't ask questions. If I had found a way for her to speak to me, for us to have shared moments together, I wanted to do whatever I could to make those moments happen again and again. I went through old hymn books and my own catalog of memory, writing down songs that I thought she would know. When I went back over to visit the next week, I sang as many songs as I could remember. First there was the favorite for both of us: "Love Lifted Me." It was an old song she had taught me during my childhood vacation Bible school mornings at her house. And she joyfully joined me in the chorus— flat and broken in parts but full of her own spirit—"Love lifted me! Love lifted me! When no-uh-thing else could help, loovve lifftedd mee." What joy! I couldn't believe it! Those visits turned into concerts of our old songs. "Jesus Keep Me Near the Cross," "What a Fellowship," "Blessed Assurance." She often just hummed along or sometimes didn't seem to listen to the verses, but when the chorus came she sang out loud and clear. Whether it was the plea of "Near the Cross, Near the Cross, Be My Glory Ever," or the staccato certainty of "Leaning on the Ever-last-ing Arms," or the resigned confidence of her own favorite, "This is my story, this is my song, praising my savior all the day long," she'd sing to the top of her voice, and we would be in unison together. Ninety percent of the time she seemed in another world, impenetrable. When we sang together, we enjoyed the same spiritual reality. In those moments of singing she seemed strong and clear—and whole.

The songs were ultimately not able to save Grandmother. The physical ravages of Alzheimer's resulting from the muscle contractures eventually led to double amputations. And while Alzheimer's nearly took her body entirely, it did not take her memory of the song. Her spirit had rested in those old melodies. As I recall now, those songs had been her salvation for a long time. She had sung out her troubles when, as a minister's wife, it didn't seem proper to resist in other ways. I had called them her "Lord, you know" songs because she always began them with those three words. She made up the rest of the words to fit her troubles as she took refuge in her kitchen, washing dishes and wiping counter tops in therapeutic circles. She had sung out loudly at church when there was no one to play the piano, and we had to "line" the songs. I still remember her voice flatly ringing out over the rest. She wasn't in the choir. She wasn't really a great public singer; she had a personal relationship with songs. It all came together as I remembered her history of singing—not showboat singing, but lifesaving singing. And here, at nearly ninety, the songs had seemed to save her spirit again.

The power of the song in my grandmother's life in those last few years humbles me still. I had heard a lot since Grandmother died about "ancestral memory," "individual magic," and "Grace." By whatever name it may be called, something wonderful happened that day when my grandmother's spirit, which I thought had been trampled by Alzheimer's, rose up in song. The songs did not prevent the continued deterioration of her physical body, but they gave her a way to articulate and bring forth her deepest inner spirit. Perhaps that is what the moans had been about all along—her recoiling to her deepest spiritual sense of herself. And maybe when she spoke out so clearly in the backyard that day, the spirit was just breaking through to affirm the words that were describing the nature of her present spiritual journey and the bedrock promise she had made to herself and to God a long time ago. When called upon to testify, she broke through the moans, the confusion, and the tangled and unconnected sentences and spoke out clearly her spiritual mission. She had a charge to keep, she had a God to glorify. It was a promise that not even Alzheimer's, the demon of memory, could make her forget.

Railing against the loss of memory is at the heart of Denard's fine essay. Paragraph by paragraph, she describes her struggle to rescue her grandmother.

In your journal, write briefly what you believe is central to each paragraph. Which paragraphs show a "step forward," some success against the Alzheimer's battle? Which paragraphs show a "step backward," a failure to slay "memory demons"?

Do you notice a pattern to the struggle? Is it chronological? Progressive? At one point Denard emphasizes "success." How does that moment echo and make the succeeding paragraphs more emotional and meaningful?

Review the essay again. Are there any details that seem

unnecessary? Or do you think Denard has been selective, using only those details which highlight her grandmother's decline and revival?

Do you have enough background to understand the relationship between the family and their elder? Highlight those details in the essay that "show" how much the family loved their elder.

Denard's grandmother, for a shining moment, finds her voice again. Where do you most clearly hear Denard's voice? Where do you most clearly hear and understand what she is testifying about?

What do you think Denard wants readers to understand most about her grandmother and herself? Even though she doesn't state it explicitly, is it clear why Denard felt she had to witness and share this story with readers?

In my experience, testifying and writing affirmations have always been a joy. But, in truth, within African American cultural tradition, all writing is in some way both testament and affirmation. As a people, literacy—the power of words (whether oral or printed)—has lifted our spirits and enlarged our freedoms. Affirmations, autobiography, memoir, even our fiction, poetry, and spirituals, have helped us as a new race of people to thrive.

To be a writer is a great calling. To be a black writer is to be part of a legacy that affirms and encourages your self-love to roar and shout, "I am."

"You are."

You are a writer if you're dedicated to witnessing your own and others' humanity, to reading, to listening to oral stories, and to devoting your time to writing words as passionately, honestly, and as brilliantly as you can.

You are the new generation making the "talking book" for all African Americans, all Americans, all people to *see* and *hear* the presence of color in this new world, this new millennium frontier!

TEN

REVISIONS AND LETTING GO

How do I know when I'm done?

In truth, the first time you think your manuscript or essay is done, finished, fini!, you probably have several weeks—possibly months or even a year—ahead of you before you are really done. Most of us are so eager to reach our goal of writing an essay or book that we rush the process. We overlook interesting possibilities, take short-cuts, or use tried-and-true techniques rather than learning better skills.

MY BEST ADVICE

Enjoy the revision process. Not only is your manuscript growing stronger, but you're becoming a better writer.

Revisions don't always come easily. Sometimes revising can be thrilling, but it can also be hard nuts-and-bolts work.

Revising takes precision, dedication, and sheer stubbornness. Below is a series of stages that can help focus your revisions. These four stages can be followed whether you're writing a memoir, an autobiography, or a personal essay.

STAGE ONE: CHECKING YOUR WORK: When you believe you've finished your manuscript, ask yourself the following:

- *Is the writing interesting? Does it explore human nature and human feelings? Is it clear why I've chosen to tell this story?*

- *Have I established my authority to tell the story? Am I persuasive in telling my personal experience, passion, and honesty about the subject?*

- *Have I chosen the best structure—the best beginning, middle, and end—to convey what I want to communicate about myself or others? Are my story's journey, turning point, and revelation clear?*

- *Does my language "show" rather than "tell"? Is my writing richly descriptive?*

- *Have I uncovered images to unify the ideas and feelings in the narrative? Have I explained the complexities of life, or have I oversimplified life?*

- *Does everything in the story contribute to what I'm trying to say?*

- *Have I made the best choices I can make as a writer?*

Don't hurry Stage One. Take as much time as you need to revise your essay or book manuscript, even though it may take weeks or months. At the very least, give yourself a week of reflecting: "How can I write, say, communicate this better?" When you feel you've exhausted your ability to develop your ideas and writing, proceed to Stage Two.

STAGE TWO: SHARING YOUR WORK:
Offer your writing to one or two trusted readers. As the author, you may have "blind spots," assumptions you've made about how well you're communicating. Remember, you already know what you want to say, but it may not be as clear to the reader. Through constructive criticism and revisions, you can mend any gaps in your manuscript.

While you're waiting for comments from your trusted readers, take an emotional and mental vacation from your writing. Read books. Take a trip. Clean your closets. Not only will this mental break refresh you; it'll also help you see your writing with "new" eyes.

Once your trusted readers begin to give you comments, you're obliged to listen, with open ears, to what they say. Yes, it may be painful. Yes, you may feel affronted because someone didn't like your baby! Or you may be suspicious if they insist that they *loved* your writing. Most writers I know (me included) tend to be self-doubtful even when they receive praise. Despite a tendency to be too defensive or to doubt sincere approval, **listen** and remain **open-minded.** A trusted reader is by definition, someone you can trust to give an honest, thoughtful appraisal of your work.

Once you've received constructive criticism, **reflect** and **consider** whether that advice is entirely appropriate. As a writer, your instincts need to be balanced against your trusted readers' comments. Often, trusted readers inspire you to add new dimensions to your writing. You may not follow their advice exactly, but it may point you to another and even better pathway that will make your writing stronger.

After you've considered readers' comments, after your emotional and mental break, it's time for more patience and persistence. Time for another round of revisions!

STAGE THREE: WORKING THE MANUSCRIPT LINE BY LINE:

Read your story aloud. Line by line, word by word.

Listen for any phrases, sentences, or paragraphs that seem flat, redundant, or strained. Do your sentences lag? Is their pace too hurried? Do you run out of breath before finishing a sentence? Do the pauses seem unnatural? Re-examine any sentence that's difficult to read.

Revise again, paying particular attention to the rhythm and flow of your words.

STAGE FOUR: SOUL-SEARCHING:

Ask yourself:

- *Have I expressed what I passionately needed to say?*

- *Have I conveyed the "emotional truth" about myself and my subject?*

- *Have I flinched from any difficult part of my manuscript?*

- *Have I paid tribute to my literary and cultural heritage?*

- *Have I written as best I can?*

If all your answers aren't "yes," consider whether you can fix the problems. Remember that not every essay or memoir you write will be a home run. Some projects may have to be abandoned; some you may need to start over from scratch; some may just remain flawed. If you've been attentive to the revision process and still can't finish, then maybe you should move on. Don't fall into the trap of revising forever. Revisions are meant to be productive, to move you closer to your goal of publishing. Once the process becomes frustrating and uninspiring, it's time to move on to another essay or life memory.

If, however, all your answers are "yes," then you should be justifiably proud of yourself! Through study and determination, you have achieved your goal of being a writer. Bravo!

PART V

BREAKING INTO PRINT

ELEVEN

PUBLISH OR PERISH?

Keep the faith.

T rust me, you won't perish if you don't publish your work. Though, I admit, trying to get published can be an emotionally draining and seemingly impossible quest. I well remember nights of crying and bouts of self-pity. "I'll never get published," I used to moan.

For over a decade, it seemed impossible for me to publish anything—whether it was a story, an essay, or a book. Everything I wrote was met with rejection. *How did I survive?* I kept writing. No doubt my writing skills became stronger. But also, luckily enough, America and American publishing had changed.

Buried in my files is a letter written in the late 1970s by an editor from a major publishing firm. This letter rejected my first novel, *Voodoo Dreams,* for many reasons, among them: 1) the novel had structural and characterization flaws; and 2) the editor believed there was no audience for my book, because, in her opinion, black people didn't buy books. Although I spent another decade improving *Voodoo Dreams,* there was little I could do to alter this particular editor's bias. But our American democracy, with its growing multicultural awareness, resulted in a flowering and, ultimately, an explosion of such best-selling African American talents as Toni Morrison, Alice Walker, Nathan McCall, Patrice Gaines, Ellis Cose, Terry McMillan, Marita Golden, Cornel West, Mary Helen Washington, John Edgar Wideman, James McBride, J. California Cooper, Bebe Moore Campbell, Pearl Cleage, and many others. Without question, the late twentieth century and the dawning of the twenty-first have confirmed not only that black people do buy books but that Americans of all ethnic backgrounds are interested in culturally specific tales. American publishing has become more inclusive because book-buying Americans want to experience the richness of being human through a multitude of cultural lenses. How wonderful!

But while market forces may have reshaped the publishing landscape, I also want to herald the African American as well as the non–African American agents and editors who have always approached their jobs with integrity and vision. "A good story is a good story is a good story," and there have been the few (and sometimes the many) who have recognized that you can't silence or hide a Langston Hughes or a James Baldwin or a Zora Neale Hurston or a Dorothy West. And today there are agents and editors who would think it unfathomable not to publish Henry Louis Gates's *Colored People,* Brent Staples's *Parallel Time,* Darlene Clark Hines's *A Shining Thread of Hope,* or Marion Wright Edelman's *The Measure of Our Success: A Letter to My Children and Yours.*

Even though it may sometimes seem as though the publishing industry has erected a gate just to keep you from entering, remember there is always someone, some agent, some editor who is looking for you. If you can't believe this in your heart, then you may waver and feel lost. You need the proper armor to buffer yourself against rejection. And rejection will come. Optimism in the face of rejection is paramount. I always call to mind the child's rhyme: "Itzy-bitsy Spider." The rain came, but the spider climbed up again!

Do you have to have a black agent or editor to succeed as an author? No. *You only need an agent or an editor who loves your work and believes in you!* Will only black publishers and African American–focused magazines publish your work? Not necessarily. Our humanity defines all of us, and though the wellspring of your memories are colored "black," you should assume that your story is suited to *Ms.* and *Good Housekeeping* magazine as well as to *Ebony* and *Essence.*

MY BEST ADVICE

Be tireless in your pursuit of becoming the best author you can be. Be equally tireless in your pursuit of finding the right agent to support and advocate your work.

Finding a good agent should be your first practical priority. Publishers will rarely read an unsolicited manuscript. Also, the best agents are skilled in matching your writing with the appropriate editor; while you may still receive a dozen rejections, an agent's job is to systematically draw up a list of editors who are most likely to value your writing. Otherwise, you might as well throw darts at a list of editors and publishing houses.

Americans like to believe that "working hard" will bring success. But if you study the dime novels of the Horatio Alger myth closely, you'll notice that the hero (not heroine!) had his share of "pluck" and "luck." Frankly, "luck" sometimes meant being poor but nonetheless white. In looking for an agent (or editor), no one can promise that you won't meet with discrimination. But your own pluck and determination can go far in your search for the right agent to support your writing.

A word of caution: It is hard to balance the dual roles of writer and advocate of your own work. Each can be a full-time job! So I advise, first and foremost:

WRITE. ALWAYS WRITE. You can't publish what doesn't exist. So write, then write some more.

When you have a manuscript you're proud of, devote several months (possibly even a year) to your campaign to find a good agent.

Step One: In the reference library or the writing section of a good bookstore, you can find various guides to literary agents. These guides give such basic information as the agent's address, fax number, years in the business, and so on. But the most valuable information is the type of material the agent is looking to represent and the names of books they've successfully placed with publishers. If you're writing nonfiction, you don't want an agent who specializes in fiction. Likewise, if cookbooks appear to be the agent's specialty, you don't necessarily want to send them a memoir.

Poets & Writers has terrific on-line (www.pw.org) and text-based resources for finding a good agent: what to look for, what to expect, explanations for why a good agent doesn't demand up-front fees. (Reputable agents make money when they make a sale for you, so you and your agent are partners in business.)

Step Two: Network. Ask other writers to recommend agents. Attend a conference at which writers and agents share their insights about writing and publishing. Hunt for agent acknowledgments inside books. Often I acknowledge my wonderful agent, Jane Dystel, of Jane Dystel Literary Management. (If you love a particular book represented by an agent, then that agent may be interested in your literary style and ambitions.)

Step Three: Based upon your research, draw up a list of ten agents to receive your query letters. What's a query letter? It's a concise letter in which you tell about your background, your book, why you were the best person to write it, and what readers your story will appeal to. If you can, cite other books that are comparable with your writing and manuscript. Some agents will want a query letter accompanied by sample chapters; some want just a query and the opportunity to decide if they are interested in hearing more from you.

Remember, a letter conveys a lot about your writing style, so take time with your query. Essentially, it is a letter to entice the agent to want to know more about you and your writing. If your letter is dry and long-winded, an agent may suspect that your writing is, too.

If you lack passion when describing your book, then an agent might not ask to see it. Think carefully about your letter, choose your words wisely, and, if possible, keep it to a page. The Writer's Market reference text often has examples of query letters. Study them, but don't hesitate to tailor your letter to suit your personality and manuscript.

If the agent requires you to submit sample chapters, then pick your best work. It may not necessarily be the opening chapters! Select the chapters with the most heart.

§ *Step Four: Wait for a response.* A good agent should get back to you within two months. Why does it take so long? Because often several readers or agents within the office may read the material. Jane Dystel, for example, has five other agents in her office: Jo Fagan, Stacy Glick, Jonas Paterno, Michael Bourret, and Nancy Stender. When a query letter and sample chapters come into the office, the agents share the work. What excites one agent may not excite another. But a good agency will encourage all staff members to take a look at the material before sending out their rejection or acceptance letter.

§ *Step Five: If an agent rejects your work, move on to the next name on your list.* Keep the faith and keep trying. If, however, no one on your list accepts your work, consider whether you need to improve your writing. Did agents cite similar problems, issues? Before you draw up another list of ten agents, make sure you go through the revision process again. It is not the end of the world if you need to do more work! Each revision strengthens your writing skills.

≋ *Step Five: If an agent is interested in your work, then send the entire manuscript.* You'll probably feel as if you're walking on air, but you still have to be patient and practical. Keep writing. This is one more step in the process.

≋ *Step Six: If an agent wants to represent you, then celebrate!* Meet with him or her. At least have a long telephone talk. Why? Because you want to make sure that this person understands your work and will represent you well. An agent's standard commission is 15 percent, and for this, they should have a plan for presenting your work to editors *and* they should be committed to getting your work published. But perhaps what is most important is to find an agent who will give you an honest assessment of your manuscript and your chances for getting it published. You don't want false promises; you want heart-felt dedication.

Ah! Now you have an agent. What do you do? WAIT.

You will be tempted to sit by the phone, weave fantasies about fame and money, and share the joy with your friends and relatives. Don't. Okay, that's not realistic. Then promise to dream only AFTER you've done a good day's work in writing your next book.

Waiting to get a publisher can take days . . . weeks. Often it can take months . . . a year, and, sadly, it may not happen.

Do you want six months or a year to pass by with all your

hopes pinned on one book? Of course you don't. It would be living in purgatory. However, if you focus on your next project, you'll stay sane. You'll also have another manuscript for your publisher to look at once your first book is accepted. If your first book isn't accepted, then you'll have another book to send to your agent.

What if you don't find an agent? If you've tried all the hundreds (literally!) available, you may want to consider self-publishing, which is an honorable way to get your work to readers. Its greatest drawback is that it will be expensive and time-consuming. And once your manuscript is published, you'll have to act as your own publicity firm to reach a wider audience. All authors should help promote their own work, but doing so without a publishing firm's assistance can absorb so much of your time, you'll find it difficult to write.

Be strategic in your marketing. For example, for my first book, I wrote letters to independent bookstores. I also sought advice from other authors, e-mailed college contacts for possible readings, and contacted local book sellers for signing appearances.

The Internet, too, can be a great tool for reaching audiences. Sites like www.pageturner.net can help you design a Web page and link you to appropriate book-selling sites. (In the Appendix, you'll find several books to guide you around the pitfalls to reach the triumphs of self-publishing and self-marketing.) Remember that the opportunities for self-promotion are endless; you'll need to decide what works best for you, your book, and your time.

* * *

If, as a self-publishing author, you have sales in the thousands, then try again to find an agent who may sell your work for re-publishing by a major firm. Publishing houses are interested in sales, and a good agent can use your book's track record to land a contract.

If you're writing personal essays, memoir pieces, or short biography, you probably don't need an agent. Instead, you should draw up a list of ten or more magazines or journals that publish similar pieces.

For example, the *Ladies' Home Journal* has a monthly first-person essay column. The May 2001 issue featured Debbie Seaman's essay "I Finally Quit Drinking." You should definitely consider that your essay on overcoming shopping addiction, a fear of heights, or breast cancer may suit this particular column. You'll never know unless you write to the magazine's editors and ask if they are interested in reading your story.

Remember, too, that each magazine or journal has its own submission requirements, but, either through e-mail or the post, you can request their guidelines. Generally, magazine and journal editors will want a query letter first. In your letter, make clear why you think your essay is suitable to their magazine and show how your experience and background led you to write the essay. If you don't yet have any publishing credits, be frank. An editor just might be willing to give you your first break!

If you don't break into writing for the more popular magazines, be sure to try the smaller journals. Dustbook's *Inter-*

national Directory of Little Magazines and Small Presses is an excellent tool for finding alternative journals and small publishers interested in publishing longer works or entire books. Likewise, their *Directory of Editors* includes names and addresses of editors at mainstream publishing houses as well as those that can assist your self-publishing.

Getting published may take time. Whatever you do, don't give up. It has been my experience that many fine writers quit trying after a few years. Don't let that happen to you. Persistence is essential. Don't focus on "no", focus on "yes." Though you may receive dozens of rejections, it only takes one "yes" to help you achieve your goals.

Find the agent, the magazine, the editor who will say "yes" to you. If they're hard to find, keep writing and improving. Self-publish if you must, but don't stop searching!!!!

Yes, it is exciting to have a book or an article published when you're twenty-two, but believe me that it's just as exciting when you're thirty-two, forty-two, fifty-two, sixty-two, seventy-two, eighty-two, ninety-two, or a hundred and two. (God bless the Delany sisters!)

You have a life ahead of you; pursue your dreams and believe your words, your writing will make a difference.

Celebrate your having finished the lessons in this book! You have improved your skills, improved your self-confidence, and improved your chances of becoming a published writer. Bravo!

Keep on growing strong. Keep on asserting your voice and identity.
Keep treasuring the memories, the thoughts and feelings that shape

you. Your choice to be a writer celebrates the African American spirit and all of humanity. Readers are waiting to share your adventures. Write. Then write some more!

The journey continues . . .

> *Love and Best Wishes,*
> *Jewell*

TWELVE

WISDOM AND ADVICE
FROM BLACK WRITERS
TO BLACK WRITERS

I asked several published writers to provide their "best advice," their best wisdom for you, the next generation of African American writers. Authors were encouraged to select their own topic and to write as little or as much as they wanted. The passion, depth, and insight of the responses have been truly gratifying. Each author provides inspiration, motivation, and insight.

Don't read these gems all at once. Instead, save them for those times when writing is frustrating and difficult. Then pull this book off the shelf and pick a selection or two or three to read. I have no doubt that one of these passages will unblock your creative energy and inspire renewed faith in yourself and in your writing.

In 1992, I took a summer sabbatical off from work to follow my dream of writing a novel in France. My laptop and I spent a wonderful July and August in a cheap hotel in Paris. I wrote the first 222 pages of a novel. Returning with exhilaration and great memories, I shopped it around to agents and editors, just to find out that I was not a good fiction writer at all. I had known this in my heart but mistakenly thought that being a writer meant being a novelist. It was an eye-opening setback, but I turned it into a comeback by starting another book—this time, nonfiction.

—Stephanie Stokes Oliver, *Daily Cornbread: 365 Secrets for a Healthy Mind*

The best writer will stand naked and without shame in front of the world. Keeping this in mind, I encourage any writer to bare his soul via the written word. The most effective and cogent nonfiction writer is one who is able to put himself in the text of a story and share his thoughts, aspirations, and foibles with the reader.

My best work as a writer occurred when I wrote a riveting and revealing personal essay about my years of battling the illness of depression. I wrote about all of the pain, tears, and hopelessness. I revealed a deep secret to more than a million people I didn't know. I took a risk. The gamble paid off. Letters, lots of them, from people with similar stories to tell poured in from everywhere.

—Glen R. Townes, author of articles and book reviews for magazines like *Emerge, Upscale,* and *Essence*

I think of writing as a spiritual process, as I do all work and art done properly. It is best done when you are connected to the source of creativity. In art, we often refer to the source as the muse. I call it the Divine One, Spirit or God.

When I sit down to write I take several deep breaths, and for me that seems to clear my mind and bring my focus to the paper and the task at hand. I also begin writing with a prayer, the smallest sentences like "Please guide me" or "Let me hear the words I need to write." Always something simple.

By this time, I am focused on nothing else—if it's a good day. Next, I try to write with honesty. This is key to successful storytelling or writing. Readers connect to honesty, and writers know when they're not being honest. Honesty feels right. Sentences flow, and at the end of the day, you know what you have written is good.

Dishonesty creeps in when we lose our focus and when we sit down with a preconceived notion of what we must write.

Follow your gut and intuition. Most often the Divine One is speaking to you through feelings. It never fails that if I don't feel good about a sentence but hold on to it anyway, then, days later, when I read over my writing, that particular sentence sounds like a bad note in an otherwise perfect song.

Readers are smart. They know a fake. But, more important, they also know the real deal when they read it. Somehow the words resonate in the deepest recesses of a reader's soul, and when you meet this stranger, he or she can recite those very sentences. I don't know any writer who isn't floored by that awesome experience of hearing their words spoken by a total stranger who took time out of her life to read those words and, furthermore, was able—with all the chaos of the world—to recall those exact words that started with a thought in the author's head. Or started with a prayer.

—Patrice Gaines, *Laughing in the Dark, Moments of Grace*

Know yourself, your core. Trust yourself enough to leapfrog over (or, more important, plod purposefully through) the obstacles and barriers that get in the way of your putting pen to paper, whatever they are. Before you sit to write, kneel and pray—for clarity of vision and for His powerful presence to touch your soul and guide your hands. Become patient and contemplative and mindful, as well as cognizant of the fact that you are a promising, talented African-American writer. And then, begin.

—Kristin Clark Taylor, *Black Mothers: Songs of Praise and Celebration; The First To Speak: A Woman of Color Inside the White House*

For me, writing is the way that I participate in the world—contain my experiences and explore ideas. When I write, my voice is heard, my vision shared, and my passion felt. Writing validates that my ancestors matter.

—Ethel Morgan Smith, *From Whence Cometh My Help: The African American Community at Hollins College*

Readers today demand authenticity. They aren't interested in reading the lofty theories of the next slickly packaged expert-in-a-box. They want to read books by real people who are sharing wisdom gained from real life experiences.

If you can deliver that information in a down-to-earth, person-to-person style, you will touch the lives of many people as well as reap the rewards in your career.

—William July, *Understanding the Tin Man; Brothers, Lust, and Love*

Write your first reactions to people, places, or things, whatever they may be, without critical constraint. In other words, write in free-style your felt-sense of life for at least fifteen minutes every day.

—Katie Cannon, *Katie's Canon: Womanism and the Soul of the Black Community; Black Womanist Ethics*

Be persistent and never give up hope. The only way to learn to write is to write. Over time, your own style, voice, and craftsmanship will emerge.

—Henry Louis Gates, Jr., *The Signifying Monkey;* co-editor, *The Norton Anthology of African American Literature*

When all is said and done, without an editor who understands, appreciates, and champions your work and your style, your project is paralyzed.

—Tavis Smiley, *Doing What's Right; How to Make Black America Better*

Research your story. If you research your story, you will never have writer's block. Research it all, then scrap the 95 percent of what you've discovered and use the 5 percent that sells your story. You just need that 5 percent. Toss the rest, no matter how precious or hard it was to come by. Not all of us can be Toni Morrison and take ten pages to describe a leaf or a room. Her gift is a flight from God. The rest of us have to use public transportation.

—James McBride, *The Color of Water*

Be a complete master of the subject matter and manage it, rather than becoming managed by the material. Second, be able to write with skill and authority. Finally, you should have the energy, discipline, and persistence to stay at the job until it is done.

—John Hope Franklin, *From Slavery to Freedom*

Treasure the most important element of your piece—the very reason why it must exist on the page for others to read and consider and discuss. Pray and prepare to, yes, proof and edit yet again—a certain word choice, that punctuation mark upon which you are certain the overall quality of your piece rests. Realize writing is rewriting. Then circulate fresh ideas, new truths.

—Eisa Nefertari Ulen, essayist and journalist, has contributed to *Ms.,* *The Washington Post, Savoy,* and several anthologies

The most important thing you'll ever share with the world besides your name is your story. Write it down! Write it down! Write it down! Write with courage, write with abandon, and write with pleasure. For this is your story to tell.

—Julia A. Boyd, *Can I Get a Witness? For Sisters When the Blues Is More Than a Song; In the Company of My Sisters, Black Women and Self-Esteem*

Most composition theorists will tell you that "invention"—ways of getting started in writing—goes back to the Classical Greeks and probably before that to the Egyptians (3000 B.C.), which should make all Black writers proud as we stand on the shoulders of ancestors.

An invention technique that works well for me is called the *snapshot/thoughtshot* exercise. Pull out a piece of paper and list five events you feel were significant in your life. These events should illustrate how you or someone you know experienced discrimination because of gender, race, class, religion, sexual preference, etcetera. After you list five topics (essay subjects), write as fast as you can for ten minutes on one of the topics. Make it visual; make it first person; make it fun. This is a snapshot, a verbal visual picture to get you started.

—Stan West, *Profiles of Great African Americans; Prism: An African American Reporter's Multi-Cultural View of the New South Africa*

I believe it is most essential for a writer to connect with and express truth—not *the* truth, but their own personal, most passionate truth—as authentically as possible. What touches the reader most deeply is that heartfelt, from-the-gut, slap-yourself-upside-the-forehead moment of revelation, not the cleverest, most impressive turn of phrase or fiercest expression of eloquence. Sometimes as writers we must get out from behind our God-given talent, wicked wit, and sharply-honed skills to dig for the nugget of pure gold that returns us to our source and stays with the reader long after the page has been turned. And, of course, we must write when we want to, when we don't want to, and at every available moment in between. Because writing, like life, is a journey rather than a destination, and if you're not writing, you're not moving forward.

—TaRessa Stovall, *Catching Good Health: An Introduction to Homeopathic Medicine;* co-author of *A Love Supreme: Real Life Stories of Black Love*

Most of the nonfiction I write is first-person essays about my very subjective reactions to topics ranging from falling in love to shutting down crack houses. In all cases, I try to remember the following five rules:

1. Tell the truth, the whole truth, nothing but the truth, especially about the stuff you'd rather lie about.

2. Pretend your mother is never going to read what you write about your personal life.

3. Pretend your father is.

4. Don't tell other people's secrets.

5. Don't forget the details.

The only other advice I have for black writers who want to write nonfiction is to read Langston Hughes's *The Big Sea.* It doesn't get any better than that.

—Pearl Cleage, *What Looks Like Crazy on an Ordinary Day; Mad at Miles: A Black Woman's Guide to Truth*

Writing nonfiction begins in your soul. It transcends your experiences and shatters all doubt that the true meaning of your life, as a person of color, manifests according to your unique consciousness. Validate your perspective by writing about it; make it impervious to scorn and doubt. Nonfiction is the ritualistic process we, as a people of color, need to establish the existence of our alternate reality. Don't think you can; know you can.

How to Marry a Black Man started out as a letter to my friend and soon-to-be co-author. It started out by saying, Remember that idea I had about writing that book called How to Marry a Black Man? Here are a few ideas . . . what do you think? Twenty pages later, this letter became the outline for our book. Of course I copied it before I mailed it, because I figured she'd lose it, and she did. So keep a journal of your musings and copies of your letters to friends and family. Inspiration for nonfiction usually strikes at the most inopportune times, so never be embarrassed to write on the side of a coffee cup, a fast-food napkin, or whatever scrap of paper is closest, so long as your fragmented ideas are captured in that crucial instant. These coveted writings may very well turn out to be the seeds of future manuscripts, as mine did.

—Monique Jellerette de Jongh, *How to Marry a Black Man*

1. Believe that your work is a contribution that fufills a divine role. In so doing, your work becomes a tool that elevates and uplifts humanity.

2. Be confident in your message.

3. Value the multi-tongued power of the word and your gift to embody and enact word traditions.

4. Search for a match between your work and the publishing venues you aspire to. Seek out those venues which are kindred to your narrative style and philosophical bent.

5. Cultivate an emergent stream of research.

6. Know that all writing is art.

7. Understand that if you have something to say, then you have something to write. Give yourself permission to write what you would say.

—S. Alease Ferguson and Toni King, co-authors, *Deep Woman Feelings: A Book of Contemplations*

Don't give up. Find a way every day to believe in the work. Support it, sustain it. Make yourself into the writer you want to be, the writer who can tell the story that you'll go crazy if you don't tell.

—Lorene Cary, *Black Ice; Pride*

When I was sixteen, I was in a minor traffic accident and required to go to court. Just before I went before the judge, he heard a case which involved a young white woman was nearly identical to mine. The judge read the details of her case aloud. He put the file down and said something like "I know this has been very traumatic for you. I can see that you're a young student and this is your first traffic violation. I'm dismissing charges and urge you to be more careful."

His words were music. Before hearing that, I had been expecting a fine. My turn came, and I was waiting to hear the word dismissed, but it never came. He leveled a small fine against me and told me to talk to the clerk. I was dumbfounded.

I sat down and wrote an essay. After I wrote and typed it, I sent copies to local civil rights groups. I didn't stop there. I went back down to City Hall and posted copies on every department bulletin board that I could access. I wanted the judge and his co-workers to read it. It was 1970, and I was accusing this judge of racism.

Within days the incident blew up large. A man from the NAACP came to our house to talk to me, and I got calls from the other organizations. The judge assured my father that he would have thrown out my case too if he'd known my father was a policeman. He urged my father to ask me if I would allow him to reimburse me the money for the fine. I'll never forget that day. I told my father NO.

The organizations I'd contacted never stopped monitoring the judge; mine was not the first complaint. His career never recovered, and he lost the next election. I know my essay contributed to his fate.

Over the next twenty years of his life, my father would periodically tease me about my story. He would tell relatives, "You better watch how you treat Jackie. You could end up in an essay!" But I know he never stopped being proud that I wrote that essay. Since then I've written many essay and op-ed pieces, most on issues less personal but none more satisfying.

—Jacqueline Turner Banks, *A Day for Vincent Chin and Me; Barely Maid, a Ruth Gordan Mystery*

Writing that counts is always a stunning achievement of memory and performance. It stretches the bare bones of truth in artfully clever ways. The most difficult task of memoir, for example, is constructing a voice that sounds authentic with respect to the experiences one hopes to recount. The voice of a memoir is difficult to make, because returning to the past normally commits one to awfully painful turns of the soul . . . carries the spirit to repressed regions where language hesitates to travel.

—Houston Baker, Jr. *Black Studies, Rap, and the Academy; Long Black Song*

Write early and write often. Strap yourself to the chair if need be. Four hours a day, every day. Let yourself get frustrated, bored, pissed-off. Inspiration will finally bubble up out of you—in dribbles or floods—it'll come.

—Trey Ellis, *Platitudes; Home Repairs*

Writer friend, please write. When you write, we're a chorus that just gets stronger, louder, deeper, richer. When you write, you bring your own candle, candelabra, flashlight, floodlight, and suddenly the rooms, alleys, bidonvils, favelas, casitas, gingerbread houses we're in just get a whole lot brighter. When you write, you come with your own African violets, magnolia blossoms, hibiscus leaves, and rose petals, and suddenly our garden blossoms and blooms with more beauty than any of us can provide alone.

Writer friend, listen to the stories around you. Life is a 3D movie spinning around the clock twenty-four hours a day. Make yourself a living sponge. Tell us about it.

Writer friend, use your memories. Make that moment in your childhood you can't seem to forget, that nightmare you have once a week, maybe that's your story. Please don't be afraid to go there. A lot of good writing comes from the most painful moments in our lives. Sometimes that sentence you can't see for all the tears in your eyes is the one that touches us most.

—Edwidge Danticat, *Breath, Eyes, Memory; The Farming of Bones*

The greatest skill that I have developed and that has brought me whatever success I have enjoyed as a writer is **listening.** I have built my career on listening.

Now this seems deceptively simple. But the basic material of my books was obtained through interviews, through going out to talk to the folk, to prisoners, to writers. Though a great deal of reading and research were required to prepare me to intelligently conduct such interviews, the critical material that would represent my unique contributions came mainly from the information that I would gather in my field work. The greatest key to success in field work is winning the confidence of the informant, who inevitably views you with distrust and suspicion and throws up all kinds of protective barriers. I have been suspected and accused of everything from being a police plant and a CIA agent to a dilettante seeking amusement among an exotic other. But somehow I managed to go among children in Jamaican yards, felons in Jamaican and American prisons and death rows, country folks in Jamaican hills and Virginia backroads, intellects, scholars, and writers all over the

Americas, and to obtain from them some of the fullest and most authentic accounts to be found. My success was due to no greater talent than the ability to **listen.**

Such informants, whether they are illiterate farmers or sophisticated writers, recognize immediately when a collector is there to reinforce his own perceptions and when he is there to hear what they have to say.

—Daryl Cumber Dance, *Shuckin' and Jivin'* and *Long Gone*

Writing nonfiction is like wearing long pants and being very formal. Too often we think about different genres the way we think of romantic affairs. I recently started writing nonfiction after establishing myself as a poet. In the beginning I thought I was secretly seeing someone who was going to lead me astray. Nonfiction was just too many words. Could I believe what I was writing? In my heart I was a poet. Suddenly I looked up and I had written a memoir. It was like marriage and raising children. How quickly it happens!

I started writing nonfiction as a way of dealing with loss. The deaths of my father and brother opened doors and windows to longer sentences. I felt a need to write more in order to heal. Poems were notes. I needed nonfiction in order to breathe again. My lungs as well as my heart needed it.

Nonfiction is linked to the reconstruction of self and voice. I am forced to determine the difference between memory and fact. When I wrote poetry, I could leave a poem behind, the experience for the moment captured on the page. Nonfiction is more like fingerprints; it's

DNA as witness. I find myself writing more essays in order to prove my innocence.

—E. Ethelbert Miller, *Fathering Words: The Making of an African American Writer*

Write because you believe your experiences and memories are gifts that bear your name and the names of others whom you will never know. Write because there is something you know to be true or wish to be true; something that you have seen or wish to see; something which resides in your viscera, waking you at night and talking to you, insisting that your words give it life and voice; something which, if not shared with others, will disappear from the screen of your memory or, if remaining there, will become a blurred and broken line you cannot read.

Write with honesty, with courage, with passion. Write with an appreciation for the sacred bonding between what you say and the how of your saying it. Write as truth inspires, not as publishing directs. This is the first step and, in truth, the only step for writers.

—Gloria Wade Gayles, *Pushed Back to Strength; Anointed to Fly*

I have two things I'd consider crucial to remember: Don't fall for the myth of "objective journalism," but remember instead that it's your particular perspective which is valuable, especially if it's deeply considered and the writing fully polished. As feminism says: the personal is political. Any significant nonfiction writer always remembers the deep personal connections we all bring to any topic we tackle. All subjects, just like all people, are connected, even if it's a topic you've never considered before in your career.

The second important point for me is to always learn something. Creative nonfiction's most rewarding gift can be to show your reader *and* the writer something she didn't really know or understand before she began.

—Jewelle Gomez, *Forty-Three Septembers; The Gilda Stories*

Allow your story to transform you. And if you do, it will transform the reader. Speak what no one will; remember what everyone told you to forget. You are not just writing a personal history; you are discovering and creating one. Expect discomfort. In fact, that should be the barometer of how effective the writing is. Don't expect your story to unfold according to your plan, for once you write the first line, of necessity, you are writing as much fiction as fact, but that is where much of the deepest truth lies. Fictional techniques and perspectives can honor the essence of personal experience in nonfiction much more effectively than trying to be objective.

—Marita Golden, *Migrations of the Heart; Saving Our Sons*

Avoid superstition. Don't convince yourself that you can only write in the morning; that you can only compose on paper because computers disrupt your creative flow. Don't convince yourself that your muse is temperamental and will only whisper in your ear after you have performed certain elaborate rituals in just the right way. Remember this: you write not because you are wearing your lucky socks, or because there is a full moon tonight. You write because you have something to say.

Maybe you have preferences; most of us do. But the writing does not require them. What the writing requires is you.

—Tayari Jones, *Leaving Atlanta*

READ. It is amazing to me that people think they can write without reading. Many people think their own personal experience is sufficient, but personal experience isn't even a beginning. You have to have perspective, and reading provides that. READ. And learn a new way of looking at your life.

—Nikki Giovanni, *Racism 101* and numerous books of poetry

First, know that you ARE a writer. As writers, all of us are continuously learning how to be truer to our craft and to our inner voices . . . but it's not that you WANT to be a writer—you ARE one. There are only published writers and unpublished writers.

—Tananarive Due, *My Soul to Keep; The Living Blood*

Maintain a distinction between yourself and the work. Regard yourself with a sense of humor; regard the work with ultimate seriousness.

—Jabari Asim, Editor of *Not Guilty: Twelve Black Men on Life, Law and Justice*

Part of any writer's challenge is learning how to tune out the praise of friends, who are too willing to accept mediocrity in the interest of friendship.

—Ellis Cose, *The Rage of the Privileged Class; Color-Blind: Seeing Beyond Race in a Race-Obsessed World*

When I wrote *Surviving the Silence,* I began in darkness. I "felt" my way from paragraph to paragraph and then from story to story. I have found that *writing* through a trauma is the one way to find the sun.

—Charlotte Pierce-Baker, *Surviving the Silence: Black Women's Stories of Rape*

WRITING RESOURCES

General Resources

The following books are all great resources for information about the publishing business. How to find an agent, how to be your own agent, how to submit your manuscript for publication, are some of the topics covered. Pay particular attention to any general information sections. Many of these books have sound advice about paying readers' fees, entering contests, writing a good cover letter, and more.

The African American Writers Handbook: How to Get in Print and Stay in Print
Robert Fleming, 2000
One World Publishing/Ballantine Books

The African-American Network
Crawford Bunkley
Plume, 1996

The Association of American University Presses Directory
The Association of American University Presses, Inc., 1996

A Complete Guide to Getting Any Book Published
William July, II
Khufu Books, 1998

Directory of Editors
Dustbooks, published yearly

How to Self-Publish and Market Your Own Book
Sara Freeman Smith, Author and Publisher
U R Gems Group/www.urgems.com

The Insider's Guide to Getting Published: Why They Always Reject Your Manuscript and What You Can Do About It
John Boswell, 1998
Doubleday & Co. Inc.

International Directory of Little Magazines and Small Presses
Dustbooks, published yearly

Into Print: Guides to the Writing Life
Poets & Writers, Inc., 1998
(also see: www.pw.org)

Literary Marketplace, 2000
R. R. Bowker, A Reed Reference Publishing Co., 1999
The Yellow Page of book publishing, and best source for finding a literary agent.

The Self-Publishing Manual
Dan Poynter
Dustbooks, 2000

2000 Writer's Market
F & W Publications, Inc., 1999

Writer's Guide to Book Editors, Publishers, and Literary Agents, 1999–2000
Jeff Herman
Prima Publishing, 1998

A Writer's Guide to Book Publishing
Richard Balkin
NAL/Dutton, 1994

Writing for the Ethnic Market
Meera Lester
Writer's Connection, 1991

More Specialized Resources

1. Agents serve an important role in helping an author find a publisher. While most writers have agents, I do know a few who have successfully managed the selling process on their own:

Author and Audience and Literary Agents
Poets and Writers, Inc.
(also see: www.pw.org)

Guide to Literary Agents: 500 Agents Who Sell What You Write
eds. Don Prues, Chantelle Bentley
Writer's Digest Books, 1998
(also see: www.writersdigest.com)

How to Be Your Own Literary Agent
Richard Curtis
Houghton Mifflin Co., 1996

How to Write Irresistible Query Letters
Lisa Collier Cool
Writer's Digest Books

Kirsch's Guide to the Book Contract
Jonathan Kirsch
Acrobat Books, 1999

Literary Agents: The Essential Guide For Writers
Debbie Mayer
Penguin, 1998

2001 Guide to Literary Agents
Donya Dickerson
Writer's Digest Books

Writer's Digest Handbook of Writing Magazine Articles
Writer's Digest Books

A Writer's Guide to Copyright
Poets & Writers, Inc., 1979

2. Protecting your authorship and ownership is discussed thoroughly in the following books:

Copyright Handbook
R. R. Bowker, A Reed Reference Publishing Co., 1982

3. What to expect once your book is accepted for publication isn't widely discussed, but Appelbaum's offers thorough and practical advice:

How to Get Happily Published (5th Ed.)
Judith Appelbaum
HarperCollins, 1998

4a. Finding quality time and a place to write is made easier by writers' conferences, colonies, and workshop retreats. Several notable workshops are cited here, along with general resources for exploring conference and workshop opportunities on your own. Also, be sure to contact your local university for any sponsored writing conferences:

Artists and Writers Colonies:
Retreats, Residencies, and Respite for the Creative Mind
Gail Hellund Bowler, 1995

Black Writers Reunion and Conference
http://www.blackwriters.org/conference

The Complete Guide to Writers' Conferences and Workshops
William Noble
P. S. Eriksson, 1995

Directory of Writers Conferences and Centers
http://awpwriter.org/wcc

The E. Lynn Harris Better Days Literary Foundation
P.O. Box 78832
Atlanta, GA 30357
(This tax-exempt organization supports new writers by

providing mentoring opportunities and workshops for aspiring authors.)

The Guide to Writers' Conferences
Shaw Guides, Inc., 1992
625 Biltmore Way, Suite 1406
Coral Gables, FL 33134

Hurston/Wright Writers Week
P.O. Box 842005
Richmond, VA 23284–20054

National Black Writers Conference
www.blackwriters.net

Voices Summer Writing Program
Diem Jones, Director; Voices Writing Workshop
Office of the Dean School of Education
University of San Francisco
2130 Fulton Street, San Francisco, CA 94117–1080
Phone: (415) 422–5488

Supportive Organizations

1. Nationally, there are many fine writing organizations devoted to fostering talent, informing writers about their craft and rights as authors, and publicizing publishing opportunities. In addition, most states have their own arts commission or council, which fosters literary events within the state via workshops, fellowships, or a reading series.

Appalachian Center for Poets and Writers
Rte. 4, Box 958
Abington, VA 24219
This center encourages a cross-cultural audience through workshops and readings. The emphasis is on abolishing Appalachian stereotypes and developing regional voices and audience.

Associated Writing Programs (AWP)
Tallwood House, Mail Stop 1E3
George Mason University
Fairfax, VA 22030
This association of university-affliated writing programs sponsors an annual conference and publishes a guide to creative writing programs. The AWP newsletter features information on grants, fellowships, awards, and publishing opportunities. It also provides in-depth articles on craft and exceptional writers.

Black Writers Alliance
http://www.blackwriters.org
The BWA is devoted to fostering talent, informing writers about their craft, and publicizing publishing opportunities. This group sponsors a yearly conference.

PEN American Center
568 Broadway
New York, NY 10012
This organization is devoted to advocating writers' rights nationally and internationally. It publishes writing guides and sponsors community and national writing programs.

PEN Center USA West
672 S. Lafayette Park Place #41
Los Angeles, CA 90057
Related to the PEN American Center, PEN West offers
tremendous support for west-based writers. They offer
readings and workshops, and their "Emerging Writers"
Program pairs young writers with more experienced mentors.

Poets & Writers, Inc.
72 Spring Street
New York, NY 10012
Poets and Writers is an organization devoted to informing
writers about their craft, agents, publishing, grants, and
fellowships. Their newsletter is exceptional—it features
updated information on contest and grant deadlines,
conferences, and publishing opportunities. Write for a
complete list of their publications.

The Writers' Center
7815 Old Georgetown Road
Bethesda, MD 20814
A membership organization that sponsors classes and
readings and publishes a newsletter, *Carousel,* and a journal,
Poet Lore. I taught at the Writers' Center one summer and
found it to be a welcoming, nurturing environment.

YMCA, The Writer's Voice Project
5 West 63rd Street
New York, NY 10023
This is a national program that sponsors community-based
writing workshops and a terrific reading series by local and

national writers. Contact your local Y for information about its affiliation with the the Writer's Voice.

2. Historically, black writers across the nation have bonded to create their own supportive organizations. Many of these organizations were founded by the vision of one person or by a community-collective. While the following list is *not* exhaustive, it provides a starting point to help you link to other writers throughout the nation. But the most important lesson, I think, is that people with commitment can create their own community-based reading group or supporting arts organization. (If you know any other organizations that should be included, please don't hesitate to contact me in care of Doubleday.)

African American Resource Center
Afro-American Studies
Howard University
P.O. Box 441
Washington, D. C. 20059
E. Ethelbert Miller directs the center and provides people with information, suggestions, and advice about scholarship and creative writing. A splendid poet himself, E. Ethelbert Miller is particularly encouraging to new writers. The center houses a fine library, which is available to the public.

The Arts Sanctuary
Church of the Advocate
1801 Diamond Street
Philadelphia, PA 19121–1590
Founded by writer Lorene Cary, this organization brings African American artists, thinkers, and activists to the heart of the Philadelphia black community.

Carolina African American Writers' Collective
5625 Continental Way
Raleigh, NC 27610
Founder and Executive Director, Lenard D. Moore, inspires this wonderfully creative organization. The collective sponsors workshops, readings, and a newsletter that provides updates about the writing craft, publishing, and community readings.

Detroit Writers' Guild
P.O. Box 23100
Detroit, MI 48223
http://www.BlackArts-Literature.org
Executive Director, Herbert Metoyer, runs a supportive organization that sponsors workshops and the annual Detroit Writers' Conference.

Frederick Douglass Creative Arts Center
270 West 96 Street
New York, NY 10025
FDCAC.org
This center has long been a haven for black writers. Besides an informative newsletter, it offers wonderful classes taught by expert instructors in a supportive community environment.

Gwendolyn Brooks Center for Black Literature and Creative Writing
Chicago State University
LIB 210
9501 S. King Drive
Chicago, IL 60628–1598

Nommo Literary Society
Kalamu ya Salaam
Box 52723
New Orleans, LA 70152–2723
kalamu@aol.com
Kalamu ya Salaam is the founder of the Nommo Literary
Society, a writers' workshop; co-founder of Runagate
Multimedia; leader of the WordBand, a poetry performance
ensemble; and moderator of e-Drum, a listserve of over seven
hundred black writers and ethnically diverse supporters of
literature. E-mail Kalamu to be placed on his listserve and you'll
receive notices about a wide range of readings, workshops, and
publications that promote African American letters.

3. Following is a listing of African American–based writing
groups across our nation.

Affrilachian Poets
Nikky Finney
English Department
University of Kentucky
Lexington, KY 40506

African American Writers Guild
Attn: Toni Asante Lightfoot
753 Fairmont Street, NW
Washington, D.C. 20011

Bambara Writers
Women's Center
Spelman College
350 Spelman Lane
Atlanta, GA 30314

Black Storytellers Association
P.O. Box 67722
Baltimore, MD 21215

Black Writers and Artists, International
P.O. Box 43576
Los Angeles, CA 90043

Black Writers Institute
1650 Bedford Avenue
Brooklyn, NY 11225

Eugene B. Redmond Writers' Club
P.O. Box 6165
East St. Louis, IL 62202
or
392 Winchester Place
Fairview Heights, IL 62208

First World Writers
Pamela Plummer
P.O. Box 5213
Atlanta, GA 31107

Harlem Writers' Guild
affiliated with the Schomburg Center
Schomburg Library
515 Malcolm X Blvd.
New York, NY 10037

Houston African American Writers' Society
P.O. Box 31478
Houston, TX 77231–1478

International Black Writers and Artists
2625 Piedmont Rd. 56–156
Atlanta, GA 30324

Multi-Cultural Romance Writers
405 West 13 Street
Greenville, NC 27834

The Nommo Gathering
Stephanie Gadlin, Founder and Executive Director
1400 W. 73rd Place
Chicago, IL 60636

Sistah's: An African American Literary Group
2829 Palomor Drive
Brunswick, GA 31520

S.P.A.R.K.S.
Attn: Patricia A. Johnson
86 Willow Oak Lane
Elk Creek, VA 24326

The World Stage Anansi Writers' Workshop
Michael Datcher
5618½ Edgemar Avenue
Los Angeles, CA 90043

Magazines and Journals

1. There are many fine magazines that discuss the craft of writing and professional issues for the beginning through advanced writer. The following journals are available nationally at most newsstands:

Writers' Digest
1507 Dana Ave.
Cincinnati, OH 45207
A popular standby. The digest has informative articles, and many explore how to make a living as a writer.

The Writer
120 Boylston St.
Boston, MA 02116
A fine magazine with helpful, practical articles. It also produces a fine annual book called *The Writer's Handbook,* edited by Sylvia K. Burak.

Poets & Writers Newsletter
72 Spring Street
New York, NY 10012
A regular publication of Poets & Writers, Inc. Articles on great writers and writers' issues make this a most informative newsletter. Also gives details on conferences, retreats, grants and submission information.

Writers' Chronicle
Tallwood House, Mail Stop 1E3
George Mason University
Fairfax, VA 22030
A regular publication of the Associated Writing Programs. Author interviews, grants and submission information, and excellent articles about craft make the Writers' Chronicle very worthwhile.

2. If you're interested in book reviews and issues related to the publishing trade, *Publishers Weekly* is the guide to have. Many

libraries carry this invaluable resource in their magazine or reference section:

Publishers Weekly
245 West 17 Street
New York, NY 10011

3. Most of the following journals and magazines offer book reviews, interviews, and examples of contemporary black nonfiction. Some of the journals are university-affiliated; others are commercial; still others are independent efforts by caring artists. You should study copies of each magazine and subscribe to the ones that most interest you. Some may provide avenues for publishing your nonfiction. Check with each for its submission policy. (Note: This is a partial listing of available publishing opportunities that specialize in black literature. For additions to this list, please write to me in care of Doubleday.) Don't forget, too, to search publishing guides and the Internet for additional titles. New journals are being created every day!

African American Review
Indiana State University
Department of English
Root Hall A218
Terre Haute, IN 47809
A mainstay journal in promoting black literature and art.

African American Literary Review
5381 La Paseo #105
Fort Worth, TX 76112
Publishes excellent work in many genres.

African Voices, The Art and Literary Publication with Class and Soul
Affiliated with the Frederick Douglass Creative Arts Center
African Voices Communications, Inc.
270 West 96 Street
New York, NY 10025
Publishes an excellent and wide variety of genres.

africana.com
Web magazine publishes nonfiction articles (reviews, op-ed, etc.) on topics of interest to African Americans.

AIM Magazine
P.O. Box 20554
7308 S. Eberhardt Ave.
Chicago, IL 60619
Publishes upbeat, socially significant works on racism and multiculturalism.

Amber Books Publishing
1334 East Chandler Blvd. #5-D67
Phoenix, AZ 85048
amberbk@aol.com
Publishes self-help books for African Americans. Has recently branched out to include more fiction and biography.

Black American Literature Forum
Parsons Hall 237
Indiana State University
Terre Haute, IN 47809
Articles, essays, and reviews of black literature.

Black Books Bulletin: Wordswork
Third World Press
P.O. Box 19730
Chicago, IL

Black Books Round-Up
c/o The Black Scholar: Journal of Black Studies
P.O. Box 2869
Oakland, CA 94609

Blackfire
BLK Publishing Co.
P.O. Box 83912
Los Angeles, CA 90083–0912

Black Issues Book Review
William E. Cox, Publisher
10520 Warwick Avenue, Suite B8
Fairfax, VA 22030

Black Renaissance/Renaissance/Noire
Journals Division, Indiana University Press
601 North Morton
Bloomington, IN 47404
Publishes fiction and nonfiction that address contemporary issues.

The Black Writer
P.O. Box 1030
Chicago, IL 60690

Brilliant Corners: A Journal of Jazz and Literature
Lycoming College
Williamsport, PA 17701
Publishes jazz-related literature.

Callaloo: A Journal of African-American and African Arts and Letters
Department of English—Wilson Hall
University of Virginia
Charlottesville, VA 22903
One of the premier literary journals devoted to diaspora literature.

Class
900 Broadway
8th Floor
New York, NY 10003

Contours
African American Studies Program
Duke University
Box 90719
121-S Carr Building
Durham, NC 27708
Multidisciplinary journal exploring experiences of people of African descent.

Cross-Cultural Communications
239 Wynsum Ave.
Merrick, NY 11566–4725
Small "alternative literary arts publisher" of multicultural works.

Dialogue
P.O. Box 4544
Washington, D.C. 20017
A fine journal devoted to promoting African American arts.

Drumvoices Revue
English Department
Box 1431
Southern Illinois University at Edwardsville
Edwardsville, IL 62026–1431.
A multicultural journal of essays, interviews, fiction and
poetry.

Ebony
820 S. Michigan Avenue
Chicago, IL 60605
Publishes a variety of genres and articles related to black life.

Essence
1500 Broadway, 6th Floor
New York, NY 10036
Wonderful magazine devoted to black life, with fine feature
writing and fiction.

FYAH.com
FICTION/POETRY@fyah.com
Fyah.com promotes black wordsmiths via articles, reviews,
interviews, essays, calenders of events, etcetera.

Gifted Voices
116 NW 13th Street, Suite 182
Gainesville, FL 32601
A monthly newsletter devoted to black literary artists.

Harmony Magazine
Pratt Station
Box 050081
Brooklyn, NY 11205–0001
Devoted to racial, cultural harmony.

Ingathering: The Literary Journal of Arts and Letters from the Black Diaspora in the Americas and the Caribbean
601 S. LaSalle Bldg., 6th Floor
Suite H-494
Chicago, IL 60605
Publishes many genres.

Konch
Ishmael Reed Publishing Company
P.O. Box 3288
Berkeley, CA 94703
http://www.ishmaelreedpub.com

Message Magazine
c/o Review and Herald Publishing Association
55 Oak Ridge Drive
Hagerstown, MD 21740
A Christian outreach magazine.

Mosaic Literary Magazine
Mosaic Communication
314 W. 231st Street, Suite 470
Bronx, NY 10463
Devoted to black and Hispanic literature.

Mosaic.com
ON-line version of *Mosaic* literary magazine

OBSIDIAN II: Black Literature in Review
Department of English
North Carolina State University
Box 8105
Raleigh, NC 27695–8105
Has an on-line counterpart that also promotes black literature.

OBSIDIAN II
http://www.ReadersNdex.com/papyrus
From this site you can link to OBSIDIAN II: Black Literature in Review, a new on-line journal.

Open City
August Tarrier, Editor
New City Press
Anderson Hall
1114 W. Berks Street
Temple University
Philadelphia, PA 19122–6090

Our Texas Magazine
Gemeral Berry, Publisher
103 N. Willomet Lane
Dallas, TX 75208
A quarterly magazine devoted to African American issues in and around the state of Texas.

Papyrus Magazine
Papyrus Literary Enterprises
P.O. Box 270797
West Hartford, CT 06127
A quarterly devoted to ideas and stories that appeal to a black audience.

Phati'tude
Chimeara Communications, Inc.
P.O. Box 214
Palisades Park, NJ 07650–0214
Multiethnic magazine devoted to writers who are politically, socially, and culturally aware.

Rhapsody in Black
P.O. Box 6296
Silver Spring, MD 20916
Devoted to diverse creative literary work and artwork.

Sauti Mpya
Sonja Haynes Black Cultural Center
University of North Carolina at Chapel Hill
Chapel Hill, NC 27599–3520
Founded to highlight the African American experience.

Skipping Stones: A Multicultural Children's Magazine
P.O. Box 3939
Eugene, OR 97403
Stories, essays aimed at children ages 8–16.

Shooting Star Review
7123 Race Street
Pittsburgh, PA 15208–1428
Publishes fine fiction, poetry, and essays.

Tameme
199 First Street, Suite 335
Los Altos, CA 94022
New journal devoted to North and South American multiethnic writing.

Warpland
Chicago State University
Gwendolyn Brooks Center for Black Literature and Creative
Writing
LIB 210
9501 S. King Drive
Chicago, IL 60628–1598
Fine journal devoted to emerging and established black
writers.

Grants, Contests, and Awards

1. Grants, contest, and awards information can be found in
many writing newsletters and magazines. However, if you want
a basic guide to grants and award opportunities, then I highly
recommend:

Grants and Awards Available to American Writers
PEN American Center
568 Broadway
New York, NY 10012

2. Following are some notable grant and award opportunities
for ethnic literature:

Fannie Lou Hamer Award
A prize of $1000 is offered to a woman "whose work
combats racism and celebrates women of color."
Money for Women/Barbara Deming Memorial Fund
P.O. Box 40–1043
Brooklyn, NY 11240–1043

Grants for Minorities
The Foundation Center
79 5th Avenue
New York, NY 10003–3050

Papyrus Writers' Showcase Contest
P.O. Box 270797
West Hartford, CT 06127–0797

Websites and the Internet

The Internet makes information readily accessible. Writers' resources are constantly changing and updating. Inquiring about information on a particular book can often lead to tie-ins ranging from an author's Web site to newspaper reviews to magazine profiles.

GENERAL TEXT RESOURCES

African American Resource Guide to the Internet
c/o On Demand Press
PO Box 6488
Columbia, MD 21045–6488

Writers.Net: Every Writer's Essential Guide
Gary Gach
Prima Publishing, 1997

The Writer's Guide to the Internet
Dawn Groves
Independent Publishing Group, 1998

WRITING RESOURCES

Black Writers Alliance
Formerly African-American Online Writers Guild
http://www.blackwriters.org/
This Web site was formed by Tia Shabazz to promote
fellowship in the African-American writing community. It
provides resources for both published and unpublished
writers. It has an on-line newsletter, author profiles, writers'
workshop, and Web links to other important sites.

AWP: Associated Writing Programs
http://web.gmu.edu/departments/awp
This is an on-line resource for many of AWP's services,
including the *AWP Chronicle* and the annual AWP conference.

Black Expressions
http://www.blackexpressions.com
A book-lovers' community, where voices and visions of
African Americans are shared and celebrated.

BlackWords
http://www.BlackWords.com
Publishes the monthly on-line publication, *wordofmouth,*
which promotes and celebrates black writing, publishing, and
performance.

The Good Book Club
http://pageturner.net
goodbookclub@hotmail.com
Founded in Houston, Texas, in 1998, this global, Web-based
group supports African American literature and produces a
weekly e-newsletter devoted to writers and readers of fine
literature.

Inkspot: Writing Related Resources
http://www.inkspot.com
A list of craft-related resources on and off the Web. Also has a section devoted to young (children) writers.

Iuniverse.com: The New Face Of Publishing
http://www.iuniverse.com/publishyourbook
Site offers options for on-demand, self-publishing.

Official Misc.Writing WebSite
http://www.scalar.com/mw/
This is the site for the miscellaneous writing newsgroup. Features include: writers' market, writing basics, recommended reading.

Papyrus: The Writers' Craftletter Featuring the Black Experience
http://www.ReadersNdex.com/papyrus
This is an on-line craft and trade publication with an exclusive focus on African American writing. It contains articles about the craft of writing, lists contests, etc. It also has a paper magazine one can subscribe to. Also at the site is OBSIDIAN II: Black Literature in Review, a new online journal.

Poets & Writers
http://www.pw.org/
Poets & Writers maintains an extensive on-line list of resources for aspiring and published authors.

Prolific Writers Network
http://www.prolificwriters.org
Prolific Writers conducts myriad on-line writing and publishing seminars.

Writer's Digest

http://www.writer'sdigest.com

A great site for books and magazines devoted to craft and publishing.

WritersNet

http://www.writers.net/

This is a resource for writers, publishers, and agents. The highlight is the Internet Directory of Literary Agents.

Writers Resource Center

http://www.azstarnet.com/writer/writer.html/

This site includes articles and such databases as a list of markets and submission guidelines.

Writers Write

http://writerswrite.com/

There is a publisher directory, job listings, and a newsletter called "The Write News."

Writers Website

http://www.writerswebsite.com/

This comprehensive site includes information on contests, retreats, and markets. Also, basic legal advice.

PUBLISHING RESOURCES

Advice and Answers about Writing and Getting Published

http://www.teleport.com/~until/faq.htm

Tara K. Harper, a professional science fiction writer, offers information and advice on query letters, agents, contacts, etc.

Bookwire: The First Place to Look for Book Info

http://www.bookwire.com

A comprehensive site about writing, books, publishing, etc.

Book Publishers Listings

http://www.arcana.com/shannon/books/publishers.html

This site lists major and minor publishers, along with guidelines for submissions.

Forward Motion

http://www.sff.net/people/holly.lisle/index.htp

Resource for people who want to make a living writing. There is advice from professional writers about topics ranging from quitting your day job, getting published, and dealing with editors and agents.

TimBookTu

http://www.timbooktu.com

A free Web site for African American writers to publish their work.

OTHER LITERARY RESOURCES

African American Literature Book Club

http://www.aalbc.com

This terrific site, founded by Troy Johnson, has an extensive listing of writing resources, book reviews, author profiles, and much more. Updated constantly, this site provides on-line guides to magazines and publishers that support black authors. It also lists community-based reading groups. To purchase books, you can use a link to Barnes & Noble as well as an extensive listing of African American bookstores.

African American Publications

http://www.aawc.com/aap.html

This site, created by William Richard Jones, provides links to Web sites of more than fifty publishers of magazines, journals, and newsletters that specialize in works by, about, and for African Americans. Many of these are on-line publications and many publish creative writing pieces.

AllBlackBooks.com

http://www.AllBlackBooks.com

All Black Books has a wonderful on-line community with chat rooms, e-newsletter, and book reviews devoted to celebrating black literature.

Callaloo

http://muse.jhu.edu/journals/callaloo/index.html

There are some editions of this literary magazine online. *A Journal of African American and African Arts and Literature, Callaloo* publishes original works by, and critical studies of, black writers worldwide. It contains a mixture of fiction, poetry, plays, critical essays, cultural studies, interviews, and visual art.

Colorado State University Libraries, African and African-American Resources

http://www.colostate.edu/Depts/LTS/research/blacks.html

This is a selected list of African-American novelists and other bibliographical and literary resources.

Essence On-Line

http://ww.essence.com

An on-line site for *Essence* magazine.

HerSPHERE

http://members.aol.com/hersphere

This is a collection of links related to African-American women. A special section is devoted to literature and writing and to magazines and newsletters.

The Literary Web: New Dimensions In Literature

http://avery.med.virginia.edu/~jbh/litweb.html

A site with extensive literary information, links to writing related sites across the Web, and bookclub and workshop information.

Mosaic Books

http://www.mosaicbooks.com

An on-line review dedicated to black and Hispanic literature. This site features an on-line literary magazine as well as link connections to bookstores and bookclubs.

PageTurner.Net

http://www.PageTurner.net

PageTurner.net provides special literary services to aid both established and novice authors project a professional image. Services include: Web site Design and Hosting, Book Jacket Design, Text Editing, and Editorial Reviews. One of their most popular literary resources is their depository of Reader Guides with African American Focus. These guides are available to authors and bookclubs on the World Wide Web.

Pentouch Literary

http://www.pentouch.com

Pentouch Literary is an African-American-owned editorial services firm that offers a pool of skilled editors, proofreaders, manuscript analysts, and literary consultants who specialize in African-American literature. Pentouch Literary's editorial services are tailored to fit the needs of African-American writers, from complex language patterns to cultural nuances.

QBR, The Quarterly Black Review

http://www.bookwire.com/qbr/qbr.html

This is an on-line literary journal, part of the larger Bookwire site. Features fiction and nonfiction by African American writers, as well as lists of black booksellers, interviews with writers, upcoming seminars, etc.

Universal Black Pages

http://www.ubp.com

This is a comprehensive list of African-American related topics, including publishing and magazine information (http://www.ubp.com/words).

Voices From the Gaps: Women Writers of Color

http://www-engl.cla.umn.edu/lkd/vfg/VFGHome

This site from the University of Minnesota is devoted to women writers of color. It includes a list of sites on which one may find general resources about women writers of color.

Web Diva Infocenter: Your Tie to African-Descendants Throughout the Diaspora

http://www.afrinet.net/~hallh

A comprehensive list of African and African-American related sites, with some literature and book information and lots of historical information for research.

Writing Black: Literature and History Written By and On African Americans

http://www.keele.ac.uk/depts/as/Literature/amlit.black.html
This is a list of reading resources by author with links to
those sites on the Web, plus information on oral storytelling
traditions and reference books.

READING LIST

There are many fine and glorious books to read. This list is my own eclectic sampling of books and anthologies that I think are historically significant to the development of African American nonfiction. Each book provides an important glimpse into our culture and illuminates the spirit of black peoples.

Autobiography and Memoir

Angelou, Maya. *I Know Why the Caged Bird Sings.* Random House, 1969.

Brooks, Gwendolyn. *Report from Part One.* Broadside Press, 1972.

Brown, Elaine. *A Taste of Power.* Pantheon Books, 1992.

Broyard, Anatole. *When Kafka Was the Rage.* Vintage Books, 1997.

Campbell, Bebe Moore. *Sweet Summer: Growing Up With and Without My Dad.* Putnam, 1989.

Cary, Lorene. *Black Ice.* Vintage Books, 1992.

Cleaver, Eldridge. *Soul on Ice*. Laurel, 1992.

Delaney, Samuel. *The Motion of Light in Water: Sex and Science Fiction Writing in the East Village*. Masquerade Books, 1993.

Dericotte, Toi. *The Black Notebooks*. W. W. Norton & Co. 1997.

Douglass, Frederick. *Narrative of the Life of Frederick Douglass, an American Slave, Written By Himself*. Signet Books, 1997.

Gaines, Patrice. *Laughing in the Dark*. Anchor Books, 1994.

Giovanni, Nikki. *Gemini*. Viking Press, 1976.

Graham, Lawrence Otis. *Our Kind of People*. HarperCollins, 1999.

Hillard, David. *This Side of Glory*. Little Brown, 1993.

Hughes, Langston. *The Big Sea: An Autobiography*. Hill and Wang, 1993.

Hunter-Gault, Charlayne H. *In My Place*. Vintage Books, 1993.

Hurston, Zora Neale, *I Love Myself When I Am Laughing . . . And Then Again When I Am Looking Mean And Impressive*. Feminist Press, 1989.

Jacobs, Harriet. *Incidents in the Life of a Slave Girl*. Oxford University Press, 1990.

McBride, James. *The Color of Water*. Riverhead Books, 1996.

McDowell, Deborah. *Leaving Pipe Shop*. W. W. Norton, 1998.

McPherson, James Alan. *Crabcakes*. Simon and Schuster, 1998.

Moody, Anne. *The Coming of Age in Mississippi*. Laurel Leaf Press, 1997.

Nelson, Jill. *Volunteer Slavery*. Noble Press, 1993.

Njeri, Itabari. *Every Goodbye Ain't Gone*. Times Books 1990.

Pierce-Baker, Charlotte. *Surviving the Silence: Black Women's Stories of Rape*. W. W. Norton and Company, 1998.

Shakur, Assata. *Assata*. Lawrence Hill Press, 1987.

Williams, Greg. *Life on the Color Line*. Dutton, 1995.

Wright, Richard. *Black Boy*. Harper Perennial, 1993.

X, Malcolm. *The Autobiography of Malcolm X*. Ballantine, 1965.

History and Social Criticism

Baldwin, James. *The Fire Next Time*. Dell, 1963.

Bennett, Lerome. *Before the Mayflower*. 6th Revised Edition. Penguin Books, 1984.

Cleage, Pearl. *Deals With the Devil and Other Reasons to Riot*. Ballantine Books, 1992.

Close, Eric. *Rage of a Privileged Class*. HarperCollins, 1993.

Cooper, Anna Julia. *A Voice from the South*. Oxford University Press, 1988.

Dubois, W.E.B. *The Souls of Black Folks.* Penguin Books, 1996.

Ellison, Ralph. *Shadow and Act.* Vintage Books, 1995.

George, Nelson. *The Death of Rhythm and Blues.* Obelisk Press, 1991.

Giddings, Paula. *When and Where I Enter.* William Morrow & Co., 1996.

Golden, Marita. *A Miracle Every Day: Triumph and Transformation in the Lives of Single Mothers.* Anchor Books, 1999.

Haley, Alex. *Roots.* Dell Books, 1980.

hooks, bell. *Ain't I a Woman.* South End Press, 1981.

Jones, Howard. *Mutiny on the Amistad.* Oxford University Press, 1987.

Jones, Lisa. *Bulletproof Diva.* Doubleday, 1994.

Locke, Alain. *The New Negro.* Scribners, 1997.

Lourde, Audre. *Sister Outsider.* Crossing Press, 1984.

Murray, Albert. *The Hero and the Blues.* Vintage Books, 1996.

Scott, Kesho. *The Habit of Surviving.* Ballantine Books, 1992.

Smith, Ethyl Morgan. *From Whence Cometh My Help.* University of Missouri Press, 1999.

Walker, Alice. *In Search of Our Mothers' Gardens.* Harcourt Brace Jovanovich, 1983.

Walker, David. *Appeal.* Hill and Wang Publishers, 1995.

West, Cornell. *Race Matters.* Beacon Press, 1993.

Wideman, John Edgar. *Brothers and Keepers.* Penguin Books, 1984.

Williams, Juan. *Eyes on the Prize,* Penguin Books, 1987.

Williams, Patricia J. *The Alchemy of Race and Rights.* Harvard University Press, 1991.

Self-Help and Inspirational

Broussard, Cheryl. *The Black Woman's Guide to Financial Independence.* Penguin, 1996.

Copage, Eric. *Black Pearls.* Quill Press, 1993.

Gandy, Debrena Jackson. *Sacred Pampering Principles.* Quill William Morrow, 1997.

Hopson, Derek and Darlene. *Friends, Lovers and Soulmates.* Fireside Press, 1995.

Jackson, Jesse Sr., and Jackson, Jesse Jr. *It's About the Money.* Times Business, 1999.

July, William. *Understanding the Tin Man.* Doubleday, 1999.

Kimbro, Dennis and Hill, Napoleon. *Think and Grow Rich: A Black Choice.* Fawcett Columbine, 1991.

Milner, Denene, and Chiles, Nick. *What Brothers Think, What Sistas Know.* William Morrow, 1999.

Taylor, Susan. *In the Spirit.* HarperCollins, 1994.

Vanzant, Iyanla. *Acts of Faith: Daily Meditations for People of Color.* Simon and Schuster, 1996.

Compilations

Bell-Scott, Patricia, ed. *Double Stitch.* Beacon Press, 1991.

Boyd, Herb, ed. *Autobiography of a People.* Doubleday, 2000.

Golden, Marita. *Wild Women Don't Wear No Blues.* Doubleday, 1993.

Gross, Linda and Marian Barnes, ed. *Talk That Talk.* Touchstone Books, 1989.

Hemphil, Essex, ed. *Brother to Brother.* Alyson Publications, 1991.

McKinley, Catherine, and Delaney, Joyce, ed. *Afrekete: An Anthology of Black Lesbian Writing.* Anchor Books/Doubleday, 1995.

Moore, Lisa, ed. *Does Your Mama Know?* Redbone Press, 1998.

Smith, Charles Michael, ed. *Fighting Words: Personal Essays by Black Gay Men.* Avon Books, 1999.

Wade-Gayles, ed. *My Soul Is a Witness.* Beacon Press, 1995.

Wade-Gayles, Gloria, ed. *Father Songs: Testimonies by African American Sons and Daughters.* Beacon Press, 1997.

Willis, André, ed. *Faith of Our Fathers.* Dutton, 1996.

BONUS EXCERPT FROM
FREE WITHIN OURSELVES:
FICTION LESSONS FOR BLACK AUTHORS

In the following excerpt from *FREE WITHIN OURSELVES:
Fiction Lessons for Black Authors* (Main Street; 1999, U.S.
$12.95/$19.95 CAN), Jewell Parker Rhodes provides excellent
advice about creating characters that are meaningful, multidimensional and unforgettable.

CREATING CHARACTER

Love all your characters.

There is no "story" if readers don't care about your characters. Before a reader will care, you need to feel passionately loyal to each and every one of your characters. Even a character who abuses and hurts others needs to be loved enough to be understood.

In Toni Morrison's *The Bluest Eye,* Cholly Breedlove is the perfect example of a despicable character who is rendered compassionately. Drunk, alienated, overwhelmed by his own self-loathing, Cholly rapes his daughter. Confusing the image of his daughter's foot with a happier memory of loving his wife, the horrible, incestuous touch occurs. But his *motive* was to touch her tenderly.

Even as readers hate Cholly, hate the brutality of his actions, they also feel sympathy, because Morrison, in prior scenes, has *shown* Cholly, as a child, abandoned by his mother and later rejected by his father; *shown* Cholly being forced to perform sexually under the flashlight glare of racists who damage his innocent first love; *shown* how money worries, falsely romantic movies, and a punitive religion drove a wedge between the love he and his wife once shared. Cholly, a "burnt-out black man," can't "breed love" because society, over a lifetime, has poisoned his life's soil. He has no nurturing, sustaining love left to give. When Cholly rapes, we won't, don't excuse his actions, but we do mourn for him as well as for his daughter. Because Morrison cared enough about Cholly to understand him fully, she reveals him with powerful empathy.

Human behavior *is* complex; it is the writer's journey to explore the human heart and in doing so you have the pleasure of discovering more about your own heart and revealing your insights through characters. It is this fundamental sharing between writer and reader—of thought, feeling, and action—which gives fiction its power and force.

Zora Neale Hurston's Janie, in talking of her dying love for her husband, Jody, says *"she wasn't petal-open anymore with him."* Characters may love, hate, be spiteful with abandon, but a good writer always remains "petal-open." If you no longer "love" your characters or feel compelled to write about them, then stop. Without love, you are almost certain to write flat, one-dimensional characters.

MY BEST ADVICE

Approach your characters as human beings.

Black people are subject to the same human foibles as anyone else. If you're writing about a strong, wondrous black woman, be certain to shade her with vulnerabilities, weaknesses. Characters, like people, are never consistently "strong," "nice," "evil," "considerate," "beautiful"—all the time. In *Voodoo Dreams,* Marie Laveau—a gifted, spiritual leader, a woman who could walk on water—struggled with self-pity and doubted she was lovable. Because I didn't want Marie to be a "character type," a one-dimensional being, I overdid her vulnerabilities. Three hundred pages later, to my dismay, I had a novel about a pathetic, victimized young woman. I revised, working to give Marie back her glory, her affirmations of self. Ultimately, there were many Maries: the warrior Marie; the spirited, questing Marie; the battered, weeping Marie; the vengeful Marie; the shy Marie. I hope my Marie expresses, often like quicksilver, as many human emotions as she could credibly hold.

Historically, in American literature and popular culture, African Americans have been presented as variations of key stereotypes: the Brute Negro, quick to violence, desirous of white women; the Mammy, nurturing, loyal to her white family, and seemingly without emotional needs of her own; the Black Matriarch, emasculating and domineering; the Tragic Mulatto, vulnerable, victimized, and more virtuous because of her white blood; the Sambo, childish, unintelligent, interested only in singing and dancing; and the Uncle Tom, obedient, desirous of emulating whites, and disinterested in the plight of his people. Stereotypes are one-dimensional characters and are a blatant attempt by society to dehumanize and oppress.

We've all heard the golden rule: "Do unto others as you would have them to unto you." In my mind, this rule applies to literature. No person should be dehumanized. An evil character, regardless of color, created with compassion is infinitely preferable to an evil character created without understanding and without potential for change.

Unfortunately, two hundred years of racism and acculturation have had their effect. Color prejudice within the black community is a result of slavery's legacy and an early literary tradition which fostered the belief that the light-skinned, straight-haired Negro would always be more tragic than her darker cousin. Likewise, standard English versus black dialect became a code by which to judge people's intelligence both in fiction and in life.

Be conscious of your characters' appearance and speech and make sure you aren't responding to outdated, harmful images. As a writer, you choose to describe characters as you see fit. The key word is "choose." Unfortunately, it's the unconscious insidiousness of racism and American schools' historic disregard for ethnic literature that force writers to be on guard.

White American writers in the eighteenth, nineteenth, and (let's be frank) twentieth centuries would announce color as though "brown," "black," "yellow," "amber," "ebony," "coffee," "café au lait," "chocolate," "cinnamon" explained all you needed to know about a character. If a color adjective was left out, then, of course, the character was white.

When I wrote my first story for a fiction workshop, classmates chastised me: "Why didn't you tell me your characters were black?" They had wanted a page one, paragraph one clarification!

Character is much more than an announcement of skin tone, and color should never be confused with cultural identity. My cultural identity is African American, but it doesn't exclude or bar me from writing about my larger human family, which is a spectrum of myriad colors.

Like jazz artists playing with variations, African American authors took the singular dimensions of stereotypes and debunked them by re-creating and replacing those images with multifaceted characterizations.

Characters are created by situations and responses, by a writer's willingness to engage in complexity. Muhdear in Tina McElroy Ansa's *Ugly Ways* fits no simplistic pattern of motherhood; J. California Cooper's mothers in the short stories "Friends, Anyone?" and "I Told Him" are living, breathing, hurting, "trying to get by" women. Ernest Gaines has a glorious record of presenting complex women—sometimes outspoken, sometimes taciturn—surviving as best they can and often far better than racism wants to allow.

Black writers have transformed the image of singing, dancing, happy slaves into musicians whose artistic power can plumb the depths of pain, as in James Baldwin's "Sonny's Blues," or praise music as joyful liberation from Western cultural aesthetics, as in Langston Hughes's "The Blues I'm Playing."

Indeed, matriarchs and musicians have a special resonance in our literature; they can be called "stock characters." Stock characters (not to be confused with stereotypes) are characters who reappear throughout black literature, uniquely drawn and reimagined by successive generations. Drawing from our oral tradition, authors have made tricksters, preachers, and badmen/outlaws familiar stock characters. It is okay to use stock characters—all cultures have them and create them to embody cultural themes and concerns. Minor characters, in particular, can be rendered efficiently as stock characters. However, as a writer, it always pays to add complexity to as many characters as you can to avoid stereotypes.

Slaves told tales of how tricksters outwitted their masters and upset the balance of racial power. In 1899, Charles Chesnutt created Uncle Julius, a trickster, who in a series of tales subversively criticizes slavery's horrors. Ishmael Reed's *The Last Days of Louisiana Red* (1974) features PaPa LaBas as a voodoo trickster detective. Some of the earliest tricksters were animal characters—Bruh Rabbit, Anansi the spider, Lizard—who survived via oral folktales and folk literature throughout Africa and the Americas. These animals, usually small and sly, used combinations of magic, wit, and cunning to outwit larger, more powerful animals. In the African American literary tradition, these animal tricksters developed into human stock characters who defended themselves against slavery's and racism's ills. Today, almost any black character who outwits the system, trumps the "master," is, in a sense, a descendant of the trickster.

The folk hero Stackolee (also known as Staggerlee, Stagolee), sung and talked about since the 1890s, is a badman who hates and lives outside conventional norms. Because he lost his Stetson hat while gambling, Stackolee kills a man. In differing tales and songs, the sheriff refuses to capture him, or the judge refuses to convict him, or the hangman refuses to hang him for fear Stackolee will get even. The badman becomes an "antihero" because he is *anti-,* against, *trying to live outside a society which typically oppressed black men.* Though their actions aren't always laudable, badmen can be envied for their audacious moments of power and control. Bigger Thomas in Richard Wright's *Native Son* is a quintessential badman. He lives outside societal norms because a racist society has made so little space for him to be a man. *The Autobiography of Malcolm X* shows the societal anger and self-hatred of a "badman" but also shows the courageous transformation of a black man re-creating himself and a space within the world for him to become the man he desires.

Preachers are often infamous stock characters, satirized for immorality, sexual promiscuity, and lack of Christian compassion. Nella Larsen's *Quicksand,* James Baldwin's *Go Tell It on The Mountain,* Ralph Ellison's *Invisible Man,* Gloria Naylor's *The Women of Brewster Place,* all have examples of preachers who don't live Christian principles or who use Christianity to encourage passive acceptance of prejudice. These stock characters become powerful tools to remind us that faith needs to be sincerely lived.

The ancestor is another familiar character in African American literature. This moral and spiritual guide can be either a man or a woman, but quite frequently in our fiction, an elderly character, a ghost, or a spirit from an African or long-ago past gives critical advice to confused, struggling characters. Baby Suggs in *Beloved* encourages black people to love themselves. McMillan's Ma'Dear is a wise old woman with good advice about life, love, and paying the bills. The grandmother in Virginia Hamilton's classic *Roll of Thunder, Hear My Cry* always supplies comfort and nurturing support to the family struggling to maintain itself in the 1950s South.

You can't always develop all characters equally, but you should try. Inexperienced writers tend to make all their characters one-dimensional. Be bold, experiment, create characters who will live always within your story and, most important, within your readers' minds and hearts.

Sometimes a character walks in the door as a gift; most times they tantalize. You have to spend enough time to know your character. You'll need to draw upon your self, your memories, your observations. Selecting a character for a story is one of the most important choices you'll make.

Who intrigues you? Aunt Sarah, who never comes to family gatherings?

Whom do you feel passionate about? The ex-lover who disappeared without a goodbye?

Whom do you imagine? The Howard student who stumbled upon a senator's body at K Street and L?

Sometimes the best characters are composites based upon people you know. But don't try to model exactly a real person (that's how lawsuits are born). A fiction writer's job is to tell great lies which make a great story. Even a real person has thoughts and feelings which you must imagine.

Remember: The stuff of your imagination is probably more promising than reality.

DUST INTO FLESH

In your journal, select a name for a character you'd like to write about.

For example, Anita. An Anita is different from a Barbara, a Lorraine, or an Elsa. A Jerome is unlike a Terrence, a Bobby, or a James.

A name makes a character real. So does history. Write down details about your character's past: When and where was she (or he) born? What are her parents' names? Was she a wanted child? Is she the only child, eldest child, or baby of the family? What are her parents' attitudes toward raising children? How much schooling does she have? Who was her first love? First enemy? What was her greatest fear growing up? Her best talent?

Write down details about your character's current life: Is she married? Does she practice a faith? Where does she shop? What's her profession? Her hobbies? Is she a mother? An activist? Is she inside or outside a network of friends?

What is a typical day like? Chances are you'll be writing about an untypical day, so decide what your character normally does. On Thursday, does your character eat at Jones's Deli? Work a night shift at the hospital? Or meet with a women's group to discuss books? What are her daily rituals? Rising at dawn for coffee and Frosted Flakes, then a bus ride with three transfers to work? Or does she sleep late, making the kids ready themselves for school, then awaken in time for aerobics and lunch with her friend Martha?

What does your character look like? You needn't list details as if you were writing a police report or printing a driver's license! Instead think of physical details which make your character striking and unforgettable. It may be her elegant hands, the way she moves or doesn't move through a crowded room, the slope of her neck or a rose-shaped birthmark on her shoulder.

What clothing does your character wear? What does she want it to say about her? That she's rich, stylish? What does it actually say about her? That she's a rich wannabe buying top-of-the-line Kmart instead of designer fashion? Colors and patterns can indicate moods and suggest fashion attitudes— black fabric has a different appeal than purple-striped silk or an indigo-and-gold batik.

Clothing tells a lot about your character's income group, self-esteem, and style, but it can also delightfully deceive. *Pierce Watson is affluent but prefers to wear Keds sneakers, Levi's, a Pirates baseball cap, and a torn green sweatshirt.*

Consider physical habits too—how your character smiles, laughs, tilts her head when she's angry. Does she sleep on her stomach? Eat her food item by item, starting with the vegetables?

Take thirty minutes and complete a character sketch.

Reread all the information you've written about your character so far. Would you know her if she walked into a room?

While all the details you've written are important in helping you visualize and understand your character, not all of the details will be directly used in the story. Using a highlighter, mark those details which might be critical to the plot—to what happens to your character in the story. For example, your character's love for exotic travel may not matter as much as her small (but, she believes, disfiguring) mole on her left cheek and her hatred of her daily ninety-minute commute on the D.C. subway (where she believes everybody stares at her and mocks her).

EXERCISE 2

BREATHING IN THE SPIRIT

Characterization is only half done until you've breathed spirit, soul into your character. Characters must have an interior life: desires, dreams, needs, fears.

What does your character desire? Love? Money? Friendship? Revenge? What does your character dream about? What are his fantasies and daydreams? What dreams are repressed? What nightmares wake him? What does your character truly need? Literacy? Freedom from self-doubt? A kind word?

Write at least two pages about the emotional, inner life of the character you sketched in Exercise 1. Pretending you are the character, you can begin with strong "I" statements or else begin with the character's name. This exercise will allow you to really feel, breathe, and experience the character.

Anita wants [I want] _____

I need _____

I fear _____

I dream _____

Desires/dreams/needs can and do overlap. But characters can also desire and dream about one thing only to discover they need something else. For example, in Alice Walker's story "The Wedding," a single mother is marrying, fulfilling her dream to give her children respectability and security. But what she desires is love and equality. During the wedding service, the character realizes her marriage will be repressive, patriarchal. What she needs is the courage to free herself from the relationship. But she can't.

Circle the overlapping desires/dreams/needs you see in your character sketch. Then underline any emotions which are at odds with each other. For example, a character dreams of being a musician but needs cocaine. Or an abused character may believe she has no desires, that she is "a speck of nothing," only to discover she needs to dream in order to survive.

Desires/dreams/needs give your characters depth and complexity. Your character's interior life will shape her motivations and how she might respond to choices and crises within your story.

Review all the information you've written about your character. What needs does she have that you're sympathetic to? Are you challenged by similar insecurities, dreams, hopes? What is your emotional stake in writing about your character? Why do you feel compelled to write about this character as opposed to any other?

In your journal, write at least a paragraph (preferably

more) about how and why you connect with your character emotionally.

Name, current life and past history, appearance, feelings and desires all create the foundation for great characterization. Add in your emotional bond and you'll breathe life into your characters, making them memorable, transforming them from "dust to flesh."

PERMISSIONS

CHAPTER EIGHT

CHAPTER NINE